THE LIVERPOOL
WELSH CHORAL UNION

Published by Countyvise Limited

The Liverpool Welsh Choral Union today

THE LIVERPOOL WELSH CHORAL UNION

THE FIRST HUNDRED YEARS

Nansi Pugh

ACKNOWLEDGMENT

TO TIM COLEMAN
OF DARKHORSE DESIGN & ADVERTISING,
42 HAMILTON SQUARE,
BIRKENHEAD, CH41 5BP
FOR COVER DESIGN

First Published 2007 by Countyvise Limited,
14 Appin Road, Birkenhead, Wirral CH41 9HH.

British Library Cataloguing in Publication Data.
A catalogue record for this book is available from the British Library.

ISBN 978 1 901231 95 3

DEDICATED

to the memory of

HIS HONOUR, JOHN EDWARD JONES
(1914 – 1998)

who during his term of office as President (1986 – 1998)
first conceived the idea of writing this history of

THE LIVERPOOL WELSH CHORAL UNION

and to the memory of

EILEEN VAUGHAN
(1905 – 2006)

who for a period of more than 60 years was a faithful member
of the choir and a part of that history

Publication of this history has been made possible as a result
of the generous gifts by the family of John Edward Jones and
the estate of Eileen Vaughan

THE AUTHOR

Although she was born in Wales into a Welsh-speaking family, Nansi Pugh's childhood was spent in Birkenhead, before the family moved in 1929 to the United States, which was to be her home for the next 28 years.

After attending school in Chicago and New York, Nansi became a student at Columbia University, graduating with a degree in History and English, and a year later an M.A. in History. She began her teaching career in Cincinnati, Ohio, while at the same time studying singing at the Cincinnati Conservatory of Music. After teaching for four years at a girls' school in Princeton, New Jersey, she spent eleven years teaching at a highly academic independent school in New York City. She returned to this country in 1957, spending five years teaching in Wallasey, followed by six years in Wimbledon. She then spent three years back in America, this time at Bryn Mawr, Pennsylvania, before returning to spend five years teaching in Croydon, followed by a period working in adult education. In 1982 she returned to Merseyside where she now lives, enjoying being part of a thriving Welsh community, which has enabled her to join a Welsh Church and to become a member of the Liverpool Welsh Club.

Wherever Nansi has lived, music (and especially choral singing) has played a large part in her life. During her childhood, leading soloists and musicians of the day would visit the family home, as her father was himself an accomplished musician. In 1929 she sang in the children's choir when the National Eisteddfod of Wales was held in Liverpool, although she cannot now recall whether the choir was conducted by Dr. Hopkin Evans. When in Chicago, she was fortunate to be a member of a children's choral group under the direction of the well-known Welsh musician, Dr. Daniel Protheroe. In the 1930s and early 1940s, she was not only a member of the University Chapel Choir, but also a member of the New York Welsh Women's Choir. Later she was for ten years a member of the choir at the famous Riverside Church. On returning to this country, she sang with the Wallasey Singers, an excellent small choral group conducted by Stainton de B. Taylor, and later in London with the choir of the City Temple and the Wimbledon Hill Singers.

Coming from a Welsh and musical background and with a long established interest in history, it is hardly surprising that in recent years Nansi has found herself a keen supporter of the Liverpool Welsh Choral Union and a ready chronicler of this famous choir's history.

ACKNOWLEDGMENTS

This history would not have been possible without the unfailing assistance of a great many members and friends of the Liverpool Welsh Choral Union.

First and foremost I must acknowledge the vision of the choir's former President, His Honour John Edward Jones, who first conceived the idea of recording the history of the first hundred years, and started the task of gathering material and information on the Welsh in Liverpool, material which is included in the LWCU Archive in the Central Library. Following the Judge's untimely death, I received every possible assistance and encouragement from his widow and daughter, Kathie Jones and Glenys Arden, who ensured that all the papers which he had collected and written arrived with me safely. On a practical level, I must record my thanks for the loan of the Judge's huge magnifying glass, which enabled me to read fading newspaper clippings and old documents written in a beautiful but minute script.

Many members of the choir have assisted my task by contributing concert programmes of which copies were otherwise unavailable, as well as other documents and information of every kind. In particular, I must mention two former chairmen of the choir, Rhiannon Liddell and David Mawdsley. At the beginning of this venture Rhiannon gathered materials from many sources and passed on the very large store of information she had acquired during the period of her choir membership. David allowed me to borrow his meticulously kept notebooks covering his two periods as chairman, was ready at all times to respond to my many questions, and provided valuable comments on drafts. The choir's archivist, Felicity Jones, has been a tower of strength in collating the enormous volume of material available.

In compiling this history I have been able to draw on the writings of many others. These include various Liverpool residents unknown to me, who took the trouble to record their memories of life in the city during World War II. Of particular assistance was the book on musical enterprise on Merseyside over the course of two centuries written by Stainton de B. Taylor, the only musician to my knowledge who has so far attempted such a task. I am also indebted to Roderick Owen and Ifor Griffith, who, within recent years, contributed the passages on the choir's visits to Germany and Ireland. These accounts appear in the Epilogue.

Finally, I must express my gratitude to all who have encouraged me to carry on with writing this history, when at times the task seemed almost unachievable. In particular, I must acknowledge the willing assistance of the choir's current President, Professor Huw Rees, and of Dr. Pat Williams, both of whom have readily read several drafts of the finished work, providing guidance and support at every step of the journey. Pat has provided invaluable assistance as to the form and appearance of the book, while Huw has been the moving spirit in finding a sympathetic publisher.

Thank you, all.

Nansi Pugh

FOREWORD

by Dr. Karl Jenkins OBE,
B.Mus., F.R.A.M., A.R.A.M., L.R.A.M., F.W.C.M.D.,
F.T.C.C.

There has been a rich tradition of fine choral singing in Wales from the earliest times. With the influx of Welsh people into England during and following the Industrial Revolution, that tradition spread to cities like Liverpool. And so it is no surprise that when the National Eisteddfod of Wales was held in Liverpool in 1900, the choirs of the numerous Welsh chapels on Merseyside were able to come together to form a united choir for the occasion.

What is perhaps more surprising is that the choir formed in 1900 has continued in existence for more than a century as The Liverpool Welsh Choral Union. This account traces the history of the Welsh Choral over its first 100 years, as it established itself as one of Britain's most successful large choirs. As it embarks upon its second century, the Welsh Choral is in good heart and going from strength to strength.

My own association with the Welsh Choral is comparatively recent. In 2005 I had the pleasure of conducting the choir in a performance of my own composition *The Armed Man: A Mass for Peace*. I was greatly honoured on that occasion to be invited to become the choir's Patron – an invitation I was delighted to accept. I look forward to working with the choir again during the celebrations to mark Liverpool's status as European Capital of Culture in 2008, with a new work to mark the occasion.

It gives me great pleasure to extend my very best wishes to The Liverpool Welsh Choral Union in the hope that its second 100 years will be even more successful than the first.

Karl Jenkins

CONTENTS

PROLOGUE: BEFORE 1900

"Praise the Lord! We are a musical nation." So spoke the Reverend Eli Jenkins in Dylan Thomas's radio drama, *Under Milk Wood.*

Whether or not this is an entirely true picture of the Welsh nation, there is certainly a perception among people of other nations that it is so. Until recent years, we may have lagged behind some continental countries in our mastery of instrumental music. There is little doubt, however, that in the realm of vocal music, our reputation has been almost unchallenged.

Giraldus Cambrensis (1146?-1223), or Gerald the Welshman, archdeacon of Brecon, traveller extraordinary and mediaeval scholar, was one of those appointed in 1188 by the government of Henry II to make a tour of Wales in order to recruit soldiers for the third crusade. Fortunately, he was an acute observer, interested in all aspects of Welsh life. Of his journey he wrote an account in which he remarked:

> In their musical concerts they do not sing in unison like the inhabitants of other countries, but in many different parts; so that in a company of singers, which one very frequently encounters in Wales, you will hear as many different parts and voices as there are performers, who all at length unite, with organic melody, in one consonance and the soft sweetness of B-flat. In the northern district of Britain, beyond the Humber, and on the borders of Yorkshire, the inhabitants make use of the same kind of symphonious harmony, but with less variety, singing in only two parts, one murmuring the bass, the other warbling in the acute or treble. Neither of the two nations has acquired this peculiarity by art, but by long habit, which has rendered it natural and familiar; and the practice is now so firmly rooted in them that it is unusual to hear a simple and single melody well sung; and, what is still more wonderful, the

children, even from their infancy, sing in the same manner.[1]

Little is positively known of the development of singing in Wales in the centuries that followed. We know that Queen Elizabeth I, following in the footsteps of her father, attempted to regulate the bardic patronage system, and graded poets and musicians according to rank. Genuine minstrels had apparently felt threatened by the competition of vagrants calling themselves rhithmers. The Eisteddfod of Caerwys,[2] called together by Elizabethan Commission in 1567, offered the authentic bards an opportunity to prove their status and abilities. Those who qualified were awarded a degree, and a licence allowing them to practise their profession and be paid for it. All others were classified as "sturdy beggars",[3] and were to be punished accordingly. Standards were set. There were obviously music critics of a sort operating in this early period.

Wales was fortunate in succeeding centuries, during years when singing for pleasure was frowned upon by Puritans. The province was sufficiently remote from the disapproving eyes of Cromwell and his officers so that singing and dancing was not so ruthlessly suppressed in Wales as in England during the era of the Commonwealth. Chiefly such singing as existed was that of individuals and small groups, most of it associated with annual and seasonal festivals. Fiddlers usually accompanied such folk celebrations. We find some prominent Welshmen, however, such as Ellis Wynne[4] in *Visions of the Sleeping Bard*, a 1703 publication, deprecating the dance, harp and fiddle as too closely identified with semi-pagan revels and vanity fairs.

---

[1] Giraldus Cambrensis, "Of their Symphonies and Songs", Bk.1, Ch. XIII *A Vision of Britain Through Time* (Oxford, 1997); http://www.visionofbritain.org.uk/text/content_page.jsp?t_:d=Cambrensis_ Desc&C_id=15 [date accessed 25/05/2007)
[2] Vaughan-Thomas, Wynford and Llewellyn, Alun, *The Shell Guide to Wales* (London, 1977) p. 129.
[3] Cheyney, Edward P., *A Short History of England* (New York, 1945), p. 368.
[4] *Y Bywgraffiadur Cymreig hyd 1940* (Anrhydeddus Gymdeithas y Cymmrodorion, Llundain, 1953), pp. 1038-1039; see also Lile, Emma, *A Step in Time, Folk Dancing in Wales* (Cardiff, 1999), p. 18.

During the early years of the eighteenth century, there is no mention of organised choirs of any sort.

If this was the state of music in Wales at the beginning of the eighteenth century, were matters any different in Liverpool, and especially among those Welsh people who had found their way to the city? For some years, interested persons have been searching the annals of Liverpool to try to discover the history of the Welsh in the city, and especially to uncover information on the origins of Welsh music making. Programmes of the Liverpool Welsh Choral during the twentieth century have on many occasions made passing references to Liverpool musical history, but one must credit Judge John Edward Jones (1914-1998), former President of the Welsh Choral, with the initiative to set on foot serious research into the past, so that a more comprehensive history of the Choral Union might be made available.

Since the city was founded in 1207 by King John, there has been some sort of Welsh presence here. As early as 1503-1515, Liverpool had a Welsh Mayor, Dafydd ap Gruffydd, and Welsh names are to be found among the lists of aldermen and other city officials. Liverpool before the period of the Industrial Revolution, however, was only a very small town, if the villages on its periphery are excluded. The entire population of Liverpool in 1700 reached only 5,000. But there was, even then, a small enclave about St. Paul's Square, which became known as Welshtown. The Welsh colony had its centre in Queen Street near the Cotton Exchange in the dock area. It was then mainly a residential enclave of tall Georgian mansions, with quiet courts tucked away behind them. It was not until the Industrial Revolution, starting about 1740, that significant Welsh immigration[5] came to Liverpool.

In 1782 a small group of recent arrivals met in the home of

---

[5] 1831: Total Liverpool population, 280,000.

a William Llwyd on Pitt Street, and later at a new chapel, one built in 1787 in Pall Mall.[6] Contributions from North Wales's chapels had helped finance its construction. In the chapels and schools of those years, the singing of hymns played an important role in all types of meetings. Few hymn-books were obtainable at first, but in 1744 a little book, a collection of the words of "hymns for all occasions",[7] had been published in Carmarthen. It cost only one penny and was therefore generally affordable. No books containing the tunes of hymns existed, but, in any case, few of the chapel-goers were as yet able to read music. Still, through attendance at Sunday Schools, the Welsh became increasingly able to read the words of the Welsh hymns, and eventually, able to handle English words too. The Welsh of Liverpool were ambitious people, who, in England, hoped and looked for a better life for their children than they had themselves experienced.

The end of the eighteenth century saw a great influx of the Welsh into Merseyside, for there was no scarcity of work in the area, and the Welsh were known to be skilled craftsmen, hard-working, thrifty and persevering. The Napoleonic Wars, that broke out in the 1790s, proved to be a period of development for Liverpool. More workers were needed in the building trade, for housing and yet more dock construction. By 1813, as the wars drew to a close, it is estimated that approximately 8,000 Welsh people, one-tenth of Liverpool's population,[8] were of recent Welsh immigration.

In 1804 the influential Welsh Charitable Society had been instituted, which encouraged Welsh participation in general city fund-raising for charitable purposes. One money-raising method was the holding of festivals in which music naturally played a part. Five such festivals[9] were held between 1823 and

---

[6] Rees, D. Ben, *Cymry Lerpwl a'r Cyffiniau* (Lerpwl, 2001), p. 4.

[7] Jenkins, R. T. , *Hanes Cymru yn y Ddeunawfed Ganrif* (Caerdydd, 1945), p. 81.

[8] Davies, John, *Hanes Cymru* (London, 1990), pp. 426-428.

[9] Taylor, Stainton de Bouffler, *Two Centuries of Music in Liverpool* (Liverpool, 1973), pp. 45-9.

1836, in all of which the Welsh participated.

By the end of the 1830s, Liverpool had become one of the chief cities of Great Britain, and certainly almost unchallenged as the chief port. To the building of canals and roads in the Northwest was now added the construction of railways. The rail link between Manchester and Liverpool was the first, not only in this country, but in the world. The commercial exchanges of Liverpool were flourishing. New business enterprises were coming into being. Good schools were established and centres of culture grew in importance. With all the acknowledged cultural growth, however, Liverpool had not yet any established choral group.

The world's first choral society,[10] the Halifax, was founded in 1817, and survives today with an unbroken record of performance. The Bradford Choral Society was established in 1836, and Liverpool was not far behind. In that same year, a subscription was opened in the city for the purpose of erecting a building suitable for festivals and other public performances. It was to be called St. George's Hall. By 1838, sufficient fundraising progress had been made so that the foundation stone could be laid as part of a ceremony held to celebrate Victoria's coronation. Shortly afterwards, in January, 1840, the Liverpool Philharmonic Society[11] was formed, with its orchestra and a choir of 200, which doubtless would have included some Welsh singers. The first stone of its fabulous new Concert Hall in Hope Street was laid in 1846. It was a hall blessed with superb acoustics, where the first concert took place in 1849.

Meanwhile, periodically, festivals for charitable purposes continued in Liverpool. Among these was one in 1840, which was known as the Grand Eisteddfod. It lasted for three days in

---

[10] Kaufman, Sarah "The Singing Century", Limelight article for *Artifact* (December, 2005), http:/www.intute.ac.uk/artsandhumanities/limelight/singingcentury.html (accessed 26/05/2007).
[11] Taylor, *Two Centuries of Music*, p.45.

August, and was not carried on exclusively in Welsh. However, it can be assumed that, in the tradition of Welsh eisteddfodau, there was a large choir brought together to sing in the evening concerts, but this still gave rise to no permanent surviving choir.

Though it may puzzle us that a people so fond of singing as the Liverpool Welsh, and endowed with such good voices, should not have formed a choral society long before this time, it is actually not surprising. The Land of Song itself had as yet no such choir. So said the musician, Brinley Richards,[12] in his speech at the Welsh National Eisteddfod held in Beaumaris in 1832. Actually the National Eisteddfodau of the 1800s were chiefly literary occasions, and though there were certainly choirs formed each year to meet the need for the singing of cantatas and anthems at the evening concerts of Eisteddfod Week, such choirs scattered once the celebrations were over.

How is it that we Welsh were so slow to establish choral societies? One answer certainly lies in the financial condition of the people of Wales. On the continent of Europe, especially in Italy, there were cities that were wealthy in the years following the Renaissance. Their merchants had money to spend on beautiful buildings, on art and other artistic pursuits. In Germany they were wealthy enough to maintain orchestras and professional church choirs. In Wales, the ordinary people were poor, and her merchants did nothing to encourage art and music. The art that flourished in Wales was of the sort that did not need much money: that is, poetry and vocal music, largely the singing of poetic compositions to harp accompaniment. The Methodist Revival of the 1730s had brought another sort of singing to take its place, hymn-singing, though, of course, folk-singing did not cease, but continued to have its enthusiastic devotees. With the coming of the Industrial Revolution, chapels

---

[12] Williams, Gareth, *Valleys of Song* (Cardiff, 1997), pp. 8-12.

were built in the new towns of Wales, and the singing of hymns formed an important part of the services. Most chapels held singing schools to learn new tunes and words, and almost every chapel had its choir. From time to time, these came together, chapel and congregation, in singing festivals. The occasional chapel choir turned to singing selected choruses from oratorios, the *Messiah,* and later, *Elijah.* Such sacred works were very popular, particularly in the industrial regions. Choirs in rural areas encountered more difficulties, since distances between centres of population were hard to bridge when it was a matter of frequent rehearsal. But in Liverpool, the concentration of Welsh people might offer hope for such a choral society. What was urgently needed was a musician of vision who could initiate such a project, and Liverpool found such a man in John Ambrose Lloyd.

John Ambrose Lloyd,[13] the son of a Baptist local preacher, was born in North Wales, in Mold, on June 14, 1815, a few days before the Battle of Waterloo was fought. He possessed what has been described as a fine treble voice and a good musical ear. He sang as a child in the Mold Parish Church choir. Though self-taught, he became a very fine musician. He was the composer of a number of hymn-tunes, the first written in 1831 when he was only 16 years of age. He was an enthusiastic participant in all eisteddfodau, local and national, and in 1845 took the composition prize at the Groeswen Eisteddfod.

John's brother, Isaac, had become editor of the *Liverpool Standard*, and, when their parents moved from Mold in 1830, Isaac asked that John should join him in his Liverpool school, in order that he might prepare himself for a career in teaching. From 1838 to 1848, John was a master at the Mechanics Institute in Mount Street, later to be known as the Liverpool Institute High School. Shortly after John's arrival in Liverpool, Isaac took a position in Blackburn, and John was left on his own. From

[13] *Y Bywgraffiadur Cymreig hyd 1940*, p.551

the first, he took an active interest in all things musical, and in 1845 he became a member of the Liverpool Philharmonic Society, recently founded in 1840. John was, however, a little unsettled in his Welsh chapel life, moving from one to another of the chapels until he finally settled in Tabernacl, the Welsh Congregational Church in Great Crosshall Street. There, very soon, he became the chapel's precentor, its *codwr canu*. It was said that the best congregational singing in Liverpool was to be heard at Tabernacl.

It happened that, in 1843, a famous Welsh preacher, the Reverend William Rees, better known among the Welsh as Gwilym Hiraethog, arrived in Liverpool. He too had an interest in music and John Ambrose Lloyd and he became firm friends. Together, they were instrumental in establishing the first Welsh Music Society in Liverpool. Lloyd gathered together a number of like-minded music enthusiasts who met regularly at his house, and this gave birth after a while to the idea of forming a choir to hold occasional concerts. The group was to be entitled *Cymdeithas Gorawl Gymraeg Lerpwl* (The Liverpool Welsh Choral Society).

At first they rehearsed in the Welsh School on Russell Street, not far from the rehearsal rooms of the current choir. Some of the early performances took place in a concert hall in Lord Nelson Street. One such concert happened on January 18, 1848, and another on January 30, 1850. There exists a copy of the cover of one programme, which dates from January 15, 1851, and which described the concert as the 'Seventh Public Performance' by the society.

Eventually, because of the increasing number of his commitments, John gave up his teaching post and became the North Wales manager for the Tea Merchants, Messrs Woodall and Jones. But the amount of travelling necessary caused him to move his home, first to Chester in 1852 and later to Conway. At some point during these years, his connection with Liverpool was broken. Dr Joseph Parry, the respected composer and teacher, had the highest regard for John Ambrose Lloyd's skill in composition. What became of his Welsh Choral Society, however, is not known.

We do know that various Welsh choral associations combined in the 1860s to form a Welsh Choral Union.[14] They gave regular concerts in the Nelson Rooms, Hope Street, and in St. George's Hall, with an orchestra whose conductorship was shared by H. Walker Jones and William Parry. The society was still in existence in 1877, when its Honorary Secretary was Llewelyn Wynne, a name important in the history of Welsh choral music on Merseyside.

There was another effort to form a Welsh choir in Liverpool. In 1880 the Calvinistic Methodist churches joined to form a large choir, with John Parry as their conductor. The choir gave regular concerts in the Nelson Assembly Rooms, the Sun Hall, St. George's Hall and elsewhere. Whether this choir formed the basis for the Eisteddfod Choir in Liverpool in 1884 is uncertain. (Or is it perhaps the same choir as the Cambrian Choral Society,[15] which is recorded as giving one of the concerts in the 1884 Eisteddfod?)

We know of the formation of yet one more mixed choir before the Liverpool Welsh Choral Union came into existence. The Douglas Road Welsh Chapel had a precentor of talent and ability, Sam Evans,[16] a grocer by trade. He formed, trained and conducted a choir of 150 voices in the singing of oratorios by Handel, Haydn and Mendelssohn. He was an expert in the sol-fa system of musical notation, and held classes to teach sight-reading to interested Liverpool singers. Much later he became deputy conductor of the Liverpool Welsh Choral Union under Hopkin Evans.

In the meanwhile, what choral progress was there in

[14] Taylor, *Two Centuries of Music*, p. 45.
[15] See Account of Eisteddfod of 1884 in the Liverpool Record Office, Central Library.
[16] Taylor, *Two Centuries of Music*, p. 45.

Wales? One problem among the early choirs was the scarcity of music sight-readers. Often in the absence of an instrument, the choristers relied on the ear and the voice of the conductor. Few before 1860 could claim any skill at sight-reading. Music published for choirs contained only staff notation or sol-fa music based on a fixed doh. The introduction of **tonic** sol-fa[17] made a world of difference to the enthusiasm of Welsh choir singers, and to their training by devoted conductors. Tonic sol-fa first claimed public attention about 1850. It owed its rapid growth in popularity to the efforts of the Reverend John Curwen (1816-80),[18] an Englishman from the north, who developed the system from a method of letter notation invented by a Miss Glover of Norwich. By adopting a movable doh for the tonic of any major key, and with a series of syllables representing the notes of all scales, the succession of intervals remaining constant, it was possible for even young children to grasp the method of reading music at sight. John Curwen first advocated the system in an article in 1842. He wrote his first book on the subject in 1843, and, much later, in 1875, he founded the Tonic Sol-fa College at Plaistow, Essex.

From the first, Welsh music teachers and choir masters seized upon the new system with delight. It was to a certain Eleazar Roberts[19] that the Welsh people, both in Wales and scattered throughout Britain, owed the spread of sol-fa. He was born in Pwllheli in 1825, but moved (or was moved) to Liverpool at two months. From the age of 13 he worked in a solicitor's office, and in 1853, became a member of the staff of the clerk to Liverpool magistrates. He eventually became chief assistant to the clerk of the stipendiary magistrate. He was elected a J.P. in 1895, the year following his retirement. Eleazar

[17] Bacharach, A. L., (Editor), "The Development of Notation" in *The Musical Companion*, pp; 43-45.

[18] Griffiths, Paul "Tonic Sol-Fa" in *Harmsworth Encyclopaedia*, Volume VIII, (London, 1905), p. 1.

[19] *Y Bywgraffiadur Cymreig hyd 1940,* pp. 809-810; Williams, *Valleys of Song,* pp. 29-32.

Roberts was a precentor at the Netherfield Road Calvinistic Methodist Chapel. With John Edwards, he conducted the first Welsh *Cymanfa Ganu* held in Liverpool in 1880. Mr Roberts was a contributor to all the important Welsh journals, and he wrote several biographies and a novel. For us, however, he is best known as an exponent in the 1860s of the tonic sol-fa system. Like John Curwen he published books of instruction for his converts: one on learning Sol-fa; a second on its more advanced uses. Realising the limitations of the system for instrumental teaching, he then wrote a book on the transition from Sol-fa to staff notation, and finally made a collection of Hymns and Tunes. He travelled much through Wales to expound the uses of Sol-fa, and to establish classes in the villages and towns. Others followed in his footsteps.

For choral conductors, the tonic sol-fa was a boon, and very soon readers of sol-fa outdistanced those able to read staff notation. It has been estimated that, of the 1130 singers that made up the seven choirs competing in the chief choral event at the 1894 National Eisteddfod, 87% were sol-faists, and the proportion among the male choirs was 96%. Supporters of the system pointed out that sol-fa was more than a system of notation; it taught pitch, rhythm and a basic harmonic sense. At Bangor Normal College,[20] in 1864, sol-fa became part of the teacher's instruction, and after the 1870 Education Act, it became the accepted method of teaching in the newly created elementary schools. It was a key factor in Welsh musical awakening in the late 19th century. Throughout Wales, the Sunday School and Band of Hope implemented the teaching of sol-fa, and all children became familiar with the Modulator. Needless to say, in Welsh circles in Liverpool too, this was the case, and every chapel had its sol-fa classes, its *ysgol gân*, 'from which young singers graduated to the adult choir, fully equipped to sing all standard choral works at sight.'[21] It contributed powerfully

---

[20] Williams, *Valleys of Song*, p. 33.
[21] Taylor, *Two Centuries of Music*, p. 45.

to the firm four-part singing that so impressed visitors to any Welsh gathering.

The development of eisteddfodau in this period was also a feature, and especially the inclusion of choral competitions in National Eisteddfodau. In 1848, the Chief Choral Competition obtained recognition. Though, at the National Eisteddfod in Aberystwyth in 1865 only one choir appeared in the competition, by 1873, in Mold, there were six entries. By 1885 one whole day of Eisteddfod Week was given over to the Chief Choral. In Aberdare in that year, six large choirs competed, each singing three set pieces. No wonder it took all day! By 1897 in Newport, the Chief Choral reached its peak: fifteen mixed and ten male voice choirs competed.

In Wales, rivalry between individual choirs and their followers became intense, especially at the National and Semi-national Eisteddfodau during the 1870s and 1880s.

Did any of this eisteddfodic fervour affect Liverpool? There had been, as mentioned before, a Grand Eisteddfod (though not a national one) in Liverpool in 1840. It was largely a literary and civic event, and competitive musical items did not play a significant part. In late September and early October 1874, the Liverpool Triennial Festival was revived after a gap of almost forty years. It was held in the Philharmonic Hall, honoured by royal patronage, and resulted in great financial success, the proceeds going as before to charity. To what extent the Welsh community participated in this Festival is not known. The next eisteddfodic event in the area was the Welsh National Eisteddfod of 1878 in Birkenhead. We are told that many Liverpudlians took an active part in the management of this Eisteddfod, and that the result was an unqualified success.

In August 1882, a meeting of the Welsh National Eisteddfod Association took place in Denbigh. Its main purpose was to decide upon a venue for the 1884 Eisteddfod.[22] The only formal

---

[22] Liverpool Record Office, Central Library, H891 660 8 WAL.

application had come from Wrexham, though it was generally understood that Ruthin had been making preparations for it. Matters took an unexpected turn. There were certain gentlemen present who, it appeared, favoured neither place. One argued in favour of Liverpool, and his proposal was seconded by a delegate from Manchester. A vote was taken, and Liverpool was the choice of a large majority. The other applicants withdrew.

The main body of Liverpool Welshmen had known nothing of the proposal. They had not even considered its feasibility. Nevertheless, they met on August 31 to consider ways and means, and after a few weeks of informal and vague discussion, they applied formally for the Eisteddfod of 1884. The names of the Mayor, 29 Councillors, and other gentlemen of the city, 300 in all, were presented as sponsors. Then came consultation with the bards, literati and musicians of Wales who directed the formation of a General Committee, and four sub-committees: Literature, Music, Arts and Finance, each with its own organisation. By July 1883, the Literary and Music Committees had completed their essential work. The locale chosen was Kensington Fields, but since the building there was not really large enough, and furthermore, since Liverpool felt that the cost of raising a special pavilion was prohibitive, the city offered the Haymarket, which was roofed over to prepare for the occasion.

The responsibility weighed heavily on the Liverpool Welsh, though it was shared among many of the growing number of Welsh residents of the time. The General Committee consisted of 12 people, the Executive Committee of 25, the Literary of 45, the Music of 30, the Arts of 12 and the Finance of 33. A subscription list of 150 was compiled, and a Special Prize list of 14 drawn up.

The Eisteddfod competitions were again chiefly literary, though there was one competition for large choirs of 150-180 voices. Four choirs competed in this division, including one from Liverpool, but it was a choir from Bethesda in North

Wales that was victorious. Day to day proceedings seem to have been conducted almost entirely in English. This was the time before the All-Welsh Rule. It has been suggested that the Liverpudlians in general looked down on the Welsh language even while they admired the Welsh ability to organise such an impressive festival as an eisteddfod. The chief concert by the residential choir was one in which *Nebuchadnezzar* by Joseph Parry was performed under the composer's direction. At another concert, the Liverpool Cambrian Choral Society under William Parry sang choruses from various oratorios. The Friday evening concert consisted of a performance of Handel's *Israel in Egypt,* sung by the Liverpool Philharmonic Choral Society, and on Saturday night the Liverpool Cymric Vocal Union presented a varied programme.

The Liverpool Cymric Vocal Union[23] was a male voice group, founded in 1882, but having its origin in the 1870s. A few young men, members of the Windsor Street Welsh Baptist Church, met in their schoolroom under their choir master, David Williams, to practise male voice music. Inspired by the fine personality of their leader and his musical culture, the group soon grew. In addition to their joy in singing, these men had a desire to serve the community, and began to give concerts in aid of chapels, churches and other good causes. It was not at first a fully organised choir; membership was a casual affair. Out of this, however, David Williams founded his Welsh male voice choir, formulated proper rules and decided on a name.

It announced its primary object:[24] the cultivation of male voice part-singing and the wish to be of service to the community. Its purpose was not to compete, though they did enter a contest in the 1884 National Eisteddfod, a competition won by the famous Arvonic Choir, led by a highly respected conductor, Dr. Roland Rogers. The latter was a well-known organist and an instructor in music at Bangor University College. Under his

---

[23] Cymric Vocal Union Programme, March 3, 1932.
[24] *Ibid.*

conductorship, his male voice choir, centred in Bethesda, had won the choral prize at three National Eisteddfodau: Denbigh in 1882; Cardiff in 1883; and now Liverpool in 1884. After 1884, the Liverpool choir returned to its original purpose of cultivating part-singing.

Rules had been framed in 1882 on democratic lines. Every member had an equal voice in decisions. The officers chosen were to vacate office at the end of every season, but could be re-elected. Each member was to pay an annual subscription. In the knowledge of the later organisation of the Liverpool Welsh Choral Union, it is interesting to examine the list of officers for the opening year of the Cymric Vocal Union.[25] The conductor was, of course, David Williams, and the Deputy Conductor John T. Lewis. The Chairman was O. J. Rowlands; the Deputy Chairman, William Evans. Gwilym Griffith was the Secretary; David James Davies, the Treasurer; Robert Wynne Jones, the Auditor; and T. Evans Hughes, the Librarian. In addition, five members were elected as a Committee, to complete the management. The Cymric Vocal Union held concerts annually, and survived as an organisation into the 1960s.

The early leaders of this choir were men of substance in their various fields. David Williams, their first conductor, later emigrated to America, where he continued his musical activities, and where he remained until his death. One of his successors, as conductor from 1890 to 1932, was John T. Jones. He was employed by the Moss Shipping Line, but among the Welsh he was known as an elder, first in the Windsor Street Chapel, and then in Earlsfield Road, where he was also the precentor. Later, for a time, at the request of Mr. Moss, his employer, he served as Choir-master for the Linnet Lane Church. A great friend of Mr. Jones was Llewelyn Wynne, who was also in shipping, and worked for the Papayanni Line. He worked diligently for several National Eisteddfodau: Flint in 1865; Birkenhead in 1878; Liverpool in 1884 and 1900. For the latter he was both

[25] *Ibid.*

its secretary and stage manager. Before the establishment of the Vocal Union, Mr.Wynne had been a member of the Welsh Choral when that choir was established under the leadership of William Parry. Another of this influential group was R. Wynne Jones, who attended the Welsh Chapel in Everton Village. He was a pupil of David Williams, and an excellent solo singer. Several newspaper critics of the time mention his highly professional performances. Still another enthusiastic member of the Vocal Union was Humphrey Lloyd. All four of these leaders were also to be active in the preparations for the 1900 Liverpool Eisteddfod, and all were on the Music Committee for that event.

In Wales, the most celebrated choral leader from 1880 onwards was Dan Davies,[26] a self-taught musician, one of fiery temperament. He was an expert in the sol-fa system and was diligent in training his choirs in that method. His first public appearance was with the Dowlais Glee Party, but he was then responsible for the formation of the Dowlais Harmonic Society, specifically to compete in eisteddfodau. In 1882, his choir was judged superior to six others, including the Dowlais Choral Society, and he repeated his success in 1885, 1886 and 1887. In 1892, he caused dismay by moving from Dowlais to neighbouring Merthyr, where he led the Merthyr Philharmonic to further victories. By 1895 he was universally hailed by critics as well as by fellow Welshmen. Then in 1896 came a reversal. At the Llandudno Eisteddfod, with the exception of one choir from Holyhead, all the choirs came from South Wales. These included the choir of Harry Evans from Dowlais. He was a young man whose name in later years was to become very familiar to the people of Liverpool. It was considered that Merthyr's main rival at Llandudno was Rhymney, but in the event, the prize was awarded to Builth, a little-known choir under a Rhymney-born conductor. The adjudication showed a change in the general perception of the elements of a good choir. The judges declared

[26] Williams, *Valleys of Song*, pp. 91-105.

The Dowlais Male Voice Choir.
Conductor: Harry Evans.
Winners of the male voice competition at the National Eisteddfod held at Liverpool in 1900

that they were looking, not merely for a body of tone or a tricky reading, but for high artistic quality, refinement and an accurate conception of the composer's intentions. Dan Davies took exception to this adjudication, as did a number of other competitors.

In 1897, Dan Davies set out for Newport, determined "that matters must be set to rights". Disappointment was in store for him, however. The adjudicators commented:

> We wished that some of the choirs would moderate their ardour just a little more. The winning choir was the one that gave the most musical reading, Abersychan and Pontypool. Its singers were trained to refinement and delicacy rather than noise.

"Terrible Dan" as he was known, continued to conduct, but he drew more adverse comment in 1899 in London and in Merthyr itself in 1901. This last was partly the consequence of his inability to manage the orchestra as well as the choir in a performance of *Elijah* at one of the week's concerts. The identical choir and orchestra, on another evening, performed *Israel in Egypt* under the baton of Harry Evans, whose performance was reported as masterly. Dan Davies, from then on, faded from the major competitive scene. He knew he had to give way to younger men who had the formal musical qualifications that he himself lacked. Of these, Harry Evans was the most distinguished.

In 1893 Harry earned the praise of the press when he became accompanist to the Dowlais Choral Society. This was a group, as we know, that set great store on winning competitions. When Dan Davies left Dowlais for Merthyr, pressure was put on Harry to form a new group. In September 1893, the Dowlais Harmonic changed its name to Dowlais Philharmonic, and in December, Harry had his first experience of large scale conducting, when he led a choir of 200 voices in a performance of Handel's *Samson,* with full orchestra. He devoted his next few years to choral competitions, and in 1897 took the chief prize of £100 in

Tonypandy. In 1898, he branched out to form a ladies' choir in Merthyr. Most of the women in his choir were young, middle-class, single women, privately educated and able to read music. This was something new in Dowlais and Merthyr. Encouraged by the success of this group, in 1899 Harry formed a male voice choir of about 100 men to compete in the Eisteddfod to be held in Liverpool in 1900. These men were chiefly ordinary working men from the iron-works, but the possibility of combining the male and female groups was present in Harry's mind. Preparation for the Liverpool Eisteddfod[27] took precedence at the moment, however, and much meticulous work remained to be done.

For two years preparations for the Eisteddfod had also been in progress in Liverpool. The pattern of preparation for 1884 was repeated, and with many of the same committees and organisers. The formation of a large resident choir was easily possible in a city with such a large Welsh population. A choir, numbering approximately 400, was brought together under the general conductorship of Mr. D. O. Parry.

At last, all the preparatory work was complete, and the long-awaited 1900 National Eisteddfod took place, not in early August, as happens nowadays, but in mid-September. Music was to play a major part in the event, and, naturally, the resident choir was very much involved. On the whole, audiences of that era were happier to listen to a variety of choruses from opera and oratorio rather than a steady diet of complete works, and so we find that on three evenings, there were variety concerts in which, of course, the Eisteddfod Choir played a major role, but at which popular soloists were also given their place. Still, there were some longer works performed during the week. On the Wednesday evening, the 400-strong choir presented Haydn's *Creation*, conducted by their regular chorus-master, Mr. D. O. Parry. On Thursday, the eminent musician and composer, Joseph Parry, led the choir in a performance of his own work,

---

[27] Liverpool Record Office, Central Library, H891 660 8 WAL.

Ceridwen. The Friday concert consisted of the presentation of Handel's oratorio, *Judas Maccabaeus,* again under the baton of D. O. Parry, with the orchestra of Thomas Shaw. The Saturday evening concluding event was the third Variety Concert, including soloists, the Eisteddfod Choir, and the band of the Grenadier Guards. Maggie Evans and Millicent Richards were the accompanists, two excellent pianists, who were later to become official accompanists to the Liverpool Welsh Choral Union.

The mornings and afternoons of Eisteddfod Week were, of course, devoted to competition, musical and literary. On Tuesday, there took place the Chief Choral Competition, in which several Welsh choirs took part, but the winners were the Potteries District Choral Society. On Friday came the Male Voice Choir Competition, the contest for which Harry Evans had been working so diligently. And not in vain! Eleven choirs competed, singing only one unaccompanied piece, although two had been prepared by the competitors. And it was the Dowlais choir that triumphed with 80 marks out of 100, defeating several well-established choirs, including the Manchester Orpheus. The choir was ecstatic, and justifiably so. Not only had they been given a glowing adjudication, but praise had also been heaped upon their conductor, still only a young man in his twenties. This too was the only competition of the week won by a Welsh choir. Otherwise, English choirs had swept the board.

So, for Liverpool, ended the Second Welsh National Eisteddfod. There was to be one other in the city. That took place in 1929, while there were still large enough numbers of Welsh men and women to sustain the work of preparing such an event. After that, and especially after the Second World War, eisteddfod devotees from Merseyside gave what help they could to the eisteddfodau of North Wales, attending day and night sessions, helping to raise funds, and supporting the eisteddfod in whatever ways they could. Eisteddfodau, local and national, still flourish in Wales.

And what of Harry Evans? He returned to Dowlais well-satisfied. His choir remained a unit for some years, giving performances of many works, and it responded to the demand for Welsh concerts at the Queens Hall in London, and elsewhere. Was it any wonder that it was to him as conductor that Liverpool turned when the decision had been made to form a permanent Welsh Choir in the city, the choir that was to become the Liverpool Welsh Choral Union?

CHAPTER ONE:
THE ESTABLISHMENT OF THE CHOIR

It was not only Harry Evans and his male voice choir who, as they returned home after their Liverpool triumph of 1900, were well satisfied with their Eisteddfod success. The Eisteddfod Choir also had every reason to feel proud of itself. The choristers had upheld the honour of the Liverpool Welsh by their stalwart performances throughout the week. They had sung two oratorios, *The Creation* by Haydn and *Judas Maccabaeus* by Handel, both conducted by their chorus master, Mr. D. O. Parry. The 400-strong choir had participated in two variety concerts, and had been on the platform to sing *See, the Conquering Hero Comes* in honour of Pedrog (Rev. J. O. Williams), the winner of the Chair of that year. They had given a performance of the cantata *Ceridwen*, a work by Dr. Joseph Parry, commissioned by the Eisteddfod Committee, and conducted at its premiere by the composer himself. The choir members certainly deserved high commendation for their week's work, had it been for their stamina alone; but it was much more than that. Every appearance of the choir had been praised by the press, and very much appreciated by the large audiences that attended each performance.

The Chairman of the closing session of the Eisteddfod was Councillor William Evans, J.P, who ended his address of the evening with these words:

> and now let me pay one tribute of praise to the ladies and gentlemen of the Eisteddfod Choir, for the magnificent services they have rendered. Under the fine leadership of Mr. D. O. Parry, they have given us a series of musical treats, which I am told, by competent critics, could not be excelled – if equalled – in any part of the United Kingdom.[1]

---

[1] Eisteddfod of 1900, Liverpool Record Office, H891 660 8 WAL.

Is it any wonder that, after such undoubted success, the choir members were reluctant to bring their organisation to an end? There were obviously in Liverpool great possibilities for the establishment of a first-class choir, if formed on a proper basis. For the time being, the choir continued to rehearse, and gave one or two performances with a chorus somewhat reduced in size. The Music Committee of the Eisteddfod continued to control the organization, but realized that positive action must be taken to prevent its total disintegration, which would be a tragic anti-climax after their two years of regular and pleasurable rehearsing. But what would be the purpose of a continuation? Would such a choir prepare for competition in future eisteddfodau? Or would it be their wish chiefly to provide a musical focus for the Welsh on Merseyside? For fifty years during the nineteenth century, one choir after another had been founded, only to cease to exist after some years. Only chapel and church choirs had remained constant. Could this Eisteddfod choir be the first to endure?

Not only the Eisteddfod Music Committee but also other friends were favourably disposed to consider the matter seriously, and this resulted eventually in the calling of a meeting[2] on July 2, 1902, when several resolutions were adopted, two of which follow: Be it resolved:

a. that as the promises of support and the interest displayed are sufficiently encouraging to warrant the formation of a Welsh Choir in Liverpool, a provisional sub-Committee be appointed to draft out a scheme for establishing the same;
b. that a Guarantee Fund be formed, and that well-wishers to the movement be solicited to sign the same.

It is interesting to note the composition of this Provisional Committee; it consisted of:

---

[2] Prospectus for 1909-1910 Season. Twenty-first Concert of LWCU.

---

a. Mr. J. T. Jones, conductor of the flourishing male voice Cymric Vocal Union, *codwr canu* in the Earlsfield Road Chapel, and later, choir master in Linnet Lane Church;

b. Mr. R. J. Hughes

c. Mr. R. Vaughan Jones

d. Mr. Humphrey Lloyd

e. Mr. R. D. Glyn Roberts

f. Mr Llewelyn Wynne, an *eisteddfodwr* of experience, and the secretary and stage manager of the Liverpool National Eisteddfod of 1900. He had been a leading member too of the Liverpool Welsh Choral of 1868.

This Committee of six formulated a scheme and issued an appeal to the public. They prepared a Guarantee Bond and circulated it, securing a favourable response. By September 24, 1902, it was possible to call a Public Meeting of Guarantors and Supporters. The assembled group took the decision to form a choir "forthwith" to be entitled The Liverpool Welsh Choral Union.[3]

There followed the election of Choir officers. Councillor William Evans, J.P., who had been Chairman of the final Eisteddfod session, was elected President. The chosen Chairman was James Venmore, J.P.; unfortunately, however, he was prevented by serious illness from acting, and Robert Roberts, J.P., was appointed in his place. The other chief officers were Mr. Humphrey Lloyd, Vice-Chairman, Mr. J. D. Jones, Treasurer, and Mr. Llew Wynne, Honorary Secretary. The remaining members of the Provisional Committee were elected members of the Executive Committee of the new Choral Union, and in addition, six other members were chosen: Mr. Richard Lumley, Mr. Abel G. Harris, Mr. R. Wynne Jones, Mr. J. T. Lewis, Mr. R. O. Williams and Mr. Robert Roberts, who ultimately took Mr. Venmore's place. Mr. H. T. Bellis became Registrar, and Mme. Maggie Evans, the accompanist.

---

[3] *Ibid.*

There remained the vital matter of a conductor. The musical leaders of Liverpool had had ample time to consider this. Many had connections with Welsh organizations and were familiar with the leading choirs of Wales and their conductors. They would have followed adjudications of conductors at eisteddfodau in North and South Wales, and would have read, if not actually heard, the remarks of leading adjudicators. Undoubtedly the name of Harry Evans would have been prominent among the possible candidates for the position open in Liverpool, even had the Committee not already been very highly impressed by his performance in 1900. Since then, the selectors had surely known of Harry Evans's conducting of the Eisteddfod Choir of 500 voices at the Merthyr Eisteddfod in 1901, when the oratorio *Israel in Egypt* by Handel was performed under his baton. The Committee might perhaps be anxious to secure a fairly young man for the new post,[4] and would be aware that a Liverpool position would appeal to the best of Welsh conductors. Doubtless, they would wisely have sounded out Harry Evans as to his readiness to accept before they issued their invitation to him, as they did in September 1902. "It was resolved that Mr. Harry Evans, F.R.C.O., of Merthyr, be invited to undertake the conductorship."

Such an offer was flattering and not to be ignored. Harry Evans responded positively. He would accept the offer with pleasure, but for the time being, he would also carry on with his Dowlais choir, and remain in his Dowlais home. He did actually compete with his Dowlais choir at the Llanelli Eisteddfod in 1903, having taught his singers the whole of Handel's oratorio *St. Paul*, and easily defeated the seven other choirs in the competition. In 1904, he took his choir to the Queens Hall in London, where its performance received overwhelming praise by the London music critics who commented that the choir's tone was pure and round, and that its execution was always artistic, never exaggerated.

---

[4] Williams, *Valleys of Song*, p. 110; also Obituary in LWCU's First Book of News Clippings (source unspecified and undated).

Harry Evans
Principal Conductor and Chorus Master
of the Liverpool Welsh Choral Union
1902 - 1914

Harry Evans, in September 1902, was prompt in taking up his conductorship of the Liverpool Welsh Choral. Choir members were enrolled and the first rehearsal took place on November 26, 1902. Where it took place is uncertain, but perhaps it can be assumed that the rehearsal rooms used for the Eisteddfod Choir were still available. From Harry Evans himself comes the information that the opening choir was made up of 49 sopranos, 46 contraltos, 38 tenors and 49 basses, 182 in all.[5]

Information about the early days of the choir, and indeed information for most of the early years of the century, is sparse. Without doubt, such a well-organized institution kept meticulous official accounts of its activities, but, as many of our readers already know, all records of the choir, up to early 1940, were destroyed in the bombardment of Liverpool in 1941. A scrapbook carefully kept by a far-seeing friend of the choir, contains press clippings of some concert criticisms dating from 1904 to 1919, but the only complete concert programmes remaining from the period of Harry Evans are a *Messiah* programme of December 18, 1909, and a photo copy of one of March 19, 1910, when Bach's *B minor Mass* was performed. Some significant correspondence has survived, but otherwise there is little authenticated information. The oldest choir member has recently died at the age of 100, but even her memory of the choir went back only to 1930, when she joined it at the age of 25. Enough documents remain, however, to put together a chronicle of an extraordinarily successful choir.

When Harry Evans came to Liverpool, though still only 29 years of age, he was by no means lacking in experience. At an exceptionally early age, he had become an organist of note, a first-class accompanist, and a successful teacher. He himself had a beautiful tenor voice, and had well-formed ideas of how to train other singers. He would concentrate on voice production and intonation. At rehearsals he would have his choir

---

[5] Introduction to the programme of the 1910 performance of Bach's *Mass in B minor*.

practise scales, pianissimo, three times up and down the scale in one breath. With his male singers, he would have the first tenors using head voice only, without forcing the chest voice at all. The result was that he had a body of tenors able to sing an effortless high B-flat. With the Welsh Choral, he favoured unaccompanied practice so that dependence on an instrument was obviated; thus, too, he made sure that any wrong intonation could be instantly corrected. When asked how he had developed his methods, he claimed it was the result of "getting about", by which he meant attendance at the Three Choirs Festival and similar gatherings, and frequently visiting London to listen to vocal and orchestral performances, and to become familiar with the wider world of music.

Harry Evans had several times explained[6] how he worked to achieve his musical effects. At eisteddfodau he had disagreed with many of his compatriots and agreed with the English adjudicators in their placing of English choirs above Welsh ones. He maintained that it was not so much a matter of national styles that brought success, as of musical technique, of accuracy, purity of tone, intelligent phrasing and a "potent restraint", in all of which English choirs excelled. He held that Welsh choirs often had better voices and a more musical temperament, but that Welsh conductors were often of insufficient technique. Harry Evans's results were achieved partly by stern discipline: rehearsals were for him a time of serious application.

By April 4, 1903, the newly formed Liverpool Welsh Choral was ready to put on its first performance, Handel's oratorio *Samson*, at the Philharmonic Hall. The orchestral role was taken by a band of forty performers. The success of the choir's initial appearance was unquestioned, the press lavish in their praise. On April 6, the *Liverpool Post* correspondent wrote:

---

[6] Obituary in LWCU's First Book of News Clippings (source unspecified and undated).

A highly finished and thoroughly enjoyable performance
of Handel's *Samson* was given on Saturday evening at the
Philharmonic Hall by the Liverpool Welsh Choral Union. The
attendance was large and enthusiastic. Under the masterly
conductorship of Mr. Harry Evans, F.R.C.O. (Dowlais),
the choir gave the utmost satisfaction. In number over 250,
(actually a slight exaggeration), their efforts were characterised
by a fine volume of tone, excellent precision, and an intelligent
conception of the work in hand. Particularly pleasing was their
singing of *Then round about the starry throne, To Man, God's
universal law;* and *Fixed is His everlasting seat.* The solos
were in good hands. Mme. Bertha Rossow displayed a sweet,
though light, soprano voice, and Mme. Juanita Jones, a local
singer, is to be commended for her artistic rendering of the
contralto music. The tenor music was admirably sung by Mr.
William Green, whose fine voice and method were universally
admired. Mr. David Hughes's sonorous bass voice was heard
effectively in *Honour and Arms*, albeit a more moderate tempo
would have been welcomed. Mr. John Henry rendered good
assistance in the bass music. A word of credit is due to the band
led by Mr. Vasco V. Ackroyd. Mr. Robert Harvey presided with
ability at the organ.[7]

The new venture was acclaimed a potent force for the future
musical life of Liverpool. In addition, always an important factor,
the concert was a financial success, the Treasurer reporting a
surplus! Writing later of this event, Harry Evans said:

The first work we gave was Handel's *Samson*, and after that
performance and two months' experience of the choir at
rehearsal, I found that there were great possibilities here and
just the right kind of people to work for Art's sake, with no
external considerations other than doing what they could do to
uphold the reputation of Wales as a choral nation. The decision
to restrict the membership of the Society to persons of Welsh
descent seemed to be attended with some risk, but now that

[7] Programme for December 19, 1914.

it has been amply justified in the results, we are proud of that restriction. We began with a membership of 150 voices, but soon the number rose to 300, each singer having to undergo a test before being admitted to the Society.

The first Annual General Meeting of the Society took place on September 1, 1903. Its main purpose was to review the work of the year, to arrange for the coming season, to agree financial matters and, crucially, to issue Rules and Bye-laws for the Society as well as tickets of membership. The earliest extant membership ticket in the Liverpool Welsh Choral Union dates from September 24, 1930. Naturally, since that time, the Rules and Bye-laws have been repeatedly up-dated, but it may be of interest to know what rules have been in force since the fairly early days of the organisation.[8]

These regulations were accepted without a dissenting vote, and, as stated above, have been amended by general consent from time to time. Previous Liverpool Welsh choirs had found it necessary to impose fines on Members who failed to obey the rules, a penalty of 3d (3 old pence) for absence from rehearsal without sufficient excuse; 1/- (1 shilling) for absence from concerts, and exclusion for four consecutive absences from rehearsals. Apparently the Welsh Choral had no need to resort to such measures, perhaps because the competition for admission to the choir was at first intense, and one would not want to risk one's place by unnecessary absence. Membership of the choir was a treasured privilege.

So the Liverpool Welsh Choral Union was firmly established. But **when** was it really established? Mr. Llew Wynne would have said 1868, since he regarded the present LWCU as a continuation of the Society that existed in the 1860s. The Centenary of the Welsh Choral was celebrated in the year 2000, which argues for 1900 as the date of establishment. A document

[8] A copy of the Rules and Bye-Laws of 1903 (as amended in 1905, 1912, 1920 and 1922) is to be found in Appendix I.

of the Joint Committee on Music Societies lists 1901 as the Date
of Formation. The book of Rules and Bye-Laws claims that the
Society was instituted in 1902. Its first concert took place in
1903 and so did the first General Meeting. So when was the
society established? Perhaps that does not actually matter.

CHAPTER TWO:
THE PERIOD OF HARRY EVANS

The Liverpool Welsh Choral was the fortunate heir of two
traditions, that of Welsh musical activities in 19th century
Liverpool and that of the choral prowess of Wales. The emerging
choir had the good fortune of securing the services of Harry
Evans of Dowlais. Though so young, he had already achieved
much. There had been successes in many eisteddfodau where
he had been consistently praised for his artistic leadership. His
fame had been by no means limited to South Wales. He had
made every effort to acquaint himself with the work of British
choirs everywhere, and had familiarised himself with the choral
works of the great composers.

Born in 1873 in Dowlais, the centre of musical activity in
the South Wales valleys, Harry Evans[1] was the fifth child of ten
in the family of John Evans, known in musical circles as Eos
Myrddin. From his cradle, Harry was given musical training,
by his father in staff notation and by his older sister in sol-
fa. By the age of five, he was able to play hymn-tunes on the
harmonium, and at seven he earned his first fee by appearing
as a soloist on that instrument. His playing was sufficiently
impressive, even in music-mad Dowlais, to enable him to be
appointed organist of the Congregational Chapel. As salary,
the congregation paid for him to have piano lessons with
Edward Lawrence, one of the town's music teachers. Lawrence
trained him in technical studies and formed his taste for Bach,
Beethoven and Mendelssohn. He passed the Associated Board
examinations with honour, but he had no piano of his own on
which to practise. The chapel people came to his rescue again
and arranged a concert for his benefit. The proceeds bought him
his piano. He was everywhere regarded as a prodigy, and some

---

[1] Williams, *Valley of Song*, pp. 105-111; *Y Bywgraffiadur Cymreig hyd 1940, pp. 220-221*

advised sending him to London for a musical education. His father, however, insisted that he should have a good general education first. He won a scholarship to a higher grade school, where he remained till he was 14.

Music was obviously his passion, but his father again decided that he must enter the scholastic profession in order to be sure of a livelihood. He must take up the position he had secured by examination, or else go into the iron-works, as almost every other Dowlais boy did. Consequently, he became, in 1887, a pupil-teacher in Merthyr Tydfil. At the same time, he became organist of Bethania Congregational Church in Dowlais, a position he held for nineteen years until 1906. He was the first organist in the district to give organ recitals, and one of Wales's first recitalists.

He continued to work hard at his scholastic duties, and passed creditably the South Kensington examinations in mathematics, science and art. At the same time, he made steady progress in his music and passed the examination for Associateship of the Royal College of Organists. Shortly afterwards, he achieved the degree of F.R.C.O. He extended his music teaching connection and built up a good clientele in the Merthyr Valley.

In 1893 Harry earned the praise of the press when he became accompanist to the Dowlais Choral Society. This was a group that set great store on winning competitions. Pressure was put on Harry to form a new group, the Dowlais Harmonic. In September 1893, the choir changed its name to Dowlais Philharmonic, and in December, Harry had his first experience of large scale conducting when he led a choir of 200 voices in a performance of Handel's *Samson*, with full orchestra. He devoted his next few years to choral competitions, and in 1897 took the chief prize of £100 in Tonypandy. In 1899 Harry formed a male voice choir of about 100 men, specifically to compete in the Eisteddfod to be held in Liverpool in 1900. For a year, preparation for the Liverpool Eisteddfod[2] took precedence over

[2] Liverpool Record Office, H891 660 8 WAL.

all other activites, for much meticulous work had to be done.

The Male Voice Choir competition came on the Friday afternoon of Eisteddfod week. There were eleven choirs competing, some from England, but most from Wales, and when the results were finally announced, it was Harry Evans's Dowlais group that secured first place, even defeating the well-known Orpheus Choir from Manchester. The adjudication was all that Harry or the choir could have hoped, and, to crown everything, it was the only competition of the week won by competitors from Wales. Harry and his choir, as can be imagined, returned to Dowlais in high spirits.

Harry Evans went on to prove himself exceptionally able in the eisteddfod tradition. In Merthyr, in 1901, he conducted the Eisteddfod Choir of 500 voices in a performance of *Israel in Egypt* with orchestra. Again, in 1902, at the Llanelli Eisteddfod, Harry Evans's mixed choir was successful in competition and took the £200 prize. His Dowlais male voice choir remained as a unit for some years, giving performances of many works, in English and Welsh concert halls, including the Queens Hall in London. Was it any wonder that the talented young conductor should be the choice of the alert Liverpool founders of the Welsh Choral Union?

When he was appointed to his new position in 1902, Harry wasted no time but called for rehearsals to begin at once. There followed the first concert of the choir in April 1903.[3] The performance was judged a great success by choir, audience and music critics. Harry Evans decided that, for the time being, he would retain his home in Dowlais, and travel to Liverpool for the weekly rehearsals. For the first few years, until he became too busy, he also enjoyed appearing from time to time as tenor soloist with other organizations. He had a beautiful pure tenor voice and was much in demand. Eventually, though, as the Liverpool choir became more important to him, he found a new

---

[3] Full report in Chapter I, pp. 44-45.

home in Liverpool, at 26 Princes Avenue. This removal was
made easier for him in that he was also installed as organist and
choir master at Great George Street Congregational Church.
Perhaps too, at that point, he was glad to get away from the
constant preparation for competition in eisteddfodau. He had
deplored the competitive approach to choral singing, though he
had himself certainly benefited from the helpful adjudications
that had been made of his choirs. He appreciated the approach
of the Liverpool Choral Union: to sing in order to make music,
and that of the best.

As already an inspiring, technically accomplished choral
conductor, he was able to introduce hitherto unattained
professional standards into Welsh choralism on Merseyside.
Though his selection of choral works was ultimately to range
widely, he wisely concentrated at first on established works,
and, as the years passed, these remained in the choir's repertoire
and were often repeated, to the satisfaction of his audiences.
During his years with the choir, the *Messiah* was sung six times,
Elijah, four times, *Samson*, twice, and Haydn's *Creation*, once.
Before Harry Evans's time, Bach's works were little known
in Liverpool and generally considered too difficult for most
choral groups. However, in 1907, Harry Evans presented the
St. Matthew Passion for the first time in the city, and repeated
it in 1912. The equally difficult *Mass in B minor* was given in
1910. In his final year, within months of his death in 1914, he
introduced the choir to Brahms's *Requiem*.

Throughout Harry Evans's period in Liverpool, the Choir
found universal favour with audience and critics alike. As one
reads through the music reviews in the press, one rarely finds
an adverse comment. The opening performance of *Samson* was
described as highly finished and thoroughly enjoyable, and
the conducting of Harry Evans as masterly. The fine volume
of tone was remarked upon, as well as the excellent prevision
and intelligent conception of the work. The large audience was

enthusiastic, and a glittering future was predicted for the choir.

This performance was followed by the first *Messiah* concert in December, 1903, on which occasion hundreds were turned reluctantly from the doors, for lack of room. This was not the only occasion on which we read of a performance which had sold out days, if not weeks, in advance. Of this *Messiah*, we learn that it was a sympathetic performance, invested with new beauty. The balance of voices was admirable, and discipline well-nigh perfect. The choir was so trained as to realise and express the precise force of every phrase. In fact, though the soloists were of the highest quality, it was difficult for them to reach the same level of excellence as that of the choir.

Elijah, given in 1904 and 1905, was received with delight by both critics and audience. A dramatic sense was maintained throughout, the voices fresh and the attack perfect. The performance evidently showed the result of conscientious preparation, with attention given to fine shades of expression, a significant sonorous tone, and scrupulous regard to marks of expression.

The Creation by Haydn did not make such demands upon the choir as the Handel and Mendelssohn works, but the critics again found almost nothing to criticise except a slight weakness in the inner parts, but, on the whole, the balance of voices was carefully maintained by Harry Evans, as he auditioned each new candidate for admission to the choir.

The introduction of Bach to Liverpool seems to have presented no stumbling block to the choir. Some Liverpudlians had doubts as to how Liverpool would receive the *St. Matthew Passion*, but eager public interest was shown by the fact that the Philharmonic Hall was sold out ten days before the concert was to take place.

The review of the 1907 performance could hardly have been more complimentary: the work of the choir was favourably compared with that of the London Bach Choir, the only other so far to have ventured to give this work in Britain. In Liverpool, it was said, here was an organization whose tastes inclined towards Bach. The choir and its talented conductor recognised that this solemn music was not an opportunity for display. Their interpretation was appropriately reticent, reverent and devotional. The critic remarked on the resonance, precision of entry, tone gradation, and balance of voices as some of the evening's features. He pointed out that the performance spoke well for the choristers' intelligence and intuitiveness in their preparation. Especially appreciated were the wonderful, restful double chorus that opens the work, and equally the concluding double chorus, an inspired requiem, sung with tranquil, quiet hope and attractive tonal effects. Between the opening and the conclusion came some spirited singing, with short ejaculatory phrases, sung with electrical effect. The chorales were delivered with admirable expression, fervour and breadth. In *The Daily Post* for March 18, 1907, we find the comment: "Few choirs are as prepared or indeed competent of grappling with music of as difficult a character." Though we have no review of the performance of the Bach *B minor Mass* in 1910, the admiration expressed by Elgar for Harry Evans's work during that year would lead us to conclude that the performance of the *Mass* must again have been a glorious occasion.

The Choral's officers were very well pleased musically with the work of Harry Evans and the choir. It was necessary, however, also to achieve financial success.[4] After the *Elijah* concert of 1904, the choir found itself at a loss of £30 on the season. They nevertheless managed to meet their expenses, and to carry over a small balance to the following season's account. For the season of 1904-5, it was resolved to give three concerts, and these, although eminently successful from a musical point of view, again left the Society at the end of the season with a debit balance of £40. The Executive Committee, still having every confidence in the future, determined to make no call on their Guarantors, and their resolve was justified by the fact that,

[4] Introduction to the Programme for LWCU's twenty-first concert, Bach's *Mass in B minor*, 1910.

as a result of the three performances given in 1905-6, the deficit was wiped out and a net surplus of £21 remained. Harry Evans was aware that he must, in choosing works for performance, please both choir members and the prospective audience. He was, at the same time, anxious to include in the choir's repertoire works new to them, and in 1904 and 1905, some of his own compositions were performed: *Hymn of Praise, The Golden Legend* and *Victory of St. Garmon.* These were works originally composed for eisteddfodau in Wales. Perhaps they were less well received than some of the more familiar choral works. It is noteworthy, at any rate, that Harry Evans did not repeat any of these in his remaining ten years with the choir. One further work of his was presented, however, in 1910. It was a cantata written for the Llangollen Eisteddfod of 1908, and was entitled *Dafydd ap Gwilym.* With libretto in English and Welsh by a Welsh minister, it tells the romantic love story of one of the most famous of Welsh poets. The cantata was sung in the original Welsh language, the choir reaching an exceptionally high standard of excellence. The comment was made that the singing had never before approximated more closely to perfection. At the conclusion of this programme, Harry Evans received an enthusiastic ovation from the large and appreciative audience, both for his composition and his conducting of it.

Other works introduced by Harry Evans into the choral repertoire included Edward German (Jones)'s *Welsh Rhapsody,* Coleridge Taylor's *Song of Hiawatha,* Arthur Sullivan's *The Martyr of Antioch, Faust* by Berlioz, and Handel's *Acis and Galatea.* Of these, perhaps, *Hiawatha* aroused most interest and most response from the music critics. It was a comparatively recent composition, having been written between 1898 and 1900. Great demands were made on the choir by the work, and successfully met. Such features as exceptionally difficult intervals and sudden changes of tempo were challenging, but the purity and fulness of tone of the choir were never lost, nor their power of expression and emphasis. The music was admired for its charm, beauty and quaintness. It was a work in which the choir had priority over the soloists, but in which all, including the orchestra, combined, under Harry Evans's controlling leadership, to present a romantic musical treat. There has been confirmation from a former choir member[5] that Coleridge Taylor himself attended the performance and was much pleased.

Exactly when Harry Evans's admiration for Elgar and his music began is difficult to determine. Equally difficult is it to know when the two first met. In spite of the fact that Elgar spent some years in London, the Elgars were too fond of their Worcestershire home in Malvern[6] to leave it for long periods of time. Elgar was intimately connected with the Three Choirs Festival, first established in 1724. Harry Evans himself tells us that he learned much in his early days by coming into contact with and learning from singers, composers and conductors, spending his savings in going about in London, especially, but also in Birmingham and Leeds, to immerse himself in all aspects of music, and that he also frequently attended the Three Choirs Festival. At the latter he had every opportunity for associating with Elgar and becoming his friend.

From the beginning of his time in Liverpool, Evans, and, through him, the choir, took a special interest in all Edward Elgar's choral works. For years Elgar had been working on the composition, *The Dream of Gerontius*, and it was ready for presentation by 1900 at the Birmingham Festival, with the famous German conductor Richter in command. This was not, as it happened, well received by the Birmingham audience, the British regarding Newman's text as doctrinal and Roman Catholic. On the continent it received a wholly successful presentation at the Dusseldorf Festival in 1902, and, following that, choirs in this country began to look at the work with more interest. We do not know whether Harry Evans or any of the

[5] The father of Myfanwy Hughes.

[6] Bonavia, F., in *Lives of the Great Composers*, ed. A. L. Bacharach (London, 193), pp. 219-238.

Choral Committee had had the opportunity to be present at an
earlier performance of the work, but the Choral decided to make
it a part of their repertoire in 1906.

The Liverpool audience looked forward to this event,
and the Philharmonic Hall was packed to capacity to hear,
for the first time in this city, *The Dream of Gerontius*. The
performance was, it is reported, an impressive one, competent
and intelligent. It was pointed out that this oratorio would not
have been possible to "the common order of choral societies",
but that it took a high degree of intelligence to bring out the
mystic and supernatural atmosphere of the work. The very able
conductorship of Mr. Harry Evans was praised for his accurate
reading and intelligent conception, as was the splendid vocalism
of choir and soloists. The second Welsh Choral performance of
the work took place in 1908, to even more enthusiastic acclaim.
One critic wrote that the Welsh choir was among the few in the
country which could do adequate justice to a choral work so
amazingly difficult. The result, he said, bore ample evidence of
devoted labour and enthusiasm spent on rehearsing. The singing
was a worthy tribute to an oratorio that dealt so powerfully and
vividly with the problems of death and the hereafter. It was an
intensely moving and inspiring experience to be present in the
Philharmonic Hall on that night.

The Dream of Gerontius has remained throughout the
century in the repertoire of the Welsh Choral. In the year of its
second performance, the Committee was ready to add to the
choral repertoire another Elgar work, *The Apostles*, composed
in 1903. It is a more austere and complex work than *Gerontius*,
and more difficult to grasp, both for the choir and the audience.
Neither, however, could fail to be impressed by the beauty of
the work, dignified, tender, and solemn, but at the same time,
vivid and graphic. The performance received every praise from
the critics, who noted the thorough understanding shown of
the text. The listeners needed to feel no anxiety as to how the

choir would deal with the difficult chromatic harmonies. There was nothing but praise for Harry Evans again. "By his forceful, watchful and tactful conducting, Mr. Harry Evans once more justified the claim to be thoroughly capable of assimilating the complexities of one of the most elaborate works of musical art, and his wide acquaintance with it was proved in the general result."

The music critic Stainton Taylor tells us that, whether by accident or design, Harry Evans was often absent from the rehearsal following a concert, but that he invariably sent a letter to be read to the choristers, thanking them and expressing his intense pleasure in their performance. We are fortunate in having the letter[7] sent after the performance of *The Apostles*. It reveals a lovable character, who could express his feelings without gush or insincerity. No wonder his choristers, as we are told, almost worshipped him.

Bangor

31st March 1908

Ladies and Gentlemen,

I am deeply grieved at not being able to attend the rehearsal tomorrow night to thank you all for the **triumph** of Saturday last. It is a curious coincidence that on two or three other occasions – momentous landmarks in my musical life – I have not been allowed to meet those who shared with me in those triumphs. But those triumphs which happened some years ago and which were then to me of much importance pale before the fine achievement of the Welsh Choral Union on Saturday. That it should have been done after an existence of only about five years is almost incredible and on Sunday last I had to pinch myself to make certain I had not been dreaming. It was all so beautiful, so pure, so true and so mysteriously grand. There was never any doubt as to the right expression, and the

---

[7] LWCU's First Book of News Clippings.

tone was always pure and chaste. Though I expected a very good performance after the hard work of the rehearsals and the great attention given to it by you all, I never expected such a revelation of beauty in music, and I shall never forget some of the things you did. It proved to me that the whole thing had been carefully stored from rehearsal to rehearsal and that it all came out on Saturday. I really believe that in one or two parts of *Turn you to the Stronghold* and in the *Ascension*, you and I got a strange feeling of exaltation such as happens rarely to anyone. Well, I sincerely hope you will take – one and all – the credit for this, for without your sympathy and whole hearted devotion, I would be helpless. You and I are one and our hearts beat in concord – may it always be so!

To the gentlemen for so bravely and successfully negotiating the pitfalls and for fine dramatic singing, Thanks. To the semi-chorus for their Heavenly Allelujas, Thanks. To the Ladies all together – for inexpressibly beautiful singing throughout and particularly for that most pathetic *Peter wept* episode, Thanks! To you all for responding so eloquently to my demands and for your glorious singing of a noble work, Thanks, Thanks, and again Thanks!!! In conclusion I wish to record my gratitude to the Committee who gave me everything I desired, and last, but certainly not least, to our most excellent accompanist for her immense assistance.

Yours sincerely,

Harry Evans.

Not only was Harry Evans on friendly and intimate terms with Sir Edward Elgar, but also with Professor Granville Bantock, Sir Walford Davies, Sir Hugh Allen, and other musicians[8] of eminence. He was held in high regard by all the musical community, not only for his superb conductorship, but for his general musicianship. We know that, at one point, Harry Evans had co-operated with Elgar in preparing a new edition of Bach's *St. Matthew Passion*. It was natural, therefore, that, at

[8] Programme of December 19, 1914.

the Musical League Festival in 1909 in Liverpool, it was Harry Evans's choir that was entrusted with the choral items. During the Festival, Elgar took the opportunity of publicly praising the choir for its "magnificent work under their great conductor." There is no doubt that Elgar thought very highly indeed of Harry Evans, and that, despite the discrepancy in their ages, their friendship was close and enduring.

The other musical associate who was to figure largely in Harry Evans's life was Granville Bantock. He was only five years older than Harry, but came from a very different background. He was the son of an eminent London gynaecologist who had forbidden him to make music his profession. He therefore joined the Civil Service, but, after he had rejected several lucrative posts, his father relented, and the son began his musical training at the Royal Academy of Music. There he soon became active in organising public performances of his own compositions and those of his contemporaries, towards whom he was always generous. He founded a musical journal, and took up conductorship. In 1906 he succeeded Elgar as professor of music at Birmingham University, a post which Elgar had resigned after only one year's tenure. In the early 1900s Bantock had already become conductor of the New Brighton Orchestra, and transformed it into one that stressed the importance of all-British music concerts and festivals. He was especially interested in the literature of the East, which led him to the composition of *Omar Khayyam*. Naturally, he spent much of his time with his orchestra on Merseyside, and it is no wonder at all that he and Harry Evans, one on each side of the Mersey, met often and became friends.

In March 1909 the Liverpool Welsh Choral Union performed *Omar Khayyam*, Part I. It was a particularly challenging work to prepare, the chorus being divided into 20 parts, 14 of them for male voices. Again this concert brought nothing but praise for the accomplishments of the choir, and above all, it brought a letter from Granville Bantock to Mr. William Evans, President of the Choir, a letter which deserves quotation here.[9]

Liverpool
March 28/09

My dear Evans,

It is altogether beyond my powers to attempt to express the gratitude that I owe to the Welsh Choral Union, and to you personally, for the beautiful rendering you all gave of my work last evening. I cannot recall any performance that moved me so much, and that brought out the subtle lights and shadings with such effective results.

I am almost inclined to believe that I must be half a Welshman (I wish it were so), for the choir seemed to grasp and realise the significance of the Poem and the music to a wonderful degree. The delicate and beautiful phrasing and the clear enunciation, together with such sincerity of expression, made this performance to me a very memorable one that I shall never forget. It will always be a great pleasure for me to recall those vivid flashes that at times seemed almost to illuminate the darkness behind that impenetrable veil, which we must all pass through.

Thanks again and again, my dear friends and comrades, for so magnificent a realisation of my dreams.

I hope it may be my privilege "to meet you and to greet you again" at some future time.

With affectionate greetings and heartfelt sincerity to you all,

Believe me,

Always gratefully yours,

Granville Bantock.

---

[9] LWCU's Archive Collection of Correspondence.

In 1911 Parts II and III of Coleridge-Taylor's *Hiawatha* were performed, equally difficult, and performed to equal acclaim, and in October 1912, the very experimental work by Bantock, *Atalanta in Calydon*, was undertaken. This brought another letter[10] from Harry Evans to be read to the Choir.

26 Princes Avenue,
Liverpool,
October 31st, 1912

Dear Miss Jones,

Will you please accept my sincere thanks, for the splendid devotion and energy, displayed in the preparation of "ATALANTA IN CALYDON". The last couple of months have been far the most strenuous in the history of the Society, and I felt that I was asking a great deal of the Members to sacrifice so many nights for the "Cause". But I am sure we all feel after last night that this unique work is worth the sacrifice.

I have always had unbounded confidence in the Welsh Choral Union, and this confidence has often prompted me to suggest works that many people considered impossible. I am glad to say this confidence has never yet been misplaced, and I need hardly reiterate, that I am proud to be the Conductor of the Liverpool Welsh Choral Union.

The splendid work of the combined choirs last night raises great hopes for the forthcoming performances at Liverpool and Birmingham, and we may all (Manchester, Liverpool and Birkenhead) congratulate ourselves in having last night made *possible* what was considered *impossible* work, as well as helping in the development of the most striking creative mind in modern choral music.

Yours sincerely,

Harry Evans.

---

[10] *Ibid.*

The final work of Granville Bantock performed by the choir had its premiere in February 1914. Again Bantock was experimenting with new ideas. The work was a setting of verses from Ecclesiastes, *Vanity of Vanities*, and was dedicated to the Welsh Choral. In a complete departure from convention, the work was set for four sets of voices, each sub-divided as in an orchestra, so that there were actually singing parts for twelve voices. In fact, Bantock used the voices as if they were an orchestra,[11] for there was no role for a traditional instrumental orchestra in the work. The composer issued strict instructions on the disposition of the choir: 2 rows of sopranos to the left of the conductor, 2 rows of contraltos to the right, 2 rows of mezzo-sopranos directly in front of him, and so forth. The whole would take superb musicianship to produce as the composer envisioned it. The assessment by the music critics was again entirely positive. The choir was congratulated on its intelligent achievement, and Mr. Harry Evans on his thorough understanding of the work, in his being able to draw from the choir such delicate phrasing and beautiful gradations of tone, causing the whole to be wonderfully flexible and elastic. Granville Bantock described it as the finest first performance of any new work in all his experience.

After this great effort, there came in March the concluding concert of the 1913-1914 Welsh Choral season. This was Brahms's *A German Requiem*, an unconventional work, which, in spite of its apparent simplicity, demands the attention of a well-trained and experienced choir. The work had been very infrequently performed up to that time. The days preceding the concert had shown that the conductor was in very indifferent health, and there was much anxiety on the day as to whether he would be able to bear the strain of the trying task before him. Happily, his indomitable will power triumphed, and he was able to direct the concert to its conclusion. We are told that Harry

---

[11] *The Liverpool Courier*, February 16, 1914; *Liverpool Daily Post*, February 16, 1914, Liverpool Record Office, Central Library News Clippings.

Evans conducted this as one inspired. Poignantly and ironically, it was to be his last concert with the Welsh Choral. The critics considered that the performance reached a very high standard indeed. The painstaking and studious attention which had been focused on the preparation by the conductor was plainly reflected in the result. It proved to be one of the most successful performances ever given by the Welsh Choral.

Two days later, on March 30, he conducted, again as one inspired, the Welsh *Cymanfa Ganu* at the Sun Hall, a fitting conclusion to his association with the Welsh people of Liverpool. He had always held that the Welsh stand alone in the glory of their congregational singing,[12] and this was singing at its best. There was still another Liverpool oratorio concert, however, a performance of *Elijah* that Harry Evans conducted for the Philharmonic Society, and even after that, a further public engagement. This took place on May 8, at the Morecambe Festival. Harry Evans conducted the combined choirs in the singing of the *Gloria* section of Bach's *B minor Mass*, a truly glorious end to a conductor's career.

Throughout the final months, Harry Evans's health had given increasing cause for concern. Many thought that he had overstrained his physical strength by allowing himself to take on more and more work. There is no doubt at all that, in the years leading up to 1914, he had gradually assumed responsibility for a vast number of organisations. He was chorus master of the Liverpool Philharmonic Society and conductor of the Liverpool University Choral Society. He was Music Organiser to the University College of North Wales at Bangor, and conductor of the Llandudno Autumn Concerts Society. He was a frequent adjudicator at eisteddfodau in all parts of Wales, and always very much in demand to conduct Welsh singing festivals. In 1914 he had been offered and accepted the conductorship of the North Staffordshire District Choral Society for the 1914-1915 season.

---

[12] Programme for December 19, 1914. p.14.

In 1909 he had conducted the Festival of the Musical League of Great Britain and in 1911 the Festival of the Empire at the Crystal Palace in London. Because of the pressure of work, he had had to give up his post of organist and choir master at Great George Street Congregational Church, and all his engagements as tenor soloist, but he still retained his connections with music in the Liverpool Welsh chapels. Most of all, however, his work with and devotion to the Welsh Choral did not in the least diminish. Indeed, in spite of his health problems, he was looking forward to a visit with his choir to Germany, where, at the invitation of Elgar, the Welsh Choral was scheduled to give a performance of *The Dream of Gerontius*.

For the ailing musician rest and treatment were ordered. All work was stopped and his wife and others ministered to his every want. Sadly, he became progressively worse. An investigation revealed a tumour on the brain. The surgeon, Mr. Thelwall Thomas,[13] performed an operation, but it was not possible to remove the tumour, and recovery was adjudged hopeless. He died on July 23, 1914 leaving a widow and two young sons. He was at the zenith of his career, aged 41.

The funeral[14] took place on July 27, and the burial at Smithdown Road Cemetery. In spite of its taking place in Liverpool rather than in his native Wales, from its nature it could have been happening in the midst of the Merthyr Valley. It was a remarkable demonstration of public sorrow. Thousands flocked to do him honour. There was first a short service at his home, followed by a service in Grove Street Congregational Chapel. Two minister friends took part in this service, at which were sung two of Harry Evans's favourite hymns, *Lead, Kindly Light* and *Mi wn fod fy Mhrynwr yn Fyw*. All the Welsh non-conformist chapels on Merseyside were represented at the

[13] *Y Bywgraffiadur Cymreig 1941-1950* (Llundain, 1970), p. 167.
[14] Collection of Obituaries in LWCU's First Book of Clippings (source unspecified and undated).

service, as they were again at the graveside. Members of the Welsh Choral formed an avenue in the cemetery, through which the cortège passed. A third minister gave the eulogy there, stressing the idea that it is intensity of life that matters and not its length. Obituaries appeared in the English and Welsh press, some of them listing the chief mourners and the societies represented. Twenty-eight wreaths were carried to his grave, including those from Granville Bantock, Edward German, and Mrs. Gladstone. Not long afterwards, members of the Welsh Choral subscribed towards a memorial to Harry Evans, to be erected in the cemetery; his two sons contributing a fund to care for the monument in perpetuity. His elder son, Sir Horace Evans,[15] became surgeon to the Queen, and the younger son, Hubert John, entered the Indian Civil Service and served as a consul in South-East Asia.

Appreciations of the achievements of Harry Evans flooded in, and some were reproduced in the December 1914 programme of the Welsh Choral. These you will find at the end of this chapter. But of course, many humble, less well-known people offered their own tributes. He was very much loved by his choristers who could never speak too highly of him.

What, indeed, were the qualities that made Harry Evans's twelve years with the Welsh Choral so memorable? Obviously his sterling musicianship and unflagging energy, but much more than this. When asked, on one occasion, about his methods, Harry Evans replied:[16]

> I always get my choir to understand the significance of what they perform and the exact position of everything they sing in a work, with the result that they sink individuality into one common whole – are animated by the sole desire faithfully to convey the composer's idea. They are always to regard themselves as actors in the drama, so to speak. I am a great believer in getting choristers to realise their importance as artistes in the performance of works.

[15] *Y Bywgraffiadur Cymreig 1951-1970* (Llundain, 1997), pp. 51-52.
[16] Programme for December 19, 1914.

Other observers pointed out that he took pains with every section of his choir, and relied on rehearsals to obtain the required detail. He insisted on the correct pronunciation and enunciation of the text in English or Welsh or whatever language was being sung. He himself had a quickness of perception in grasping the general character of a work, and a thorough understanding of the particular alliance between the text and a passage of music. He had a strong individuality, and that individuality seemed unconsciously to be transferred to his singers. Audiences noticed the sway he had over the choir, how he seemed to hold them in thrall. He was at all times master of the situation, controlling all the music makers with his graceful gestures. The correspondent of *The Manchester Guardian* wrote that "in the course of twelve years, Mr. Evans developed the choir into one of the greatest choral forces in the United Kingdom."

APPRECIATIONS OF HARRY EVANS

It was a very great shock to me to hear of the great loss the musical world has sustained in the death of Mr. Harry Evans. I had the honour to be associated with him in several important musical matters. I held him and his abilities and qualities in the highest esteem.

Edward Elgar.

* * * *

Evans's death is grievous. It is a great and irreparable loss both to English and Welsh Musical Festivals. Liverpool loses a sure-handed, indefatigable choral conductor, who brought inspiration to his fellows. But the aspect that forces itself most upon me is the loss of an invaluable judge at our Competition Festivals. When penetration such as his conspires with kindliness such as he loved to bestow, a good judge was likely. When these are combined, as they were in his case, with strength and facility of expression, an excellent judge stands complete, and this he was. ... One loves to think of the hundreds of obscure village choralists who will remember him with love and gratitude. He could tell them their faults when they won, and give them encouragement and a working policy when they lost. You will miss him terribly, you who knew and loved him so well. I knew him less, but I would not willingly believe that I loved him less than his nearest friend. He went about from Festival to Festival doing good. And how delightful he was to work with. Perhaps we may hope that his memory will provoke other men to good works, for the Competition movement can ill spare so gifted and amiable a leader.

H. Walford Davies, in a letter to Dr. McNaught.

* * * *

Wales lost one of the ablest and strongest of her musical
personalities when Harry Evans died on July 23. I knew him
well and was greatly attached to him, and I have every reason for
the belief that he was attached to me. We were kindred spirits in
so much of our life-work. He had a fine musical temperament:
there was in it that intensity of emotion so characteristic of
his race. But unlike so many of his compatriots, he was able
to control this inward ferment by a strong intellect. He made
it his servant; he never allowed it to become his master. His
musical sympathies were broad, embracing all the best things in
music from Bach – for whom, like many of us, he had a special
veneration – to Brahms, and the later developments of choral
idiom exemplified in the chief works of Elgar and Bantock. ... He
possessed that peculiar, fascinating magnetism that focussed the
attention of performers and compelled obedience. Conducting
was sheer joy to him. I have seen his great eloquent eyes beam
with anticipation when he left me in the adjudicators' box and
mounted the platform. As an adjudicator at eisteddfodau and
British competitions he was unique. I often sat with him and
admired, if I did not envy, his electric alertness, his power of
seizing all the points of a performance, and duly relating their
importance in the whole scheme of judgment. I have known less
experienced and less vigilant listeners say that Harry Evans was
too casual and too much of an impressionist, simply because
they could not follow the operations of his quick mind. In
adjudicating he was lucid and, before all things, educational. No
one had a keener ear than his for discovering technical faults,
but he never regarded these faults as being all important. The
message of the music, the rhythmic treatment of the phrasing,
and all that makes for fine interpretation were the factors that
counted. Evans was greatly in demand at competition centres
all over the British Isles. If I may say so without in any degree
disparaging other eminent adjudicators, he was becoming, if

he had not already become, the most powerful individual force in the progress of the Competition Festival movement in this country. Why he should be taken at the age of forty-one, just as he was coming into his rightful inheritance, is among the perplexing mysteries of things.

W. G. McNaught

* * * *

It was as a choral conductor, and especially as the conductor of the Liverpool Welsh Choral Union, that he really set the seal upon his fame, and the writer of this memoir has no hesitation in describing him as the greatest of all choral conductors in his time in England. Harry Evans had undeniable genius. He was what we call a "born" conductor, or as the Germans would say, "a conductor by the grace of God". He had a most winning personality, full at once of great mental strength and of a rare genial sympathy. He was full of ideas, which he clung to with the utmost tenacity, but he was always open-minded, nevertheless. As a companion I have only too rarely met his equal, for he was full of the milk of human kindness; his chiefly self-acquired knowledge was of the widest, and he could and would talk with a perennial freshness. He was a man of the rarest qualities, not one of which had been hardened by the rough and tumble of a life well spent, however strenuous it may have been. He was of the small tribe of all men friends and never an enemy. His loss is so great to choral music that its magnitude will only be fully realised as time passes.

Robin H. Legge (*Daily Telegraph*)

* * * *

Many of our musicians have found their way from small and humble beginnings to positions of importance, and not a few could be mentioned who have equalled Harry Evans in his accomplishment as a choir-trainer, and still more as a composer. But it was as a conductor that he achieved exceptional distinction, and though he lived to make the Welsh Choral Union known far beyond the boundaries of Liverpool, it was the opinion of many who knew him that he had by no means reached the summit of his career. For reasons into which it would take us too long to enter, British conductors have hitherto not, as a general rule, been a brilliant success, but Harry Evans was a prominent exception. He had, as a typical Welshman, the fire which is lacking in most Anglo-Saxons, he had also a far wider outlook than most of his countrymen, he was in equal sympathy with choral and orchestral music, and he possessed the genial, sympathetic, enthusiastic temperament that is so essential to a leader of men. Those who were present at the first and only Festival, at Liverpool, of the Musical League, will not soon forget how brilliantly he accomplished the task of conducting a number of complex, difficult new orchestral works by young and ambitious composers, a feat which well deserved the public tribute paid to it by Sir Edward Elgar on that occasion. Combining, as he did, the virtues of a first-rate choir-trainer and a really able conductor, he may without exaggeration be said to have occupied a unique position among British musicians, and, for the present, it seems impossible that his place can be filled.

Mr. Herbert Thompson (*Yorkshire Post*)

* * * *

It is hard to believe that the lovable and generous Harry Evans has passed away from us so suddenly, and I know that I am only one of many who feel this loss as a personal bereavement. There is but little consolation to be derived from the conviction that his memory will endure, while we, his fellow-workers and comrades, are left behind for a little time longer. The place of the departed friend must and will remain always vacant.

He was a brilliant conductor, and was respected by all who sang or played under his beat. He was one of the greatest interpretive musicians that I have ever known, and he was able to infuse his forces with the spirit of the music, and the fire of his own enthusiasm. Under his direction I have heard choral singing attain to heights of expression beyond description. I have never yet met a man who so easily earned and so richly deserved the affection and esteem of all the members of his choir. As an adjudicator at the Musical Competition Festivals, he achieved signal success and the almost impossible task of satisfying audience and competitors alike. His judgment was sure and reliable, his criticisms convincing, and he had the happy gift of kindly speech that cheered the heart of the loser and made the decision appear inevitable.

I shall always cherish his memory, and feel a pride in the knowledge that for many years we held ideas in common, and shared mutual hopes with never a dissentient note to cause a jar in the harmony of our friendship.

Granville Bantock.

CHAPTER THREE:
THE FIRST WORLD WAR

The Welsh Choral's beloved conductor, Harry Evans, died on
July 23, 1914, and his funeral took place on the twenty-seventh.
Eight days later, on August 4, Great Britain was a leading
protagonist in the war called, during that time, The Great War,
but which we know as World War I. Could the Liverpool Welsh
Choral survive under the double blow of war and the loss of the
only conductor it had known since the choir's inception? It was
a problem calling for anxious and careful consideration.

Within a few days, the Executive Committee met to assess
their situation. A heavy programme had been planned for the
1914-1915 season. One project already mentioned was a visit
to Germany at the invitation of Sir Edward Elgar to sing his
oratorio *The Dream of Gerontius*. Another scheme was a visit
to London at the invitation of Sir Henry Wood, who was to
conduct the choir in a work of his own choice, to be performed
later in Liverpool. During the same visit, Mr Evans and the
Welsh Choral would repeat in London their performance of
Bantock's *Vanity of Vanities,* the work dedicated to the choir
by Sir Granville. Both visits, of course, would now have to be
cancelled.

Though the general expectation, in 1914 in Britain, was
that the war would be over by Christmas, it was inevitable that
the numbers of the choir in the immediate future would be
depleted, especially in the male sections, so much so that the
balance of voices might be difficult to maintain. On August 3,
Lord Grey, Britain's Foreign Secretary, had famously observed:
"The lamps are going out all over Europe; we shall not see them
lit again in our lifetime." But members of the LWCU had no
intention of seeing their own lights extinguished. They were
determined that the choir, which had been built up to such an

eminent position during their twelve years under Harry Evans, should not fade into nothingness. It was decided, at any rate, to carry on normally for the time being, if only to honour the work of their departed conductor. They would give a Christmas performance of *The Messiah* in memory of Harry Evans.

The question of who should conduct the Christmas concert naturally was of immediate concern. It was far too soon to consider the appointment of a permanent conductor. It would surely be best to carry on with a series of guest conductors, with the thought that perhaps one of them would impress the Committee and members more than the others, and lead eventually to a permanent appointment.

The Executive Committee of the Welsh Choral was composed of very remarkable men, men who put their considerable talents and energies at the disposal of the choir. There had been exceptional continuity of committee membership since 1902. In 1914 the chief members of the Executive[1] had been leaders since the choir's foundation: Robert Roberts, the President; Richard J. Hughes, the Chairman; R. Vaughan Jones, the Vice-Chairman; John D. Jones, the Honorary Treasurer; and Llew Wynne, the Secretary. In addition, Mme. Maggie Evans had served as chief accompanist throughout the period. There were also on the Committee several promising new members, including Mr. H. Humphreys Jones.

From the foundation of the choir, the Committee had had to make vitally important decisions. It had had to be the guiding force in the choice of conductor, soloists for each concert, and venues for rehearsal and performance, and, with the conductor, had had to select the music for concerts and decide upon appropriate accompanying orchestras or bands. Above all, difficult financial decisions had had to be taken: fees for conductor and soloists, rental payments for practice rooms and instruments, and agreement on such necessary items as

---

[1] Back cover. Programme for December 19, 1914.

CHAPTER THREE: THE FIRST WOLD WAR

choir members' subscriptions and the prices of concert tickets. The officers had made a full accounting for all dispursements to the Annual General Meetings, at which their decisions were endorsed or rejected by democratic vote. Despite the occasional setback, the Choir had come through the twelve years with an admirable, smoothly-operating system of administration.

Rehearsals were resumed in the Autumn of 1914. Mr. John Watcyn of Dowlais,[2] a former pupil of Harry Evans, was invited to conduct the opening concert. In South Wales his reputation as a choral conductor was high. Doubtless, in responding to the invitation, John Watcyn hoped to impress the choir and committee sufficiently to warrant further invitations, and possibly to emerge as Harry Evans's successor. Permanent conductorship of the choir would be a much sought-after post, both from a monetary point of view, and that of prestige.

The soloists for the 1914 *Messiah* were Miss Evans-Booth, Miss Hilda Cragg-James, Mr. John Booth and Mr Herbert Brown. Of these, Mr. Brown was an especial favourite with Liverpool audiences, and had been bass soloist on many occasions under Harry Evans's directorship. The printed programme for December 19, 1914, was an extraordinarily interesting one, in that it included the Welsh Choral Union's Roll of Honour,[3] of 14 tenors and basses serving with the armed services. It also included, surprisingly, a notice that Members of the Choral met for rehearsals every Wednesday evening during the season in the Small Lecture Hall, behind the Library, William Brown Street, at 7:45; and that there were vacancies for good voices. The names of those desirous of joining would be received by the Secretary. This last announcement is puzzling, in that it was the practice of the Welsh Choral to audition any applicants, and that, in 1914, there was no permanent conductor whose function it would be to carry out this procedure.

---

[2] Variously spelled, Watkyn and Watkins. Williams, *Valleys of Song*, p. 189.

[3] Programme for December 19, 1914. p. 9.

The concert was held in the Philharmonic Hall, which was crowded for the performance, the proceeds of which were to be in aid of the Prince of Wales Relief Fund. It was a solemn evening, beginning with the *Dead March* from *Saul*, played in memory of the late conductor. *The Messiah* was, of course, a work the Choir knew very well indeed, having sung it almost every year under the baton of Harry Evans. The critics wrote that this performance showed the guest conductor to have an intimate knowledge of the work, and that it was an eminently sane reading without any sensationalism. The work of the soloists was commended; most outstanding was the singing of Herbert Brown, coupled with which was the finished playing of the trumpet obligato by Mr. A. Hall in *The Trumpet Shall Sound*. Under Mr Watcyn the choir and soloists had shown that the traditional standards of the LWCU were still upheld.

We are fortunate in having a surviving copy of the printed programme of this concert, for it is here that the appreciations of Harry Evans's career first appeared. Harry Evans would, without doubt, have been pleased to be reassured that the traditional Christmas performance of the *Messiah* was being continued, despite wartime restraint. For the next four seasons, this custom was maintained unbroken, the Merseyside audience regarding the annual performance as a permanent feature of music making in Liverpool. During these years, since several different conductors took their places on the podium, choir and audience were able to judge and to come to a decision as to which of these Welsh leaders would be best fitted to succeed Harry Evans.

The 1915 *Messiah* performance was conducted by another South Wales guest conductor, Mr. T. Hopkin Evans[4] of the Neath Valley. Like Mr. Watcyn, Mr. Evans did not attempt any unusual reading, but strove to create a broad, generous and disarming interpretation of the work. Though the time

---

[4] *Y Bywgraffiadur Cymreig 1941-1950*, p. 88.

for choir and conductor to come to understand one another had been limited, it was evident, from the concert result, that a good relationship had been set up, and that Hopkin Evans had placed his individual stamp on the singing. Mr. Evans had evinced studious care throughout, and the plaudits of the large audience were a fine tribute to conductor, choir and orchestra. The soloists were commended on their efforts, and again Mr. Herbert Brown, accompanied as before by Mr. Hall, aroused the audience to a high pitch of enthusiasm.

Performances of *The Messiah* took place in the month of December in 1916, 1917, and 1918. In 1916 the work was conducted by Mr. Vincent Thomas, who had worked with Sir Thomas Beecham. It was noted with admiration that he managed to impart a devotional character to a work that might have been regarded as humdrum and over-familiar. It was a reading that showed choral grandeur and sublimity. There was beautifully impressive singing in some choruses, along with solidity of tone, and Mr. Thomas's wonderful precision added to the success, shown also in his efficient control of the orchestra. One critic commented upon an aspect of the performance that was beyond Mr.Thomas's control. Apparently fog somehow penetrated into the hall, proving no small hardship to the singers.

The December 1918 performance took place a month after the Armistice, and was accepted by the large audience as homage to the new reign of world peace.[5] For the last four years, *The Messiah* text had reflected a certain strain of mockery, but now the old oratorio had become a great thanksgiving hymn of "warfare accomplished". Mr. Hopkin Evans was once more the conductor. There was some criticism of galloping tempi in the early choruses, but only praise for the Passion music, which was arresting in its restraint and its poignant qualities. In spite of the continued depletion of the male sections of the choir, the balance of voices and sureness of pitch were remarked upon as

[5] Treaties of Versailles, St. Germain, Neuilly, Trianon, and Sevres, 1918-1919.

exceptional. The solo work in this performance was less than perfect. The women soloists apparently were both suffering from colds, and the aging tenor, Mr. Ben Davies, was no longer at his best. However, as in every wartime concert, Mr. Herbert Brown's bass singing was superb. But the transcendant feature of the performance was the singing of the Hallelujah Chorus, so impressive that the audience insisted on an encore.

Though all the music criticisms of the Liverpool Welsh Choral Union during the war referred to the depleted sections of the choir, it is obvious that recovery at the war's end must have been sudden and immediate. Numbers exist for 1910, and, at 10-year intervals, to the end of the century:

DATE	SOPRANOS	CONTRALTOS	TENORS	BASSES	TOTAL
1910	75	75	57	65	272
1920	119	90	54	94	357
1930	98	67	48	64	277
1940	82	71	54	65	272

How Welsh the choir remained is interesting to speculate. A present choir member[6] has looked into the names of members for 1910. The choir then included 64 of the name of Jones, 28 with the surname Williams, 18 Robertses, 16 Hugheses, 13 Davieses, and 10 Edwardses, a total of 149, or more than half the choir. Presumably the claim to Welsh descent was at that time still a prerequisite for joining the choir.

It is a pity that, so far as is known, there is no photograph of the choir before 1920, and no mention of one having been taken. We can, however, to some extent, picture their appearance. As in most choirs of the time, the women wore long, loose white frocks. Whether there were any additional accessories we do not know. In choirs in Wales, back in the 1890s, the women wore sashes[7] during eisteddfodic competitions, one colour for

[6] Rhiannon Liddell, former Chairman of the Welsh Choral.

[7] Williams, *Valleys of Song*, p. 100.

sopranos and another for altos. In 1897, the year of Victoria's sixtieth Jubilee, the women choristers of one choir went so far as to wear sashes with colours of the British flag. The men invariably wore evening dress, in choirs in Wales and in England, though at one point the LWCU added white silk scarves.

It is regrettable that, rather than call the period of 1914-1918 the War Years, there is not some happier appellation, something equivalent to the word 'Inter-regnum' for 'Between Two Reigns'. For the Choral Union it was primarily the period between two Evanses as conductors, Harry and Hopkin. In 1919 the decision was made to offer Hopkin Evans the post of permanent conductor, and it was the choir's good fortune that he was pleased to accept.

CHAPTER FOUR:
THE PERIOD OF T. HOPKIN EVANS

"Imitation", says an ancient adage, "is the sincerest form of flattery." A 19th century dictionary expresses it somewhat differently: "Imitation is the copying of an admired model".

When, in 1919, the Executive Committee decided it was once again time to appoint a permanent conductor for the Welsh Choral, it is clear that the committee was actually seeking someone who was as like as possible to Harry Evans, their model. Since his death, several conductors had appeared as guest conductors of the depleted choir in their annual *Messiah* performances. In 1915 and again in 1918, that conductor had been Thomas Hopkin Evans, whose work had pleased both Choir and audience.

Some very striking similarities exist between the background of Harry Evans and that of his namesake. Both were born in the 1870s in neighbouring South Wales valleys, at a time when the chief choral activity in Wales was centred in those valleys. While Harry Evans had been born in Merthyr Vale in 1873, Hopkin Evans was born in 1879, in Resolven, in the Vale of Neath. Both areas were centres of the mining industry, Merthyr more so than the Neath Valley. Both boys were born into musical families, and showed exceptional talent from a very early age. In both cases, their first music teachers were their fathers. Harry Evans, as we know, had become proficient on the harmonium and piano. Hopkin as a youngster[1] learned to play the flute and was a member of the village band. He took lessons on piano and organ, and showed a keen interest in composition. Like most ambitious young Welsh boys, Hopkin Evans entered competitions at national and local eisteddfodau, and often carried off the first prize, especially in composition.

---

[1] *Y Bywgraffiadur Cymreig 1941-1950*, p. 88.

Hopkin Evans began his advanced musical education under Professor David Evans[2] (1874-1948) at Cardiff University, and later studied in Birmingham and in London. While still in his teens, he had become organist of the Presbyterian Church, London Road, Neath. Before he turned twenty, he had organized and conducted the Neath Choral Society, a choir that gave, under him, many concerts, including the singing or performing of choral and orchestral works that brought him and the choir to favourable notice. In 1911, at the Crystal Palace in London, he accompanied the Welsh National Choir at the Festival of Empire. Since the overall conductorship of this festival was in the hands of Harry Evans, we can assume that Hopkin Evans and Harry Evans spent time in each other's company. In the years following, it was Hopkin Evans who organised the South Wales Music Festivals,[3] which took place in 1913, in 1914, and again towards the end of the war, in 1918 and 1919. The Festival of 1913 included an adventurous production of Bantock's *Omar Khayyam*, a work not previously heard in Wales, though it had been performed by the Liverpool Welsh Choral under Harry Evans. Many had prognosticated disaster, but the result was a brilliant success, and showed what Hopkin Evans might do to advance music culture in the land of his birth.

In December 1918, the Welsh Choral gave their usual *Messiah* performance, and dedicated it to the memory of Harry Evans. Details of this concert are given in Chapter III of this memoir. It is significant that it was Hopkin Evans who was selected to conduct this important concert. Former members of the choir, absent during the war, flocked back, and large numbers of singers put in applications to be auditioned for the choir. A consequence of this renewed interest was the appointment of Hopkin Evans to the vacant position of permanent conductor of the revitalised choir, the conductorship to begin with the

[2] Professor and guide to many young men who later came to prominence.

[3] *Who Was Who, 1929-1940* (London, 1941).

Hopkin Evans
Principal Conductor of the Liverpool Welsh Choral Union
1919 - 1940

1919-1920 season. The prospectus announced three concerts for the season: on November 15, 1919, Scenes from *The Song of Hiawatha*, followed by other miscellaneous selections; on December 20, 1919, the annual performance of *The Messiah*; and on Saturday, March 13, 1920, Mendelssohn's *Elijah*. Well-known soloists were engaged for each concert, and the programmes printed the names of Band and Chorus, 350 performers in all - or so the programme stated. In fact, if one goes to the trouble of counting the names, it is obvious that 350 is an under-statement. In the programme[4] are the names of 53 bandsmen, 120 Sopranos, 90 Contraltos, 54 Tenors and 94 Basses, and in addition, 12 soloists, over 50 Honorary Members and 100 Guarantors. As in previous programmes, there is a notice that there are vacancies for good male voices, and that the names of those desirous of joining will be received by the Secretaries. What had happened to the limit of 300 singers originally prescribed in the Rules of 1902? In 1919, the Liverpool Welsh Choral Union was, without doubt, in a flourishing condition.

Hopkin Evans's period with the Welsh Choral coincides almost exactly with that of the years between the end of World War I and the outbreak of World War II. While, in 1919, Hopkin Evans was signing his contract with the Welsh Choral, the leaders of Europe and America were engaged in completing and signing the treaties[5] that made up the Peace of Versailles. The 1920s and 1930s were years of comparative peace in Britain. The chief concerns here were those of the economy. Unwise treaty provisions led in this country to unemployment and poverty, and it was not until the Second World War loomed that war industries and the building of munitions brought increased employment and a measure of security to Britain's industrial regions. It was a depressing time for the ordinary man. Music was, for many, one of the uplifting influences of an otherwise uninspiring era. In Liverpool, participation in the singing or

[4] Philharmonic Hall, Liverpool. Saturday Evening, November 15, 1919.

[5] Versailles, St. Germain, Neuilly, Trianon and Sevres.

enjoyment of singing in such organizations as the Philharmonic Choir and the Welsh Choral, played an important role in the daily lives of its inhabitants.

Though documentation for the first forty years of the choir's existence is difficult to find, it is certain that, throughout the period, the Welsh Choral was guided by an Executive Committee of very exceptional quality. If we postulate that their activities followed similar patterns to those of post-1940, their work, while absorbing and varied, was also demanding and exacting.

Except for the period of the Great War, the Choral gave three to five concerts a year, and there was much planning to do for each. With the advice of the conductor, the works to be given were selected, and music purchased or rented. The dates and venues for each concert had to be arranged, and, if required, an orchestra engaged. The Welsh Choral sang in the Philharmonic Hall up to 1933 when there was a disastrous fire,[6] caused, it was thought, by careless workmen. It reduced the hall to ashes. The Central Hall on Renshaw Street was then the choir's venue until 1938, after which they were able to return for their Christmas concert to a new Philharmonic Hall. Its stark exterior appalled some concert-goers, but the lush interior and near perfect acoustics delighted everyone who attended a performance there.

Soloists had to be chosen for each performance, usually four, either from among singers known personally to committee members or through a music agency such as Ibbs and Tillett in London. The prices for tickets had to be agreed. These prices might perhaps be of interest to readers. In 1911-1912, Boxes for six cost 35/- or 30/-, Stalls, 6/- or 4/6, Gallery, 3/- or 2/-. By 1939 the price of Boxes had, surprisingly been reduced to 27/-, while the Stalls had been lowered to 4/6 or 3/6, but the Balconies had been raised to 3/6 or 3/-, with 2/6 for standing room. An

---

[6] Taylor, *Two Centuries of Music,* page. 22.

interesting change of nomenclature had also taken place. The
Gallery had become a Balcony, later to change again into the
Upper and Rear Circle.

Apart from the work involved in concert planning and the
financing of each project, there was the routine work of the
Executive Committee: Rules and Regulations for the Choir to
be made or revised, matters of attendance at rehearsals to record,
discipline during rehearsals and concerts to be emphasised, and
subscriptions from members to be collected. Many decisions, of
course, were taken finally in the Annual General Meeting, which
was meticulously prepared by the Committee. As a general rule,
the Executive Committee would meet once a month, but often
an emergency arose, making an exceptional meeting necessary.

The remarkable thing is that so many members of the
original Committee served so long and so faithfully. Mr. Robert
Roberts, who served as Chairman in 1902, became President
by 1911, and was still in that position in 1930-1931.[7] Mr. Llew
Wynne, elected Hon. Secretary in 1902, served until the 1920s.
Mr. J. D. Jones, Treasurer in 1902, served equally long, and then
became one of the Vice-Presidents. Mr. Humphrey Lloyd, who
was Vice-Chairman in 1902, was still on the Committee in 1912.
Mme. Maggie Evans, accompanist in 1902, remained in that
post into the 1920s, when she was replaced by Miss Millicent
Richards. William George, the Librarian, served through to the
1930s. Mr. R. Vaughan Jones, who was on the 1902 Committee,
was by 1930-1931, the Chairman. A vitally important Choral
member too was Mr. Tom Lloyd, who, when necessary, served
as Deputy Conductor.

A well-known Liverpudlian, Mr. H. Humphreys Jones,
had joined the Choral as a singing member in 1903. In 1910
he was elected to the Executive Committee; by 1919, he was
Vice-Chairman, and remained in that position until he became
President of the Society in 1934. He served as President, highly
honoured, until his death when he was in his nineties.

[7] Programme for Saturday, March 21, 1931, p. 11.

The Liverpool Welsh Choral Union at the Queen's Hall, London, 1923
T. Hopkin Evans conducting

The Welsh Choral has been happy in having as an active, and later, an honorary member, Miss Eileen Vaughan. In June 2005, she celebrated her one hundredth birthday. Until her death in January 2006, she retained an active interest in the society, and, what is more, a retentive memory and a delight in talking about the early days of her participation in the Choral. She became a member in 1930 at the age of 25. Having had from childhood an interest in music, she wondered, on her arrival in Liverpool, whether there might be a choir that she could join. Apparently her sister worked in the Central Library, and she reported to our Miss Vaughan that she had, on Wednesday evenings, heard the sound of singing emerging from the Little Picton Hall behind the library, sounds that indicated the existence of an able singing group. Eileen Vaughan therefore made enquiries, and discovered that the group was, of course, the Welsh Choral. As a person of Welsh ancestry she could at least qualify on that score. Could she pass the audition held by the conductor, Hopkin Evans? She admitted that it was an ordeal, but at its conclusion Mr. Evans said, "Well, your voice isn't a big one, but it is true, and it is evident that you can read music. I shall be glad to have you in the choir as a contralto." From that time on, Miss Vaughan became an active member of the choir, enjoying rehearsals and performances, and eventually serving as Treasurer and in other capacities over many years. It is she who was able to supply a photograph of the Welsh Choral as it was in the early 1930's. The hall shown is the old Philharmonic Hall, where the fire, previously mentioned, happened in 1933.

Though no official Welsh Choral records from this inter-war period have survived, there are in the archives some concert programmes, and the Liverpool Record Office[8] is able to provide micro-film copies of press music critiques of the period. Except for a photo-copy of the programme for November 15, 1919, none from Hopkin Evans's period exists for the years before 1928.

[8] Central Library, William Brown Street.

It is recorded elsewhere, however, that on several occasions Hopkin Evans conducted the choir away from its home ground. In 1923 he took the choir to London[9] to perform Holbrooke's *Dramatic Choral Symphony*, a work that he later repeated here in Liverpool.

In general, early concerts under Hopkin Evans's direction consisted of works already familiar to those who had been members of the Welsh Choral under Harry Evans. As had remained the Christmas custom since the war period, *The Messiah* was presented on December 15, 1928. The hall was full to overflowing on that occasion, with many Welsh 'fans' coming from as far away as Anglesey. It was, the critics judged, an outstandingly good performance; the chorus was in fine form with its sonority of tone and cleanness of attack. At times dramatic and impressive, at others appropriately moving and inspiring, the choir received its usual enthusiastic acceptance by the audience. The principals were well chosen, Horace Stevens, the bass, especially selected for commendation. The playing of the orchestra was less reliable, though the trumpet part in *The Trumpet Shall Sound* was flawlessly rendered by Mr. C. Britles. Hopkin Evans was masterful in his control and was able to draw an intelligent response from all his forces.

Not every concert received unqualified commendation. In March 1931, the Choral risked presenting Bach's *B minor Mass*. The response of the critics was mixed. The *Mass* had not been performed for twenty years by the choir, so that obviously many in the choir would not previously have been acquainted with Bach's great work. The Choir's approach was adjudged to be less assured than in the singing of more familiar Handel works. The choristers tended to sing in too staccato a way, and not to appreciate the elaborate sweep of the work, though the singing did gather assurance in the latter part of the *Mass*. The performance, however, was not helped by the fact that the

---

[9] Taylor, *Two Centuries of Music in Liverpool*, p. 47.

A Welsh Night at the old Philharmonic Hall, 1933
with the Liverpool Welsh Choral Union and H.M. Welsh Guards
T. Hopkin Evans conducting.

orchestra was underweight and the inner parts submerged. The soloists retrieved the balance somewhat with their professional expertise, and Dr Hopkin Evans conducted throughout with dignity and restraint.

March 1934 brought a well received concert. It is obvious that the choir was in excellent form. *The Daily Post* critic was most impressed with the performance of the Verdi *Requiem*, and said, "Vocally this was the best performance I can remember." Dr. Hopkin Evans managed to secure an impressive and gripping rendering without its being blatant. There was no unnecessary striving, and the result was a performance that showed real eloquence. There was a fine range of colouring and expression, and, though the *Sanctus* could not be called perfect, the closing pages, it was noted, were especially beautiful, Isobel Baillie taking the soprano solos. The remaining artists were also praised for their attractive and earnest singing.

In November 1936, a performance of *Elijah* took place, dominated, apparently, by the bass singing of Mr. Horace Stevens. This was announced to be his last appearance before retirement. It seemed that the opening of the oratorio "had not gone above mere efficiency", but with Mr. Stevens's upbraiding of Ahab, the whole company was galvanised, and from then on the programme was one of inspired singing "as good as any oratorio singing Liverpool is likely to hear for years." It was passionate singing, telling a grand story. The other soloists all sang well, and Dr. Evans had probably never conducted better or been so well rewarded by his choir.

Apart from the works already discussed, in his twenty years with the Welsh Choral, Hopkin Evans conducted performances[10] of *Gerontius, The Apostles, King Olaf, The Banner of St. George* (all by Elgar); *Omar Khayyam* (Bantock); *The Choral Symphony, The Mass in D* (Beethoven); *The Passion according to St. Matthew* (Bach), *The Choral Symphony* (Holbrooke);

[10] Performances listed in *The Times* Obituary on T. Hopkin Evans. (undated).

The Sea Symphony (Vaughan-Williams); *The Mass of Life, Sea Drift* (Delius); *Requiem* (Mozart); *The Veil* (Cowen); *Prince Igor* (Borodin); *Requiem, Song of Destiny* (Berlioz); *Pagliacci* (Leoncavallo); *Cavalleria Rusticana* (Mascagni); and the oratorios of Handel, Mendelssohn and Haydn. He was also held in high regard for his purely orchestral conducting.

As a youth, Hopkin Evans had competed and then adjudicated in Welsh eisteddfodau, and this activity he carried on almost without a break. His fame also spread to America.[11] In 1927 he toured the United States as conductor, adjudicator and lecturer. In 1934 he was engaged to conduct the song festival in Cleveland, Ohio.[12] Hopkin Evans travelled to Palestine, lecturing at the Jerusalem Conservatoire, and he broadcast in Syria and Egypt. He served as conductor-in-chief for the Harlech Castle Music Festival in 1926, 1927, 1928 and 1933, and was one of the conductors at the King's Command Jubilee Concert at the Albert Hall in London in 1935. With regard to the National Eisteddfodau in this country, he was music adviser and chief conductor in Birkenhead, 1917, Neath, 1918, Liverpool, 1929, Wrexham, 1933, and Denbigh, 1939. Of these, for the Liverpool Welsh Choral, naturally the Liverpool Eisteddfod was the most important.

The Eisteddfod Choir for the Liverpool Eisteddddfod may not have been identical with the Liverpool Welsh Choral Union, but one may be sure that there were few members of the Welsh Choral who would not also volunteer to sing in the Eisteddfod Choir. The choir played a large part in the Eisteddfod proceedings. *The Liverpool Daily Post* correspondents covered all the six days of the Eisteddfod very thoroughly indeed.[13] On some days, as many as four broadsheet pages were devoted

[11] *Who Was Who, 1929-1940.*
[12] An assertion found in several obituaries and in *Who Was Who, 1929-1940* is mistaken. It is stated that he was an adjudicator and conductor at an eisteddfod held in the New York World's Fair in 1939. There was no such eisteddfod. The present writer was a resident of New York at the time, and involved in Welsh musical affairs.
[13] To be found on Micro-film in Liverpool's Record Room, Central Library.

exclusively to articles about aspects of the Eisteddfod, results of all the competitions, and photographs of activity on the platform and in the grounds.

Monday was the day of brass bands, with the children's concert in the evening. Tuesday was the day of the Crowning of the Bard, Caradoc Pritchard. The evening concert, in a rain-drenched Sefton Park, was a performance of Handel's *Israel in Egypt*, Hopkin Evans conducting. Particularly selected for praise was the chording of the short 8-part choruses, not easy to perform with such a large volunteer group.

On the Wednesday of the Eisteddfod came the Chief Choral competition, for which Hopkin Evans was one of the adjudicators. Thursday was, for years, the day of the Chairing, and was, in addition, the day when Lloyd George would be present to deliver the President's speech of the day. An audience of over 10,000 attended in 1929 to hear him. The evening brought a variety concert, in which the choir participated, but which met with criticism for not including more typically Welsh music.

On Friday evening came another opportunity for the Eisteddfod Choir, the singing of *Faust* by Berlioz. Though no real fault could be found in the performance of this work, there was adverse criticism on the choice of the work for an eisteddfod concert: so delicately sung were some passages that they could not be heard because of the hammering of rain on the pavilion roof. On Saturday, the Eisteddfod concluded with the Male Voice Choir competition. Again the competition piece, *Cataract*, by Harry Evans was adjudged to be an unsuitable work for the occasion. It had been chosen to honour the Welsh Choral's first conductor, but it was thought to be rather old-fashioned, calling for and receiving too much bombast, and not enough precision and detail in the more lyrical passages. Harry Evans would have been disappointed. However, the evening performance, another Eisteddfod Choir concert under Hopkin Evans's direction, would have surely gained his approval.

Presentations were made to Dr. Evans, Mr. Tom Lloyd, and Miss Millicent Richards, the accompanist, "to whose labours the choral work of the Eisteddfod owed so much."

The resemblance of Hopkin Evans's background to that of Harry Evans has already been noted. As time passed, the similarity heightened. Both were dynamic choir-trainers and conductors, equally energetic in fostering modern British music. As Harry Evans had introduced the works of two modern choral composers, Elgar and Bantock, to Liverpool audiences, Hopkin Evans did the same service for Frederick Delius. While music director and choral conductor for the Wrexham National Eisteddfod in 1933, he prepared and conducted the Eisteddfod Choir in a performance of Delius's *Mass of Life*. In the September 1933 issue of *Y Cerddor*, W. Albert Williams, an organist and composer from Liverpool, has this to say of the event:

> My most vivid impression of that memorable week at the Wrexham Eisteddfod is of the astonishing success of the performance of *A Mass of Life* by Delius. The performance proves what can be done when the right spirit of determination and enthusiasm is infused into the venture.
>
> Dr. Hopkin Evans has enhanced his reputation as a choral conductor to a degree far beyond the limit of his past achievements. To attempt such a stupendous undertaking with a choir of local singers, utterly devoid of any choral experience in the exacting technique and style of Delius, demanded qualities of faith, confidence and perseverance to an extent which few men would care to assume. Yet Dr. Evans's faith was fulfilled, his confidence justified, and his perseverance richly rewarded. *A Mass of Life* was successfully performed and reflected enduring credit upon all who accepted the responsibilities which its presentation entailed.

News of the performance reached the blind and paralysed Delius, who wrote Dr. Evans a letter of thanks. He said:

The Liverpool Welsh Choral Union at the new Philharmonic Hall in 1938
T. Hopkin Evans conducting.

I have just heard from Norman Cameron what a wonderful
performance you gave of my *Mass of Life*. How I regret I
was not able to hear it. Let me thank you from the bottom
of my heart for the loving care with which you prepared the
performance and for the glorious final achievement.

Hopkin Evans was a leader in Welsh and English musical
life for many years, a man of enterprise and vision. After his
Delius performance, his fame was even further enhanced. The
Delius Society honoured him by making him a Vice-President,
and the many invitations showered upon him, to conduct and
to adjudicate, increased it yet further. An Honorary Doctorate
from Oxford was awarded him. Not only could he look back
upon a successful career as conductor and adjudicator, but he
also had a number of compositions to his credit, among which
were: *A Cymric Suite, A Brythonic Overture, Three Preludes on
Welsh Hymn-tunes for Orchestra;* for choirs and orchestra were
two works: *Kynon* and *Psalm to the Earth;* and many songs for
solo voice, anthems, part-songs, and piano pieces.

By the late 1930s Hopkin Evans, again like his predecessor,
had assumed more and more responsibilities, and, no doubt,
overstrained his physical strength, despite having a very
competent deputy in Sam Evans, who did all he could to lessen
the strain. Hopkin Evans was fortunate in enjoying a happy
domestic life in his Liverpool home, with his wife, Adelina
Powell, and his two sons, who by 1939 had become seriously
worried about his health. In early 1940, his doctor insisted that,
after the *Elijah* performance in March, he should go to Wales
for a holiday. It was a performance of Berlioz's *Faust* that
had been announced in the Prospectus, and it may be Hopkin
Evans's increasing ill-health that was responsible for the switch
of programme to the old favourite, *Elijah*. On that occasion,
the last oratorio concert to be conducted by Dr. Evans, the
performance was judged to be a thoughtful reading. There were
moments of dignity and impressiveness, firmness, balance and

solidarity of tone. The chosen soloists, though not altogether an effective quartet, it was thought, all sang wonderfully well individually.

Hopkin Evans, as instructed, went for a Welsh holiday, but he could not resist invitations to conduct singing festivals at that Easter time, and he accepted engagements for Llangranog on Good Friday and Ammanford on Easter Sunday.[14] He fulfilled the Llangranog engagement, but, feeling seriously unwell, he then returned to the home of his brother, in Neath. Realising the severity of his illness, his Neath family summoned his wife from Porthcawl, where she had been visiting her parents. She arrived in time to see her husband and to exchange some words with him, but sadly, he drifted into unconsciousness and died later that same evening. It was March 23, 1940.

On Easter Sunday a memorial service was held in Ammanford, where he had been expected to conduct their Cymanfa, and his death was commemorated at services throughout Wales and, of course, in Liverpool. The funeral was held in the Neath Valley, in his native Resolven.

Whether many of the Choral members attended the funeral is not known. On Sunday, May 5, 1940, however, a Memorial Service for Dr. Evans was held in the Catherine Street English Presbyterian Church in Liverpool. This service was arranged by the Liverpool Welsh Choral Union - "In memory of a beloved Conductor for over twenty years". Two years later, at a concert that took place on the anniversary of Dr. Hopkins's death, the Liverpool Welsh Choral Union, under Dr. Malcolm Sargent's baton, gave a performance of Verdi's *Requiem*, and the choir had an opportunity to pay its own tribute to their cherished conductor:

---

[14] Obituary, Monday, March 25, 1940, *Liverpool Daily Post.*

The Liverpool Welsh Choral Union at the Philharmonic Hall, post 1938

The LATE THOMAS HOPKIN EVANS
a TRIBUTE by Mr. H. Humphreys Jones
Liverpool Welsh Choral President

The irreparable loss which music generally, and Welsh music in particular, sustained by the death of Thomas Hopkin Evans has already been publicly acknowledged. It is our desire here today to pay personal tribute to his memory.

That he was our Conductor for an unbroken period of 20 years is sufficient testimony to the value we placed upon his services, and words themselves do not express the bond of friendship between Choir and Conductor which mellowed and ripened into affection during those years. This was the natural outcome of his many qualities, none of which he spared in his efforts to establish the Choir in the foremost rank of British Choral Societies, which under his direction it undoubtedly achieved.

The "Welsh Choral" was his particular vanity. To it he devoted the skilful guidance and judgment which he possessed and with which he mingled a cheerfulness and humour which made our rehearsals a pleasure and our concerts a real joy. He was no less wanting in his exertions to maintain a high standard of repertoire and to perfect the quality of our performance.

The outbreak of the war put a suspension (happily only temporary) on public concert-giving, and our performance of Bach's *Mass in B minor,* then in course of preparation, had to be abandoned. Bitterly disappointed at the enforced interruption and convinced that music had a distinctive part to play in war-time, he concentrated his energies on rectifying the position by arranging for a performance of *Elijah* in March, 1940, and those who heard it adjudged this concert to be one of his finest with the Welsh Choral; it was also his last. He had overtaxed his own strength and within the week he had passed to the fuller life.

One of his best loved works, which it always gave him particular pleasure to produce, was Verdi's *Requiem,* and for this reason we are dedicating today's performance to his memory.

He was also very fond of Elgar, whose *Nimrod* variation from the *Enigma* will be played at the opening of this afternoon's concert; the fervent emotional spirit embodied in this short piece would seem to be a fitting portrayal of the life and character of the one whose memory we revere today.

CHAPTER FIVE:
THE SECOND WORLD WAR

By the time of Hopkin Evans's death, England had been at war with Germany for six months, and naturally, what concerned England was of vital concern to Liverpool, as the prime Atlantic port. There was, however, no mention of war in the Welsh Choral Prospectus for 1939-1940, nor, indeed, in *The Messiah* programme of December 16, 1939, or the *Elijah* programme for March 16, 1940, Hopkin Evans's final concert with his choir. One might almost think there was a conspiracy to ignore facts that were unpalatable, or any suggestion that daily life was fundamentally altered.

In 1937 the Civil Defence Services[1] for the Merseyside area had been established, and in 1938 came the detailed planning of the evacuation of the city. A special committee was set up on "Procedures for Civilian Evacuation",[2] which issued a report in July 1938. Authorities believed that war with Germany would lead to massive bombing of industrial areas throughout Britain, that up to 600,000 people in the whole of Britain would be killed and over twice that number injured. Civilians were issued with gas masks, identity cards and ration books. All was ready by August 1939, to deal with an enemy attack.

On September 3, 1939, with 1103 civilian passengers on board, the S.S.Athenia[3] was sunk, the first casualty in the War of the Atlantic. The ship had sailed from Liverpool the day before and was the victim of an attack by a German U-Boat. On the same day, a Sunday, 95,000 children were evacuated from Merseyside, many of them travelling by train from Birkenhead

---

[1] Chambré Hardman Archive, *Liverpool Blitz Time*, http://www.mersey-gateway.org/server.php?show=ConWeb.1201 [accessed 26/05/2007]

[2] Boyce, Joan, *Pillowslips and Gasmasks* (Birkenhead, 1989) p.5.

[3] *Ocean Waves, Merchant Navy Heritage, Merchant Navies*, http://scholar.google.com/scholar?q=www.+ocean+waves+merchant+navy+heritage+merchant+navies&hl=en&um=1&oi=scholart [accessed 26/05/2007].

to North Wales. Before Christmas, however, two-thirds of these had returned to their homes, not to leave again until conditions became worse in late 1940, and intolerable in the Spring of 1941.

To what extent the war conditions affected members of the Welsh Choral in late 1939 and early 1940 we do not know. But the Executive Committee of the Choral was not slow to respond to the emergency that the death of its conductor, Hopkin Evans, had brought upon them when he died suddenly in March, 1940. On March 28, 1940 the Committee, sixteen members being present, met at the Royal Institution on Colquit Street, under the Chairmanship of Mr. J. R. Jones. The atmosphere was sombre. Their first action was naturally to pay tribute to Dr. Evans. They stood for a moment of silence, and then unanimously supported a motion that his work must be carried on as a monument to him. It was natural that, in the subsequent discussion, reference should be made to the death of Harry Evans in 1914, and of how it was then thought best that concerts should, for the duration of the war, carry on with Guest Conductors. The same was seen to be the situation now in 1940, particularly as there was no conductor in Wales who was sufficiently outstanding to be recognised as an obvious successor to Hopkin Evans. Perhaps, too, the Committee would rightly hesitate to persuade any conductor to leave the somewhat more peaceful land of Wales, for residence in a city expecting devastation at any moment. Important decisions were made at the March 28 meeting,[4] and confirmed at a second meeting a fortnight later. Granville Bantock and Dr. David de Lloyd of Aberystwyth would be asked for advice. The choir, for the 1940-1941 season, would carry on, as far as possible, with plans already formulated: Bach's *B Minor Mass, The Messiah,* and *The Creation* were to be the works for the coming season, and it was decided that a

---

[4] For much of the Choral information in this and subsequent chapters, I am indebted to the carefully inscribed minutes of successive Honorary Secretaries, of whom Mr. E. H. Edwards is the first. The entries were a delight to read.

conductor of repute, such as Sir Henry Wood, would be invited to conduct the Bach work. It was hoped that the presence of such an eminent musician would ensure a packed house. Mr. Tom Lloyd, who had at Dr. Evans's request, acted as conductor for some rehearsals during the previous season, was now to be appointed the official Chorus Master.

With the account of the March 28, 1940 meeting of the Executive, the first surviving book of Minutes begins. It is interesting that, during the next five years, the word "war" does not appear at all in any account. There seems, indeed, to have been a decided reluctance to acknowledge the existence of war, or to concede anything to its demands. In later entries in the Minutes, the nearest we come to its mention is the use of phrases such as "Because of difficult times", "In view of the international situation", and "In these trying days".

The chief task of the committee meetings of April and May, 1940, was the choice and appointment of conductors and soloists for concerts of the coming season. Sir Henry Wood accepted for the first concert "on terms considered to be very reasonable"; William Rees of Manchester was to conduct *The Messiah*, and Dr. Malcolm Sargent was to be approached to conduct *The Creation*. It was an age of highly accomplished singers of oratorio. Among those booked for the season were Isobel Baillie, Joan Hammond, Joan Cross, Gladys Ripley, Astra Desmond and Nancy Evans, sopranos and contraltos; Heddle Nash, David Lloyd, Trevor Jones, Norman Walker, Roderick Lloyd, and Tom Williams, tenors and basses.

Performances by the Welsh Choral had, from the beginning, taken place in the Philharmonic Hall, with orchestra, but, in the time of Harry Evans, the names of orchestral players were not printed in the concert programmes, though we find there the names of committee members, honorary members, and choral singers fully listed, as well as those of the conductor and soloists.

The concert programme of December, 1914, allotted a page to the orchestra, and members' names were given individually, with the "principal" of each string section set apart. The orchestra as yet had no name, however. This format was the one followed for the next twenty-five years. By the time of Hopkin Evans's final concert on March 16, 1940, the orchestra consisted of forty-six listed players, and, though it still had no official name, it seems to have been referred to under the name of its Leader, Louis Cohen.

With the advent of Malcolm Sargent as guest conductor in April, 1941, a change could be seen. The orchestra had been reorganised and had grown in size to fifty-eight. It was now the Liverpool Philharmonic Orchestra, the names of players again listed individually. Most of the players from the 1940 orchestra remained in that of 1941, but there were considerable acquisitions in the string sections. It has been suggested that many of the added players were incomers from the south of England, where there was little work for purely orchestral players. The new leader, Henry Holst, and the deputy, H. S. Cropper, were both newcomers, probably previously known to Sargent, who, until the war intervened, had been chiefly working in London and its environs.

In 1941, concert programmes of the Welsh Choral (still costing 6d.) were printed just as in peace-time, with the usual references to the closure of doors and the required behaviour for late-comers. Refreshments, by Messrs Reece and Sons, Ltd., were to be served in the interval, as had always been the custom at the Philharmonic Hall.

On August 9, 1940, the first bombs were dropped on Merseyside at Prenton,[5] Birkenhead, and the first casualties of the war were registered. On the tenth, bombs were dropped on Wallasey, and on the seventeenth, on Liverpool, damaging the overhead railway. On August 19, Walton Gaol was bombed,

---

[5] *Liverpool Blitz Time,* http://www.mersey-gateway.org/server.php?show=ConWeb.1201 [accessed 26/05/2007].

killing 22 prisoners. It was on September 5 that the Anglican Cathedral was damaged by bomb-blast. On September 6, the Children's Convalescent Home in Birkenhead was bombed, and on the sixteenth came the first heavy raids on docks and warehouses. By October, Merseyside had suffered two hundred air raids in all.

In November of the same year occurred the heaviest raids to date: 200 people in total were killed as the first land mines were dropped on Merseyside. When a shelter underneath the Junior Technical School on Durning Road collapsed, 164 people were killed. December was to bring even worse devastation. On the third, 180 people were killed in an attack on a packed air-raid shelter. Several minor raids occurred during the next days, and on the twentieth came the start of the Christmas raids, with 365 people killed over three nights. Again children, 1399 of them, were evacuated out of Liverpool. The Christmas raids finally came to an end on December 22.

The concerts planned for October and December did not take place. For the first time in years, there was no *Messiah* performance at Christmas. Whether rehearsals continued on a regular basis is doubtful. The normal rehearsal room was unavailable, having been taken over by lectures for allotment holders. The Executive Committee, however, met in August and again in September and October.

When the Committee came together in January, 1941, they reported public complaints that the annual *Messiah* performance had not been given. This was to be regretted, and it was felt important that rehearsals for the *Creation* should be resumed as soon as possible. Regular meetings of the choir had obviously been difficult in the dark days of winter with air-raids threatening every evening. On February 8, 1941, rehearsals began again, now held at 3:00 o'clock in the afternoon.

During January, bad flying weather had resulted in only three air-raids having taken place. On February 7, the Western Approaches Command Headquarters[6] were transferred from

---

[6] Garnett, Ron, *Liverpool in the 1930s and the Blitz* (Preston, 1995), p. 99.

Plymouth to Liverpool, and there were only two air-raids on Merseyside during the month. In March, on the twelfth and thirteenth, heavy bombing was resumed. Wallasey suffered its heaviest raids as 174 people were killed. In April, the Luftwaffe limited the raids on Merseyside to just three, conserving their forces for the May Blitz of the following month. The severe bombing began on May 1, and before the end of the week, 1741 people had been killed and 114 seriously injured. The worst night was May 3, when the cargo ship, Malakand exploded in Huskisson Dock, and on the same night an ammunition train was blown up. On May 13, 550 "Unknown Warriors of the Battle of Britain"[7] were buried in a common grave at Anfield Cemetery. The statistics for the casualties of Liverpool are chilling, worse than those of Birmingham or Clydeside. Liverpool had been the prime target in Britain, after London.

An aspect of the wartime Choir that is unrecorded is whether the numbers singing in the Choral were, indeed, as announced in the programme. The list of members is very little altered from that of March 1940. Nor indeed were other features altered. The members of the Philharmonic Orchestra were listed in full. The programmes still cost sixpence, and the prices of tickets were unchanged from those of 1939. Problems had arisen with regard to dates for the use of the Philharmonic Hall, and although the matter was sorted out on this occasion by the intervention of Mr. Humphreys Jones, the President of the Welsh Choral, the difficulties about concert dates and, later, about the sale of tickets, were again to cause problems in future years.

It was during the hiatus of bombing in April 1941 that the performance of *The Creation* took place. Dr. Malcolm Sargent was the Guest Conductor, and the soloists were Isobel Baillie, Trevor Jones and Tom Williams. The programme for this concert is the first which contains an announcement about a possible air-raid alert:

---

[7] *Liverpool Blitz Time,* http://www.mersey.gateway.org/server.php?show=ConWeb. Doc.1201 [accessed 26/05/2007].

> In the event of an air-raid 'Alert' taking place during a Concert, the audience will know of such an 'Alert' by the continuous burning of an amber light on the base of the Conductor's Rostrum. Members of the audience may leave the auditorium if they wish. As the music will continue without interruption, will those who are intent on leaving do so as quietly as possible.

Malcolm Sargent mentioned this arrangement in a radio broadcast some years later, when he spoke of frequent alerts during the performance. He was proud to add, "Nobody in the audience stirred."[8] It is surprising also to note that light refreshments were still being served by Messrs S. Reece and Sons.

The concert of April 1941 marks the first appearance of Dr. Malcolm Sargent as conductor. During the following Executive Committee meeting, the concert was assessed by the assembled members: it was considered to have been musically an unqualified success, but the results financially were less good. The suggestion was made that possibly this was owing to the air-raids that had taken place a few days previously! There was little doubt that Dr. Sargent had been a most satisfactory Guest Conductor in every way, though gratitude was also due to Mr. Tom Lloyd, who had prepared the work and to Dr. West, the organist and accompanist, who had been supportive in every way. Encouraged by the response of the Choir, the Committee planned three concerts for the 1941-1942 season, the third to be the Verdi *Requiem* in March, an evening set aside as the second anniversary of the death of Hopkin Evans, and a tribute to him. This important concert was to be conducted by Malcolm Sargent.

The latter half of 1941 and the beginning of 1942 were comparatively free of bombing, light air-raids registered on only four occasions. A performance of *The Messiah* took place under Dr. Sargent in October and another under William Rees of

[8] Reid, Charles, *Malcolm Sargent*, p. 186.

Manchester in December. The October programme celebrated the 200th year of Handel's composition of the oratorio. In the programme notes, Dr. Laurence West supplied a timely joke about Handel's attempts to find good sight-readers in Chester Cathedral, where he was anxious to try out his oratorio before sailing to Ireland. A singer was sent who did not acquit himself well. Handel expostulated: "Did I not understand that you could sing at sight?" "So I can, Sir", replied the man, "but not at *first* sight."

The main problem encountered by the Choral with regard to these concerts was the realisation that, in the May bombing of 1941, all the Choir's good copies of *The Messiah* had been destroyed in the old choir room, leaving only the tattered copies. It was agreed that the Librarian should be authorised to purchase a new supply, and that any members who could buy their own, should do so. In the same choir-room disaster, there disappeared other possessions even more valuable. Most of the Choir records up to early 1940 were destroyed, making the collection of documents for the assembling of the history of the Liverpool Welsh Choral very difficult indeed. Oddly, in the Minutes for this period, there is absolutely no reference to this major loss of early Choral documentation.

In their discussions of the forthcoming Verdi *Requiem,* the committee agreed to accept Sargent's opinion on any additional items to be included in the progamme, and his judgment on the inadvisability of having individual solos by the artistes before the performance of the major work. The occasion was all that the choir and audience had hoped it would be. The printed programme was a worthy one too. It contained the Choral's tribute[9] to Hopkin Evans, analytic notes by A. K. Holland on Gluck's *Alcestis* and Elgar's *Serenade for Strings*, both played by the orchestra, and full notes on Verdi's *Requiem*. The evening began with Elgar's *Nimrod* from the *Enigma Variations*, during

---

[9] Printed at the conclusion of Chapter IV, pp. 97-98.

which, after the singing of the National Anthem, the audience remained standing in memory of Dr. Evans. The *Requiem* was regarded as an act of tribute, and, because of its devotional character, the audience was asked to refrain from applause.

The printed programme also contained the now familiar Air-raid Precaution notice, and in addition another, announcing: "The Committee regret to announce that owing to war-time difficulties of staff and supplies, refreshments will not be available at these concerts until further notice."

The critics[10] were universally enthusiastic about the event. Said one, "War or no war, the Welsh Choral Union managed to put up a fine and impressive performance of the *Requiem* of Verdi". Although below strength, he said, the fire was still there, and they responded to Dr. Sargent's inspiring conducting. Another called it a deeply moving performance.

In 1941, while discussing works to be performed in the coming season, one committee member had objected to the choice of *Judas Maccabaeus*, "as the words were not suitable for the present times". It is not clear whether he objected to the passages of lamentation which open the oratorio, or the savage triumphalism in the concluding passages, and the determination to exact revenge from the defeated enemy. He might possibly have objected to the assumption that God took sides in war. The performance of this oratorio in 1941 was in any case rejected. It found a place, however, in the plans for 1942-1943, when war conditions in Liverpool were less severe.

There was much consultation over the works chosen for this season. Any demand for division of the Choir was to be avoided. Works chosen must, however, for the sake of the Choir, be sufficiently challenging. The audience too must be considered. It was important to choose works that made a direct appeal, and some considered it vital to keep off "high-brow"

---

[10] Music criticisms are based on the comments of daily newspaper critics. The originals are to be found in LWCU's Second Book of Clippings (source unspecified and undated).

works like Bach's *Mass* and the Verdi *Requiem*. Another matter
had to be given weight. Concerts were now cut to two hours
in duration, to take place from 3:00 to 5:00 in the afternoon,
and certain oratorios would suffer from injudicious cutting. The
works chosen were *Elijah*, a Christmas *Messiah*, and *Judas
Maccabaeus*.

Soloists had to be voted on for each concert, and, because
the Committee had been warned by Ibbs and Tillett[11] that some
artistes would be unavailable because of having taken war work
or become members of ENSA (Entertainments National Service
Association), the Committee took the precaution of drawing up
preferred lists of soloists for all three concerts, with alternatives
for each. These lists were handed to Dr. Sargent, who then
conferred with the agents. It was, of course, a particularly rich
period in oratorio singers of quality and experience. Many of
the soloists later became, and remained, family names for years
to come.

In spite of war, or perhaps because of it, sale of tickets
for these concerts surpassed all records. The booking for the
Christmas concert opened early one November morning, and in
less than three hours, every seat was sold, and many were turned
away, disappointed. It was probably *Judas Maccabaeus*, of
these three concerts, which drew most unrestrained praise from
the critics. The dramatic choruses were, it was reported, after
the Choir's own Welsh hearts. There were stirring moments of
splendidly vital and powerful singing, with thrilling climaxes.
Malcolm Sargent, who had recently spent some time conducting
choirs in Wales,[12] seemed to enjoy this concert as much as the
Choir, and the soloists[13] also were at their artistic best.

Concerts in the Autumn of 1943 were described as thrilling,
stirring and touching, performances in which the choral singing
never faltered. Dr. Reginald Jacques, who conducted the 1943

[11] London-based Concert Agents
[12] Reid, Charles, *Malcolm Sargent* (London, 1968), pp. 234-237.
[13] Ruth Naylor, Muriel Brunskill, Parry Jones, and Norman Walker.

Christmas *Messiah*, was very much impressed by the Welsh Choral. He remarked that the Choir was so highly trained and so manageable that a visiting conductor had a comparatively easy task of it. It was to the credit of the Chorus-master that this was so, since new singing members had recently been incorporated into the Choir.

From time to time, the Choral had had requests from other bodies to participate in supplementary events. The Choir had been invited in 1942 to help out other societies in a performance of *Cavalleria Rusticana*, but felt there was too little time to learn the work. Neither could they take part in a concert planned in the Picton Hall for February, 1942. Late that year, the Choir was asked to put on a performance for the troops, but with so many of the Choir involved in Home Guard or fire-watching duties, no extra concerts could really be considered.

In late 1943, several outstanding problems arose to confront the Executive Committee. There was trouble over tickets, some having been sold outside the Philharmonic Hall on the evening of the concert, while earlier in the week, the ticket office of the music shop Rushworth's had had to refuse applications for tickets. This had led to some financial embarrassment, settled by generous subscriptions from Choir members and Honorary members. A more disagreeable matter to settle was that of Choir members who avoided rehearsals, except those immediately prior to the performance. One offender had been particularly culpable in this matter, and was now excluded. Some misunderstandings had arisen with regard to seating arrangements at rehearsals and concerts. The question of allotting definite seats had many times been postponed, but now two Committee members were prepared to draw up such a seating plan, and were authorised to proceed.

By early 1944, there was a general feeling that the war was sure soon to be over. No bombs had fallen on Merseyside since early 1942, and air-raid shelters in private gardens were being converted into garden sheds.[14] Food rationing and other restrictions were the chief sources of complaint. In the Committee's discussions of plans for the 1944-1945 season, it was thought that four concerts a year would now be possible, and Committee members began to offer suggestions for works and soloists. Perhaps Elgar's *The Kingdom* could be revived, or *Acis and Galatea,* and certainly a performance of *Hiawatha* would be welcome. *The Apostles* of Elgar might be too hazardous because of the extra rehearsal time that would be necessary. It was also decided in February 1944 that it was high time to appoint Dr. Malcolm Sargent as the permanent conductor, if he would accept the position. He was, of course, already conductor of several other choirs.

Dr. Sargent's first concert as permanent conductor, a Spring performance of *The Messiah,* was in April 1944. There was a packed hall, and the choir gave a thoroughly satisfactory performance, despite the disparity in numbers that had developed between men's and women's voices. The critics gave the Choir high praise, as usual, but what was especially notable about the concert was the outstanding solo work, especially that of Kathleen Ferrier, who "sang with a combination of vocal beauty and simplicity of style." Another welcome debut with the Liverpool audience was that of the bass singer, a Pole, Marian Nowakowski.

Later in the same month Dr. Sargent conducted a curtailed version of Bach's *Passion according to St. Matthew,* again requesting that no applause be given except at the end of each part. Because of the cuts made necessary by the time allowed for a performance, this concert did not meet with universal favour. The soloists were Elsie Suddaby, Astra Desmond, Edward Reach, Frank Phillips and Robert Easton. The October concert, *Hiawatha,* brought another three excellent soloists, Joan Hammond, Peter Pears, and Tom Williams. As usual,

---

[14] Garnett, *Liverpool in the 1930s,* p. 120.

the audience welcomed a performance of the Red Indian tale of "braves and squaws" as an old friend, and, to add to their enjoyment, once again, after three years of restrictions, they had in their hands programmes in which there was no mention of the possibility of an Air-raid. In addition, the prospect of once more having refreshments served during the interval must have given assurance of the return of normality to their lives.

It was felt, by some of the most musical Choral members, that the last three Christmas *Messiah* performances had fallen below the Choral's former standards, and a special effort to improve the situation must be made in 1944. Since Sargent was not going to be available on the date selected, the decision was made to invite Sir Henry Wood. He replied, however, that he was unable to undertake provincial engagements till the end of the war. Ibbs and Tillett were consulted, and they suggested Richard Austin, who accepted the Choir's invitation. From then on, Austin became one of the Choir's preferred guests, especially when a substitute for Sargent was required.

Ever thoughtful, in December 1944, Malcolm Sargent had let the Choral know that he would be flying to New York in February and March, 1945, and that there was a possibility that he would not be able to get back in time to conduct the *Creation* on March 17. The weather for flying would be a factor. The question arose as to whether a substitute ought to be found, or gamble on Sargent's being able to return. Sir John Barbirolli did not conduct choral works. Sir Thomas Beecham was nowhere to be found. What about Boult? By early February the matter was urgent. Sir Richard Austin was again approached, and was free to accept.

As the Choir, under Austin's leadership, had pleased the audience in the Christmas *Messiah,* in the singing of *The Creation* this was no less the case. The critics remarked that the oratorio performance was full of freshness and vitality, overflowing with innocent delight. The hopeful news from

Europe, it was felt, was reflected in the singing of Haydn's jubilant thanksgiving choruses, ringing out to a generation embittered by an experience of the Chaos Man had made of God's world.

For the last wartime concert, Dr. Malcolm Sargent had returned from America. Normality was returning to the world, and to Britain. The Welsh Choral, now numbering 300, were glad to have an opportunity to do another Springtime *Messiah*, and particularly with soloists who had recently delighted the Liverpool audiences, Kathleen Ferrier and Marian Nowakowski. They were joined by two who had pleased in previous years. Sargent himself was apparently so carried away by enthusiasm as the Choir approached the Hallelujah Chorus that, with an expansive gesture of his baton, he struck an overhead light, momentarily startling himself, the soloists, and the Choir.

On May 29 the Executive Committee held its last meeting of the season. The war in Europe itself was over, and, though areas in the South of England had suffered from the ravages of the flying bombs, the North-West had been too far distant to be reached by the V-1s,[15] with their range of 150 miles, or even the V-2s, with an estimated range of 200 miles. To be sure, the war in the Far East was still being hard fought, but few had doubts of the ultimate outcome. A review was given in committee of the last season's concerts: a good result, musically and financially, at each performance. The Welsh Choral could congratulate itself on having survived the war with more than reasonable success, and could now begin what the Committee hoped would be a long, peaceful and happy association with its renowned Permanent Conductor.

---

[15] *Ibid.*, p. 121.

CHAPTER SIX:
SIR MALCOLM SARGENT

PART I: TOWARDS THE GOLDEN JUBILEE

The Liverpool Welsh Choral's first two permanent conductors had both come from South Wales, and, while both had arrived in Liverpool after having had valuable experience of conducting Welsh choirs, it cannot be said that either was widely recognised outside his native country. Both early conductors were ready to make the Liverpool Welsh Choral the centre of their musical lives for the foreseeable future. Malcolm Sargent came to the Welsh Choral after having had a relatively full and varied life in music. He was, throughout Britain, a well-known personality, recognised for his outstanding musical qualities, as well as for his flamboyance, his reputation with women, and, by 1940, his well-advertised disagreements with orchestral players. At the same time, he had his advocates, his warm friendships, and his iconic position as a trainer and conductor of choirs.

Harold Malcolm Watts Sargent was born on April 29, 1895, at Ashford[1] in Kent, while his mother, a matron at the Stamford High School for Girls, was on a visit to a former school-friend. Malcolm's father, Henry Edward Sargent, described himself on Malcolm's birth certificate as "organist", but his daily work was that of a clerk, later manager, in a coal merchant's firm in Stamford. Though theirs was a humble home, Henry's passion for music, and the organ in particular, was such that there was no sacrifice too great for his parents to make in order that Malcolm and his sister Dorothy should have every educational and musical opportunity. From the first, Malcolm responded positively, and he was lucky to be taught by an excellent music teacher, a Mrs. Tinkler, known to all as Tinkie.

Malcolm Sargent devoted himself whole-heartedly to

[1] There is some dispute about this. See Aldous, Richard, *Tunes of Glory, The Life of Malcolm Sargent* (London, 2001), p.2.

piano and organ study, and sang in a number of choirs. At the age of 14, he had an unusual opportunity to try out his skill in conducting at an orchestral and choral rehearsal[2] of an amateur operatic society. He found it enjoyable, and all who saw him remarked on his extraordinary authority and ability, and predicted a bright future for him. At 16, he became assistant to Dr. Haydn Keeton, the organist of Peterborough Cathedral. At 19, he became titular organist at Melton Mowbray Church. Next, he studied musicology at Durham,[3] and earned his doctorate there. In February, 1921, he made his mark with Sir Henry Wood as a conductor, when he so manoeuvred matters as to conduct in his presence in Leicester.[4] As a consequence, Sir Henry Wood invited him to conduct at the Promenade Concerts in the Queen's Hall. From that time on, Sargent devoted himself exclusively to conducting, adding, in 1923, a lectureship in that field at the Royal College of Music in London.

He began to make a name for himself as an interpreter of British music, and in 1924 took over Robert Mayer's Children's Concerts, becoming lastingly popular with young audiences for introducing words and phrases to illustrate musical themes. He continued to conduct these concerts for fifteen years, until war intervened. During the 1920s and 1930s, his work was wide and varied. With the Royal Choral Society in the summer of 1928, he staged a remarkable performance of Coleridge Taylor's *Hiawatha* at the Albert Hall, and in 1931, at the Leeds Triennial Festival, he turned a possibly failing performance of Walton's *Belshazzar's Feast* into a triumph. He was acknowledged to be the most exciting choral conductor in the country. Even Beecham[5] conceded that Sargent was the greatest choirmaster

[2] Reid, Charles, *Malcolm Sargent* (London, 1968), p.43.

[3] *Ibid.*, p. 347. Sargent was later awarded doctorates at Oxford and Liverpool also, but valued Durham's more highly, if we are to believe his biographer, because he preferred the colour of its doctoral gown.

[4] Aldous, *Tunes of Glory*, p.23.

[5] Reid, *Malcolm Sargent*, quotes Beecham's words: "He is the greatest choirmaster we have ever produced. Choir conducting is one of the most difficult arts. Myself, I can only bring it off occasionally – sometimes in the last Act of *Die Meistersinger*, for example. But Malcolm always does it. He makes the beggars sing like blazes!"

ever produced in England.

As his fame grew, he deliberately altered his image. He had always been meticulous about his person and dress, a fact that had led to his sobriquet of Flash Harry[6] while he served briefly in the army in 1918. He now went further. No longer did he sport a mop of thick bushy hair, but he slicked it back with Brylcreem. His dress became formal, expensive, and dapper. He encouraged his showman's image, and delighted both in the company of the aristocracy and in the applause of ordinary people. He became, as he remained, attractive to and attracted by women. One affair in the 1920s led to a shotgun wedding with a servant girl, but this did not at all distract him from his conducting ambition.

In 1927 and 1928 he was principal assistant to the Ballets Russes in London, and was recommended to Elizabeth Courtauld as conductor of her series of concerts combining traditional and contemporary music. By July, 1929, the Courtauld-Sargent Concerts were established as a popular subscription series. Some expected of Sargent the slipshod method of a dilettante, but the reverse proved to be the case. Exceptional detail was demanded by him in rehearsals, and he outlawed the old deputy system in his orchestra, a practice that had led to indifferent playing. In 1932, the sub-standard LSO was replaced by the LPO[7], an orchestra shared between Beecham and Sargent.

Then disaster struck! In 1933, Sargent collapsed physically, and tuberculosis was diagnosed. He was forced to take a two-year period of rest and withdrawal from the musical world. His inability to work made apparent to himself and to others his financial bankruptcy. In order supposedly to save money on an agent's percentage, and to have the freedom to decide on his

---

[6] Reid, *Malcolm Sargent*, p. 394. Sargent said, "I have never enjoyed being called 'Flash' very much. Curious how the nickname was given me. I was on the air in a Brains Trust in London. Then the announcer introduces me conducting the Hallé in Manchester. There was a character called 'Flash' in a strip cartoon at the time. He could flash from pole to pole. Well, I flashed from London to Manchester in a second. So I became known as 'Flash' ".

[7] London Symphony Orchestra and London Philharmonic Orchestra.

own engagements, he had never employed an agent, but relied for everything on his secretary. Although making every effort to persuade him otherwise, she never prevailed on him to cut down on his extravagant life style. Sargent had delighted in his status among London's party-going, county-image group, and had become embroiled with some titled women, without ever having estimated the consequences. He had taken on a great deal of enjoyable work, for which he was willing to accept particularly low fees. Sargent was now, in 1933, in need of an expensive operation and care, which he was unable to afford. Friends rallied to his help, and there were whip-rounds among choral singers and orchestral players, as well as substantial cheques from wealthy supporters. That is what made the crucial event of 1936 so painful. By then, he had recovered sufficiently to go on a money-making Australian tour. On the eve of departure, he gave a very ill-judged press interview, in which he said that, in his opinion, orchestral musicians had 'no job for life' but should receive pensions only when each had poured out ungrudgingly his whole strength.[8] Sargent's orchestras never forgave him for his harsh words, since they had done all they could to support him in his need. In 1936, an informal poll named him the least liked of all conductors. Only when the second World War came and he toured tirelessly with the LPO did orchestral players soften towards him.

When, in 1939, war was declared, Sargent was fortunate in having recently been appointed to the conductorship of the Hallé Orchestra, in order, it was hoped, to revitalise it. His appointment had been announced while he was again on tour in Australia, and his engagement there had not yet terminated. Although he had a further sixteen concerts to conduct, three days after the outbreak of war, he asked to be released from his existing tour[9] and put his name down for the first available flight

[8] Reid, *Malcolm Sargent*, pp. 224-226.

[9] Aldous, *Tunes of Glory*, p. 98.

home. He arrived back in London on November 27, after a long and risky flight, but glad to be back in Britain. Actually, Sargent was then the only conductor of stature remaining in London. Beecham and Barbirolli were in America, Boult with the BBC in Bristol, Sir Henry Wood was ageing and had only a few years to live, and Sir Hamilton Harty was already terminally ill. Very little work, naturally, was possible in South-East England for any conductor, and Sargent was relieved to have appealing work waiting for him in the North. Though not happy in Manchester, he remained conductor of the Hallé Orchestra until 1942, when he switched to the Liverpool Philharmonic Orchestra, a post he retained until 1948.

It was the good fortune of the Liverpool Welsh Choral that, during the war years, Malcolm Sargent was spending so much of his time in northern cities, and that he was able, as early as the Spring of 1941, to give attention to the Welsh Choral. It was also fortunate that, during the 1930s, Sargent had developed a very high regard for Welsh singing voices.

The Three Valleys Festival had begun in South Wales in May, 1930, and continued for the rest of the decade, with Dr. Malcolm Sargent as a very popular guest conductor. Sargent exulted, it is reported, in the lustre and power of his Welsh voices. With his 3000-strong Festival Singers, he had tackled the standard choral repertoire, as well as Bach's *B minor Mass* and the Verdi *Requiem.* Unlike many of his contemporaries, Sargent became acquainted, either during this period or later, with the tonic sol-fa system of sight-reading music, and realised its value, even using it sometimes in his later work with the Liverpool Welsh Choral when confronted by a particularly difficult passage. Like one of his predecessors, Harry Evans, Sargent had boasted, "Listen to my tenors – every one of them has a top B flat." He had set about improving and refining Welsh choralism, striving slightly to quell the native enthusiasm, and to teach his choristers to sing sensitively while losing none of their old fire. He had also managed to improve audience behaviour in Wales, and had gone some way towards preventing audiences from breaking into enthusiastic applause before the end of the big *Messiah* choruses. He had attempted, with some success, to suppress the chatter that occurred in the purely orchestral passages. Thus he taught the Valleys much, even while they also taught him.[10]

The conductorship of the Liverpool Philharmonic was by no means a sinecure. During the years 1942 to 1947. Malcolm Sargent conducted more than a hundred concerts each season,[11] often with difficult contemporary works dominating his programmes, though he retained a sufficient number of popular works to fulfil his ambition of bringing live classical music to the working classes. Early in the war, too, Sargent was involved with a scheme to bring music to cities that were in greatest danger from bombing, cities that were ports or armament centres. In 1940 and 1941, Sargent took the LPO to six cities: Birmingham, Liverpool, Coventry, Glasgow, Manchester and Sheffield.[12] In December 1940, Sargent joined fire-watchers in Manchester as the Free Trade Hall, the orchestra's home, was destroyed by fire. Back in London, too, Sargent continued to be active. On the afternoon of May 10, 1941, he conducted a performance of *The Dream of Gerontius* with the Royal Choral Society at the Queen's Hall. That night, among many other fine buildings, the Queen's Hall was completely destroyed by enemy fire.

It is almost unbelievable that Sargent was able to give as much time and attention as he did to each of his organisations. He was principal conductor of many choral societies. From 1928 to 1967, he conducted the Royal Choral Society in London; from 1932, the Huddersfield Choral Society; from 1941, as we know, the Liverpool Welsh Choral. He was always ready to do all he could for his choirs, and in return, his singers admired and were devoted to him.

---

[10] Reid, *Malcolm Sargent*, pp. 234-237.
[11] Aldous, *Tunes of Glory*, p. 108.
[12] Reid, *Malcolm Sargent*, p. 276.

Sir Malcolm Sargent
Principal Conductor of the Liverpool Welsh Choral Union
1944 - 1967

Sir Malcolm Sargent not only declared his pleasure in his choirs, but found a practical way of showing his devotion to them. The following tale is told of his action with regard to the Bradford Choir, his first in the provinces.[13] His fee for them at the time, in 1925, was to be 150 guineas a season, a little less than £13 a date. Those were the hard days of struggle and depression. Because of reduced public support for the choir, the singers had agreed to increase their annual subscription from 5/- to 7/6. Hearing of this, Sargent said, "That's very generous of them. I must do something to help. I'll reduce my fee from 150 guineas to 100 guineas a season. All I ask in return is that my rehearsals be cut to one per concert – the final one, that is." When Sargent later became Conductor of the Welsh Choral, he kept his fees far below those of his contemporaries. For years, he charged £40 per choral concert, when other conductors were receiving four or five times as much.

Increasingly the Welsh Choral's Executive Committee turned to him for advice, and not only was he helpful in the matter of programme building, but he would offer to negotiate with Ibbs and Tillett, the concert agents, on the choir's behalf, to secure the best possible soloists for his northern choirs. His help was also sought by the Welsh Choral Executive Committee to intervene in the question of arrangements between the Liverpool Philharmonic Society and the Welsh Choral, especially with regard to the use of the Philharmonic Hall. Surprisingly, perhaps, it was not until 1944 that Sargent was actually appointed the Welsh Choral Society's permanent conductor.

Throughout the war years, Welsh Choral concerts conducted by Sargent were never less than enthusiastically reviewed. Words used about his choral conducting, and, of course, about the choir's performance, were impressive, inspiring, moving, stirring, thrilling and passionate. Always, too, the Choral, under Sargent, was described as well-balanced and well-prepared.

[13] *Ibid.*, p. 200.

Indeed, it is seldom that one comes across even slightly adverse comment. Sargent had every reason to be satisfied with his reception in the North of England.

His personal life, however, was less satisfactory. His relationship with his wife, never happy, brought distress to them both. Added to that sorrow was grief over the declining health of their daughter, Pamela, and the failure of Sargent and his son to communicate adequately with each other. In 1937 there had been a family holiday in Italy, a holiday that had been cut short when Pamela, aged fourteen, developed poliomyelitis. From this she never fully recovered. In 1942, Sargent and his wife Eileen agreed to separate, and their children were told that they must choose between the parents. Peter chose to spend his school holidays from Eton with his mother, but Pamela chose her father. Her Kensington school had been evacuated in 1939 to Hartland Abbey in the West Country, where Pamela was happy and was sympathetically treated. When, in early 1944, it was apparent that her health was seriously failing, she asked consent to return to the Abbey. For the first time in his musical life, Sargent took time off from his duties to spend a final week with his daughter. Both were aware that death was imminent, but were glad to be together. On August 23 Pamela died peacefully. Her father was not with her at the time, but was reached by telephone in Liverpool.[14] For five days he surrendered to his grief, and though he never recovered emotionally from his daughter's death, pressure of work came to his aid. His very fine recording of *Gerontius* in 1945 was a tribute to Pamela's memory. This HMV recording, sponsored by the British Council, was the first ever complete performance of the work to be put on disc. It was made with the Huddersfield Choir and the Liverpool Philharmonic Orchestra, Heddle Nash singing the title role.

During the war years, Sargent had also become well-recognised in another field. On June 29, 1941, he took part

[14] *Ibid.*, p. 305. Aldous, however, maintains that he was conducting in Leicester when news of Pamela's death reached him.

in the BBC programme, *Any Questions,* later to become *The Brains Trust.* He found himself associating with the intellectual leaders of Britain, people chiefly of high academic standing and of political leadership. He perhaps surprised himself as well as others by how completely he fitted into their company. He became a popular member of the group, and an almost permanent guest. He had, as a conductor, been famous, but now he became what the present generation would call a Celebrity. The story is told of a time when, after conducting a concert in the Potteries district, a girl was waiting outside the stage door, holding an autograph book. She enquired, "You Dr. Sargent?" He nodded, smilingly. She asked again, "**The** Dr. Sargent?", and again he nodded. "Dr. Sargent of the Brains Trust?" she persisted. He nodded a third time. "All right, I'll have your autograph", she conceded. It says much for Sargent's sense of humour that he delighted in telling this story. He came to realise that, while he had reached thousands with his music, he had reached millions of radio listeners with his wit, his repartee, and his ability to debate with others in his inimitable fashion. The Brains Trust lasted throughout the war years to 1945, and was considered at home and abroad to be the best of Britain, something of which this country could with good reason be proud.

More than was perhaps realised by many at the time, Sargent was by nature a deeply patriotic person, even twice flying through enemy air-space to Sweden, in November 1942 and September 1943, and once to Portugal in January 1943, as musical ambassador, to conduct their native orchestras. It was an aspect of the British Council's 'cultural war.' On the continent he was received with ecstasy by enthusiastic audiences. At the same time, Sargent was a sincerely religious man. Very soon after the conclusion of the war, Sargent persuaded the National Federation of Music Societies, to which the Welsh Choral belonged, that it would be appropriate to hold a Thanksgiving For Victory concert at the Albert Hall. The date was to be April

20, 1946. Among others of Sargent's choirs, the Welsh Choral's Executive Committee, in due time, received a notice of this proposal, and, at the next rehearsal, it was made known to the members, so that those who wished to participate could take up the offer of the limited number of seats allotted to each choir. The letter of invitation was read to the choir, and the names of interested members taken.

How many of the Welsh Choral members responded to this opportunity is not known, but among those who made the journey was Miss Eileen Vaughan, by this time an established member of fifteen years' standing. It was a significant enough event in her life for her to recall it with pleasure and enthusiasm sixty years later. Unfortunately, no list of the works performed at the concert could be found, nor, indeed, a complete list of the choirs taking part, but all had sung previously under Dr. Sargent's baton, and their combined voices must indeed have made it an occasion to be remembered.

Eileen Vaughan had other personal reasons for remembering her London trip.[15] She travelled alone to London for the Thanksgiving For Victory Concert, and returned alone. On the journey home, a change of trains at Crewe was necessary. The railway station was less comfortable then than it is now, and, as she was walking up and down the platform, she became aware of another traveller doing much the same, and realised it was Malcolm Sargent. Wondering whether it would be fitting to speak to him, she hesitated, but then as he came towards her purposefully, she ventured to tell him she was on her way back to Liverpool after the Albert Hall concert. "Oh, so you must be a member of the Welsh Choral", said he, and from then on it became easy to continue the conversation. The two discussed the Choral, Sargent speaking of their need to find a professional musician soon to take over the choral training.[16] The day following the train journey, a Welsh Choral rehearsal was held, to

---

[15] Personal Interview.
[16] Not long after this encounter, Dr. Caleb Jarvis was appointed to the post.

prepare for an imminent concert. When all the Choral members were ready in their places, Dr. Sargent entered, and there was a pause while his eyes roved the assembled choristers until they came to rest on Miss Vaughan. He gave her what might pass for a wink and followed it with a wave, saying, "Good! You got home safely then". Such friendly informality, in contrast with his highly regulated rehearsal, was surely part of his charm, and was why he became, as the two Evanses had been before him, much loved by all who sang under his direction.

It was not only his charm, however, that made Malcolm Sargent so attractive to his choirs. Even in his earliest appearance before a professional choir in 1922, two seasoned musicians had remarked, "The young man's fervour for the music, his transmitting of this fervour to every singer on the platform and his supple technical control of the choir mark him out as a great choral conductor in embryo."[17] All his choralists would be "lost in admiration of the lucid professionalism that underlay his charm."[18] From the beginning they felt, too, that "when he arrived for rehearsals, he made everybody feel enormously glad to be alive simply because he looked enormously glad to be alive himself."[19] One woman singer wrote of him, when he returned to them after his illness of 1933, "I've often gone to rehearsals tired after my day's work, wishing I hadn't to go. But once you get there, every bit of tiredness disappears. His enthusiasm makes us enthusiastic. And he's so gentle. I feel I could sing for Dr. Sargent even if he didn't beat time at all. His expression itself is enough to tell us what he wants. The chorus gets more out of it than those who just sit and listen."[20]

A present member[21] of the Welsh Choral recalls how he would arrive in rehearsal, wearing a grey suit with a jacket, and a flower – not a carnation for rehearsal, but a different flower –

---

[17] Reid, *Malcolm Sargent*, p. 106.
[18] *Ibid.*, p. 200.
[19] *Ibid.*, p. 94.
[20] *Ibid.*, p. 217.
[21] Irene Lockwood

in his buttonhole. The choir would have risen on his entrance, but as soon as they were seated, the rehearsal would get under way without delay. He did not, as some conductors do, first sing straight through a work, but he would stop at each error to correct it at once. It would be hard work, but at the same time he enjoyed the "fun" of it, and he expected everyone else to enjoy it equally.

He also, of course, expected concentration on and response to every correction or suggestion that he made, and, having made a point, he would say, "Mark it in" and expect it to be done and remembered ever after. A story is told of one occasion, while rehearsing an Elgar work, he had asked the contraltos to make a slight breath pause in the middle of a certain phrase which was marked *legato* in the copies. Some unfortunate woman failed to pull up, and her voice sailed through the gap. Sargent paused and said, "If any one of you hears your neighbour make this mistake again, give her a good kick, like this," and he demonstrated.[22] With this touch of humour, he made his point, and any humiliation was overcome by his droll response.

He was occasionally questioned about his conducting technique. He replied, referring back to his earliest conducting days, "I found myself using a natural stick technique. I have been using the same technique ever since. When I say 'natural', I mean something I was born with. My conducting gestures were entirely unconscious, as they are to this day. No gesture for gesture's sake."[23] Many years later an Australian critic described what he could observe. "While the right hand beat time," he said, "the left hand painted in the picture, put in the highlights, delicately applied hairlike lines, made broad sweeps of colour, fashioned delicate traceries and applied dainty touches, all with the surety of a master."[24]

---

[22] Reid, *Malcolm Sargent*, p. 223.
[23] *Ibid.*, pp. 43-44.
[24] *Ibid.*, p. 249.

At one point an oratorio chorus had, in rehearsal, sounded to him unnecessarily dull and flat. Sargent just laid down his baton and stopped the singing. He spoke quietly to the rapt choristers, pointing out the beauty of the words and how the music was perfectly fitted to their meaning. Then he said, "Now, let's try that again," and there was an instant response to his mood.

One Saturday afternoon in mid-April, at the Welsh Choral final rehearsal with orchestra, he announced the first piece to be sung, and lifted his baton to begin. Instantly the orchestra broke into an enthusiastic playing of "Happy Birthday To You", in acknowledgment of Sargent's birthday, and no one enjoyed the gesture more than he. In the evening concert, however, decorum would reign, and he would walk on with his ramrod-straight back, dressed immaculately, and sporting his white carnation.

During the twelve months that elapsed after the cessation of war, the Welsh Choral and its Executive Committee did everything possible to restore normality to their organisation. The achievements of the Committee were not inconsiderable. During their dozen or so meetings, a variety of subjects had been discussed, some matters settled, by majority vote as required by their constitution, and other more thorny problems had been deferred for further consideration.

Some problems were naturally financial. It was recognised that inevitably, after the removal of wartime restraints, costs would rise. The cost of hiring rehearsal rooms increased, as did the cost of the Philharmonic Hall for concert-giving. The Committee members at first protested at an unexplained additional £50 fee, which had appeared on their account with the Philharmonic Society, feeling that the charge, possibly for the sale of Choral tickets, was not commensurate with the amount of work done. The Welsh Choral had rejected, at least for the time being, an increase in the price of tickets, but there was necessarily a rise in the cost of soloists. While Ibbs and Tillett had been able to expand their roster of artists available, they had regretfully to inform all their clients that fees must go up. In spite of increased expenses, however, the Choral's treasurer managed to show a healthy balance sheet, and the Choral could relax in press and public approval.

Sargent had, upon becoming permanent conductor, insisted on the appointment of a professional musician as choir-master. Tom Lloyd had filled the position while the war continued, but when he resigned, Dr. Caleb Jarvis, an established Liverpool organist and musician, was offered the post, which he immediately accepted. Sargent was pleased with the choice, and thereafter the two musicians worked together in complete harmony. During Jarvis's first season as choir-master, it was arranged that auditions be held, for both new and old members. The choir had increased in number, and it was feared that standards would fall unless a thorough test of each singer were carried out. It was agreed that Jarvis's decision on each person's competence should be final and unchallenged. The auditions proved to be a lengthy process. At its completion, Jarvis reported to the Committee that, to his surprise, he had found the standard of sight-reading "frightfully low".[25] However, in spite of a few inevitable dismissals, and his insistence on the necessity for re-auditioning some candidates during the following year, the current voice levels were high. It was to be hoped that, before long, younger members could be added to the choir, especially in the male sections.

As usual the Executive Committee began to make plans for five concerts per year. Of those for the 1946-1947 season, Sargent was to conduct four and Richard Austin had already been retained for the fifth. In the later 1940s, Sargent regularly conducted the majority of concerts, with Jarvis leading at least one every year. Without exception when at home in Liverpool,

---

[25] Is it possible that some older members, brought up in Welsh chapels and Sunday Schools, would have been familiar with tonic solfa, but less able to read staff notation?

all concerts took place in the Philharmonic Hall, and of course, the wartime practice of afternoon concerts was abandoned, with an eight o'clock starting time favoured for evening concerts. Dr. Sargent and the Committee alike felt the need to introduce new works into the repertoire. Elgar's *The Apostles* and Verdi's *Aida* were both added, though, with each requiring six soloists, their inclusion would naturally bring further expenses, whenever they were performed.

The concerts of the post-war period were very well attended, and the choir and soloists received almost universal praise for their work. Indeed, it must have strained the vocabularies of the critics to find suitable and original phrases to describe the performances. Of the annual *Messiah* performances, we learn about the "magnificently vital singing and electric atmosphere created"; the choir "sang with conviction"; and was "assured in attack, impeccable in response". There was "clarity of enunciation, and unwavering response to Sargent". Finally, familiarity had bred not contempt, but admiration and affection. Of *Israel in Egypt,* mention is made of "the realistic Hailstones chorus". "Inspiration and restraint" were words used about the presentation of *The Apostles,* as well as "exaltation, tenderness and compassion", and again in the Brahms *Requiem,* the "restraint" is commended, as well as "moments of telling power". There are some critical comments about lack of clear enunciation in *Elijah*, and more so in the concert version of *Aida*. Of the other Verdi work, however, the *Requiem,* it was recorded that soloists, choir, orchestra and conductor were well coordinated from beginning to end, and the gradations in dynamics were particularly beautifully done. But it was the singing of *The Dream of Gerontius* that drew the warmest response. Three performances of this oratorio took place between 1946 and 1949. In 1946 it was a performance of "fine and at times very moving quality". An atmosphere of angelic innocence was conveyed. Perhaps the critic thought this was carried a little too far, for he remarked that the Demons sang in rather too "gentlemanly" a fashion. With Heddle Nash, as usual, in the role of Gerontius, the 1948 performance was "so moving as to become at times almost unbearable, especially in the beauty of the pianissimo singing". In 1949 the critic commented, "I wonder whether there is a finer choir and choral conductor in Britain. Sargent's control over the large choir and large orchestra is remarkable."

There is little doubt that Malcolm Sargent valued his association with the Welsh Choral as much as any one of the members cherished him. During these busy years, further honours were accruing to Sargent's name. 1947 was a key year for him. Early in the year, he was named conductor of the Leeds Philharmonic Society. In June he received his knighthood in the King's Birthday Honours, and in the Autumn he took over the Promenade Concerts, which, since Wood's death in 1944, had been conducted, without enthusiasm, by Adrian Boult. This appointment brought him greater public exposure than ever, especially as the Last Night of the Proms was shown on television. In 1948 Sargent was put in charge of all concert music for the Olympic Games in London. At the end of the decade, he became Chief Conductor of the B.B.C. Symphony Orchestra, again succeeding Boult in this position, and later he took Wood's title of Conductor-in-Chief of the B.B.C. Proms. More than one foreign tour was fitted in between other obligations. Is it not remarkable that Sargent is never known to have reneged on any commitment to the Welsh Choral? The Choral's Jubilee Concert on June 6, 1950, in which he conducted the performance of Elgar's *The Kingdom*, was actually Sargent's thirtieth Welsh Choral performance, and he postponed his departure on a foreign tour, in order to be able to conduct it.

Much of the Committee's time in 1948 and 1949 was spent in planning an ambitious series for the fiftieth anniversary. It was agreed that five works should be performed during the Jubilee season, and that the choir would not stint on obtaining the best possible soloists. Four works were quickly agreed upon: *The Dream of Gerontius, The Creation, The Messiah* and the Verdi *Requiem.* The choice of a fifth work led to some debate. In the end, the Executive Committee took a vote: *Israel in Egypt,* 4 votes; *Elijah,* 2 votes; *Faust,* 3 votes; but *The Kingdom* by Elgar won with 8 votes.

In such a memoir as this, a memoir chiefly to celebrate the music of the Welsh Choral in Liverpool, it is not possible to discuss the very many singers of note who were soloists with the choir during the 1940s. It was an era of great singers, many of whose names will not quickly fade from the memory. For those who like statistics, it may be of interest to know that, among those who sang with the Choral between 1919 and 1950 are: Isobel Baillie, five times; Gladys Ripley, six times; Elsie Suddaby, five times; Kathleen Ferrier, five times; and Ena Mitchell, six times. Among the most popular of the men soloists were Heddle Nash (as Gerontius); Norman Walker (especially as Elijah); Peter Pears (particularly as narrator in the Bach Passions), and Harold Williams in many bass parts. Other favourites with audiences to the Welsh Choral concerts were Joan Cross, Nancy Evans, Mary Jarred and Marjorie Thomas; David Lloyd, Trefor Anthony, Roy Henderson, Richard Lewis, and Owen Brannigan, whose career was only just starting in those years. Some were particular favourites of Malcolm Sargent, and most especially Kathleen Ferrier, whose career was so tragically cut short. Sargent claimed the honour of having introduced Kathleen Ferrier to the agents, Ibbs and Tillett, who were delighted to put her on their books.

For the Golden Jubilee of the choir, perhaps influenced strongly by Malcolm Sargent, the Choir, as previously mentioned, had chosen to present *The Kingdom* by Elgar. A very special effort was taken with the printed programme for the celebration. It had to be worthy of a choir whose status was secure. It is extraordinary that it was still possible to produce

such a souvenir programme, a programme full of interest, for a
price of ninepence. In addition to the usual listing of the Choral's
Officers, the programme contained the impressive list of Vice-
Presidents, 34 in all. We also find that there were 80 members
in the Orchestra, 238 Singing Members, and 390 Honorary
Members and Subscribers. A brief history of the Choir up to
1950 was written by Mr. David J. Lewis, the Chairman of the
Choral, and, of course, the Libretto of the evening's oratorio
was given in full. Future concerts of the 1950-1951 Season were
advertised. Best of all are the excellent full-page photographs
contained. They are of Sir Malcolm Sargent, who conducted on
that special evening, Mr. H. Humphreys Jones, J.P.; F.R.I.C., the
President at the time, Mr Lewis, the Chairman, and the Honorary
Secretary, Mr. E. H. Edwards. Also pictured are Dr. Caleb Jarvis,
the Choir-Master, and Mr. Ernest Pratt, the Accompanist, as
well as the two former conductors, Harry Evans and Dr. Hopkin
Evans. The Souvenir programme was indeed one worth having
and keeping.

    The critics were united in their judgment of the quality
of the concert. Following is the review of the renowned critic,
A.K.Holland:

Welsh Choral Jubilee

"The Kingdom"

    Elgar's oratorio, "The Kingdom", which the Welsh Choral
Union chose for their Golden Jubilee concert on Saturday,
is not perhaps so formidable a work as its predecessor, "The
Apostles," but it is a more gracious and human one.

    Its themes, many of which are taken over from the earlier
oratorio, are treated with great imagination and tenderness. The
tone of the two works, indeed, is quite distinct. "The Kingdom"
is bathed in purely Elgarian sentiment to an extent not exceeded

even by "Gerontius. " It has not quite the mystic rapture of that work at its highest moments, but it contains many pages which are among the most affecting that Elgar ever wrote: ravishingly lovely closes, a beautiful phraseology, memorable and haunting motives, and some truly magical orchestral touches.

It was the unity and cohesion of the work that struck one most in the fine performance the choir gave on Saturday under Sir Malcolm Sargent, making his first appearance since the appointment on which the Lord Mayor (Alderman J. J. Cleary) congratulated him – and we were glad to learn from the president, Mr. H. Humphreys Jones, that the new post will not involve the severance of his ties with the Society.

It was, by and large, the most satisfying and organic performance of the work that we remember in Liverpool. "The Kingdom" took some years to become popular, but when it does come off as completely as it did in this performance, there are few oratorios which make a more deeply moving impression. We had not perhaps previously realised so fully that it also contains its dramatic moments and the choir rose nobly to them. They gave us some very brilliant as well as some very melting singing and they, their conductor and their chorus-master (Dr. C. E. Jarvis) merit the highest praise.

The solo work is interwoven with the choruses with the subtlest art but there are two superb solo passages – the address of Peter which Mr. Harold Williams sang with fine spiritual fervour (throughout he was a dominating personality), and the lovely solo of Mary, "The sun goeth down," which Miss Ena Mitchell treated so tenderly. The contralto recitatives are of great beauty and expressiveness (Miss Gladys Ripley sang them sincerely) and to complete the quartet Mr Richard Lewis brought a lyrical charm to his singing of the tenor role. Everywhere there was a touch of inspiration.

A. K. H.

H. Humphreys Jones
President of the Liverpool Welsh Choral Union
1934 - 1971

CHAPTER SIX: SIR MALCOLM SARGENT

PART II: A NEW HALF-CENTURY

In telling the story of Sir Malcolm Sargent and the Liverpool
Welsh Choral, it would be ungracious as well as inaccurate not
to mention the singular good fortune of the Choir in once again
having, as in the early years, an exceptionally able, loyal and
hard-working Executive Committee. They gave generously of
their time and talents to the service of the Choral. The personnel
and the execution of its work was a pattern to the Committees
of future generations.

The President, Mr. H. Humphreys Jones, was a man of
standing in the city, honoured by the Welsh of Merseyside,
and often referred to in his later years as the Prime Minister
of the Liverpool Welsh.[26] Born in Wales in 1878, he had come
to Liverpool in 1897, and here he held many high offices.
From 1908 to 1950 he was Principal of the Liverpool School
of Pharmacy and in 1961 was awarded an honorary degree by
the University of Liverpool. In 1936 he became a Justice of the
Peace and in 1951-1952 was High Sheriff of Carnarvonshire.
He was for years President of the Liverpool Welsh Society, and
there were few Welsh occasions in Liverpool at which he was
not a familiar figure. He had sung with the Welsh Choral since
1903, was elected to its Executive Committee in 1910, and, in
1934, became its President, a position he held until his death
in 1971 at the age of 93. It was he, of course, who presided
over the Choral during the whole of Malcolm Sargent's period,
and was present at the Executive Committee's meeting in late
1967, to speak glowingly of Sir Malcolm's contribution to the
Society.

In mid-century the Chairman of the Welsh Choral Union
was Alderman David J. Lewis, J.P., A.R.I.B.A. Originally from
Aberystwyth, he was active in Liverpool City affairs, and served,
during 1962-1963, as Lord Mayor of Liverpool. He was almost

---

[26] Rees, *Cymry Lerpwl*, pp. 102-103

always present at Executive Committee meetings, despite his busy schedule, and was ready to do anything in his power to smooth the path of the Choral when any difficulties emerged. His Chairman's reports at the Annual General Meetings showed a comprehensive grasp of all aspects of the Society's concerns, as well as a droll method of presenting them.

The Society was blessed in having a succession of excellent Secretaries. When Malcolm Sargent became the Permanent Conductor, he found Mr. E. H. Edwards as the Choral's Hon. Secretary, but in early 1954, Mr. Edwards was forced to resign on grounds of ill-health. He had been in the position for 41 years. The first existing Book of Minutes is almost entirely his work, and no-one could have improved on the pattern he set. In 1954, on the resignation of Mr. Edwards, Mr. Gerald Ashmore was elected to be the new Hon. Secretary. He remained in this position for almost ten years. It proved an ideal appointment. Not only did Mr. Ashmore keep meticulous records of all that happened, but he made a habit of privately collecting documents of all kinds and of writing full notes upon all events concerning the Society.[27] In 1963 came Gerald Ashmore's resignation and the election of Mr. David ap D. Jones. Mr. Jones carried on the tradition of his predecessors. His beautifully written minutes, noted in his attractive, easy-to-read calligraphy, take us through to the end of Volume II of the Choral Records. Very unfortunately, after the end of 1971, there is a gap in the records, a gap not of Mr. Jones's making, and one only partially filled by consultation of the printed programmes of the period.

The Hon. Treasurers of the time are to be no less congratulated on the clarity and comprehensiveness of their reports, and also offered our sympathy for the many financial crises with which they had to contend. The multiplicity of their

---

[27] These notes, through the kindness and care of Gerald Ashmore's son, Commander Brian Ashmore, have been passed down, first to Judge J.E.Jones and then to the present writer. After the death of Commander Ashmore, his wife has continued to send documents which will remain in the Choir's archives.

duties is frightening to contemplate. A balance sheet of Income and Expenditure shows indeed a startling lack of balance, with five sources of income, but 37 items of expenditure on the debit side. Yet most Annual Reports of the period conclude with the cheering entry: Excess of Income over Expenditure.

Other offices also demanded much work and much responsibility, those of Hon. Librarian and his Assistant, and those of the two Hon.Ticket Secretaries. Their titles are self-explanatory, but of course, the War and its aftermath put extra strains on their efforts. Problems of loss or destruction of music were to some extent solved by the readiness of some choristers to purchase their own copies, but throughout the period, the Librarians had to deal with the apparent reluctance of some singers to return their music promptly after a concert.

One of the most persistent problems that the Welsh Choral had to contend with was, of course, that of the sale of tickets, and of the delicate balance to be maintained in pricing tickets so as to retain the less affluent members of the audience, while still ensuring a profit for the concert. Again and again the matter was raised in Committee, and the ticket secretaries were to be congratulated on having dealt tactfully with so many awkward situations. There were irritating disagreements with the Philharmonic Box Office and with Rushworth and Dreaper with regard to the percentage to be charged by them for the sale of tickets. Also, more than once, there were unsold tickets returned from agents, causing a considerable loss on those concerts. Some of these matters took years before a settlement could be finally agreed. At the same time, of course, with inflation playing its part, the cost of tickets had to be raised somewhat, but this happened only very gradually indeed, and only when absolutely necessary. Choir members, when informed of any shortfall, were always generous in offering to make up deficits, and they were almost invariably compliant to suggestions of increasing their own yearly subscriptions.

From its earliest days, the Welsh Choral had joined the

National Federation of Music Societies, and had, in bad times, relied on the Federation to help them obtain a grant from the Arts Council. In 1951, in communication with the Federation and the Arts Council, the Choral found that a promised grant of £250 was not forthcoming, and the reason given was that the choir had in their recent concerts made a small profit. Since the Choral had depended on the grant, this put the treasury into some difficulty. An offer of an interest-free loan of £300 was made, but that was not regarded with favour by the Committee members. Some members present at once contributed £50 to a Fund, and it was decided to put the matter to the AGM, when it was decided to accept the loan. The General Meeting also decided upon a special effort to raise funds. This happened towards Christmas, 1952, with the result that £577-19-2 was raised. The Welsh Churches of Douglas Road and Heathfield Road were warmly thanked by the Committee for making their halls available for a Sale of Work and for a concert performance of *The Messiah*. The raising of the Choir subscription was also discussed, but it could be seen that this would involve a revision of the Rules of the Society. Arrangements were thereupon put in hand for a complete overhaul of the Rules, which finally happened in 1955.

At a Committee meeting, it was suggested that changes first be made in several of the Bye-laws.[28] In Rule One, '8 o'clock' should be changed to '7 o'clock', wherever it occurred, and '8:30' to '7:30'. In Rule Two, the word 'Conductor' should be altered to 'Choir-master'. In Rule Six, the 'Orchestra' should become the 'Platform', and in Rule Seven, rather than "No member shall be permitted to take part in any concert who has not been present in the General Rehearsal", the Bye-law should read "who has not been present in at least one of the two rehearsals".A new Bye-law, Number 10, should be added: "Copies of music loaned to members must be returned to the Librarian within 14 days after the concert performance. Any

[28]A copy of the Bye-laws will be found in Appendix I.

member not complying with this rule shall be required to pay the purchase price of the copy." In the Annual General Meeting subsequent to this Committee meeting, Rule 7 was discussed. Members present failed to come to general agreement, and the change was deferred until further discussion had taken place. The remaining changes were accepted. One further alteration occurred in the Choral's constitution. As so many applicants for membership could not clearly show their Welshness, it was decided, in 1959, no longer to refuse new members on the basis of their inability to speak or understand Welsh. At the same time it was agreed that Tonic Sol-fa sight-reading would be acceptable on a par with that of staff notation. These points, though agreed and understood, were not entered in the Rule-book.

In the history of the period, the Choral was honoured to have had for so long the services of Dr. Caleb Jarvis, Chorus Master from 1946 onwards, and of Mr. Ernest Pratt, Accompanist since 1945. Dr. Jarvis's importance to the success of the choir was incalculable. Press critics remarked repeatedly on how carefully the choir had been trained and prepared. How very wise Sargent had been in 1946 to insist on the appointment of a choir-master, and how very fortunate the Choral was to secure one of the standing of Jarvis! Sargent and he worked closely together, Jarvis always ready to attend to Sargent's suggestions on every aspect of choral preparation, but at the same time, having a mind of his own. More than once he had his differences with the Committee, objecting to the declared preferences of the Committee in their choice of music for a concert, sometimes on the very reasonable grounds that there was not sufficient time to prepare properly a tricky work. The Committee had, in the last analysis, to defer to his judgment.

At each Annual General Meeting, Dr. Jarvis and Mr. Pratt were warmly thanked, and then Jarvis would give his report on the year's work. It was a report to anticipate with pleasure. He would review each of the Season's concerts in turn, would administer reproof where he thought it was deserved, and praise when appropriate. He would follow this with his plans for the future. Only once, in 1959, was there reason to call a special meeting to discuss problems arising during any of Dr. Jarvis's rehearsal sessions. A strategy for dealing with lateness to rehearsals, a constant complaint, was devised. An attempt was made to ensure better discipline, less unnecessary talking, and orderly seating. Two members were appointed to draw up a seating plan, for both rehearsals and concerts. Of course, as new members joined the Choral in later years, and old ones left, the problem of seating was bound to rise again, but certainly matters were more easily resolved as time went on.

With the Golden Jubilee of 1950 safely over, the Choral could not afford long to rest on its laurels. 1951 was the year of the Festival of Britain, and it was essential to consider what part the choir would play in the Festival. Planning for the usual concerts proceeded as usual, *The Apostles* in November, *The Messiah* in December and *Israel in Egypt* in tandem with the *Faure Requiem* for the Spring of 1951. The Choral initially planned an adventurous foray into Walton's *Belshazzar's Feast* for the July Festival programme, but then it emerged that the Liverpool Philharmonic Choir had fixed on the same work, and the Welsh Choral was not averse to preparing a further performance of *The Apostles* by Elgar. Indeed, the Choral was becoming especially well-known for its interpretations of Elgar's works, and the July performance was followed in the following November with a presentation of *The Dream of Gerontius* along with Brahms's *Four Serious Songs,* sung this time by Marjorie Thomas.

Even then, as 1951 became 1952, there was no end to special occasions. The death of George VI in February, 1952, led to the accession of Elizabeth II, and to her Coronation in 1953. This brought another event to be marked with special concerts. In the summer of 1953, Malcolm Sargent was very much involved with events in London and with a variety of musical celebrations throughout Britain and the British Commonwealth. Here in Liverpool, therefore, it was Hugo Rignold who conducted a massive Coronation Concert at the Stadium on June 3. The Welsh Choral joined in concert with the Liverpool Philharmonic Choir and Orchestra, and the trumpeters of the Royal Signals Corps in a huge out-of-doors celebration.

Though all appeared to run smoothly during these years, there still remained some perennial matters that caused friction. For years there had been problems with the overcrowding of the Green Room after each concert. Enthusiastic audiences flocked to obtain Malcolm Sargent's autograph and those of the soloists, and the number of signed programmes now in the archives testifies to the generosity of the performers in this matter. Apart from the discomfort occasioned to the willing victims, however, such overcrowding could become dangerous. The Committee decided it must engage temporary commissionaires to direct the traffic and to act as a restraining force to the over-eager petitioners for signatures.

Another danger point which needed to be handled firmly but diplomatically rose from the mad dash that took place at the Interval, of those making for the refreshment rooms. This rush, it was pointed out, took place even before the performers on the stage had had a chance to take their bows. Notices requesting an orderly exit from the auditorium were inserted into the programmes, time and again, but years later, the same stampedes were still apparent. Has it entirely subsided even today? It is certainly questionable.

Within the Committee itself, the atmosphere was usually one of harmony and tranquillity. Occasionally, however, there arose a matter on which opinion was divided, or one that could lead to disagreements, unless tactfully dealt with. Shortly after the triumphant conclusion of the 1950 Jubilee celebrations, the secretary reported in Committee that he had received a disturbing letter from two friends of the Choral. The relevant sentence read, "We are always cognisant with all that goes on in the Society, having numerous friends on the Committee and in the Choir." All those present in Committee regarded this communication as a matter for concern, and the Chairman spoke very strongly about the responsibility resting upon each member of the Executive Committee to keep the deliberations private and not divulge them until such times as they became accomplished facts and ready for publication. So far as is known, never again did any question of this kind surface, to disturb the confidence with which Committee members were able to make known their opinions in the knowledge that they would go no further.

Very occasionally, there was lack of agreement between the Choral and the Liverpool Philharmonic Orchestra.[29] In 1955, in a final orchestral rehearsal before a performance of the *Elijah*, it appeared that some members of the orchestra had behaved inappropriately. They had shown disrespect to the Choral conductor, displaying such behaviour as was apparent to all present. An official complaint was sent by the Executive Committee to the Philharmonic, and a meeting was arranged to discuss the matter with representatives of the orchestra. In the end, no apology was forthcoming. However, Alderman Livermore, on behalf of the orchestra, was willing to tell Alderman Lewis, who spoke for the Choral, that he recognised that the statement made to him was made in good faith. Exactly what this meant towards a reconciliation is not clear, but it is known that, by the end of the next year, 1956, the Philharmonic Society proposed, in a friendly exchange, that the Welsh Choral give a concert during the Promenade season of June 1957, and the Choral accepted the invitation, provided all costs were met by the Philharmonic. After this episode, relations resumed their usual tenor, until ten years later. At that point the complaint came

---

[29] In 1957 the Liverpool Philharmonic Orchestra became the **Royal** Liverpool Philharmonic Orchestra, the RLPO.

from the orchestra. Apparently, in fear for their instruments, the orchestral players requested that the Choral remain seated after a concert until the orchestra had had a chance to leave the platform, and the choir acceded to what seemed a reasonable request.

It will be remembered that, at that time, the Choral was in general reluctant to sing away from its home ground of Liverpool without firm assurance that it would not be to its financial disadvantage. In June, 1965, an invitation came from the London Welsh Trust to sing in December a performance of *The Messiah* at the Royal Festival Hall. The London Welsh Trust would arrange everything, including the conductor, soloists, organist, etc., and would pay the Welsh Choral's travel expenses, as well as arrange a meal on their arrival in London and refreshments after the performance. There were to be no fewer than eighty singers in the choral group. It seemed too good an offer to refuse. The Choral accepted with delight, and with a recommendation that Caleb Jarvis be engaged to play the organ. In September a slight hitch in the arrangements was revealed. Dr. Terry James had been appointed conductor and his name published without at all consulting the Choral committee. The Committee was not happy, and it was decided that the Chairman would visit London to discuss matters with the Trust secretary. By October, however, the Welsh Choral had been given full details of Dr. James's qualifications, and had, for the omission that had occurred, received an apology from the London Trust. Matters were amicably settled, and in December the expedition took place, and was, it seems, enjoyed by all. A generous letter of thanks was later received by the Welsh Choral.

At home in Liverpool, between the Jubilee Concert of 1950 and Malcolm Sargent's death in 1967, over sixty concerts in all took place, almost all of which could be called successful. Some, however, must be singled out for special mention here. There were, as always, many performances of *The Messiah*,

The Liverpool Welsh Choral Union at the Philharmonic Hall, 1967

some conducted by Sargent and others by guest conductors. David Willcocks conducted the Christmas, 1959, concert. Two contrasting views of this performance were expressed: one critic called it restrained, thoughtful and dignified; the other spoke of it as a masterpiece of dance and merriment rather than of pomp and ceremony, an occasion for singing of airiness and buoyancy. One wonders whether the two were at the same performance, though both mention the meticulous preparation by the Choir-master, Caleb Jarvis. Sargent himself conducted the Christmas 1965 performance. This time three press accounts appeared, but there was general agreement among them. Malcolm Sargent exerted his "personal magic". It was a performance of "radiant piety", and of strength born of long understanding. It was remarked that the singing was beautiful and compelling in its unfailing clarity and perfect balance.

The two works of Haydn in the Welsh Choral repertoire, *The Seasons*, performed in April, 1959, under Sargent's baton, and *The Creation*, under George Hurst in February, 1965, were described as having been approached with affection which spread to the audience. The critics spoke of smiling **with** Haydn, rather than **at** him. They commended the lightness of touch and freshness of tone, as well as faithful adherence to Haydn's dynamics.

Performances of Verdi's *Nabucco* during the 1960 Diamond Jubilee and in 1962, both under Charles Groves, brought moments of touching beauty. There was powerful chorus work displaying passion and drama. It was obvious that the choir was enjoying every moment, whether rejoicing as conquering Assyrians or lamenting as the defeated Hebrews. The other Verdi work, the *Requiem*, was, in 1961, performed in a way that went right to the heart of its emotional depth. Sargent's confidence in all his performers was shown in his allowing an unusual degree of freedom, while remaining fully in charge of the whole conception.

Bach's *B minor Mass* was performed under David Willcocks in 1966, after meticulous preparation by Jarvis. The great choruses of the work were given vigorous life by invariably firm attack and resilient rhythm. It was a performance of beauty and exaltation. Willcocks was, at this time, the conductor of the Bach Choir of London, and a specialist in the works of that master.

Elgar's oratorios, favourites of Sargent and of the Welsh Choral, as well as of the audience, were performed frequently during the period under discussion. In 1951 and 1952, all three works of his were performed, *The Apostles* in July, 1951, *The Dream of Gerontius* in December, and *The Kingdom* in the following year. The critics remarked that the Choral sang these difficult works as confidently as they did *The Messiah*. They sang always with sensitivity, but invariably paying scrupulous attention to the careful markings of the composer. Elgar oratorios were almost always conducted by Sargent himself, though once in 1960, Myers Foggin conducted *The Apostles,* when it was said that his was a performance of which Malcolm Sargent could have been proud.

As can be seen, press criticism of the Welsh Choral was almost universally complimentary. There arose an occasion in early 1957, however, when the music commentaries in both the *Post* and the *Echo*, reviews of *The St. Matthew Passion*, conducted by Sargent, were incomprehensibly offensive and insulting. This was so unusual as to arouse the ire of the Committee. Their disgruntlement was intensified when it was rumoured that neither critic had actually attended the concert, but had based their comments on secondary information and on the programme notes. The newspaper editors were informed that the critics would no longer be welcome at Welsh Choral concerts, and no complimentary tickets would be sent for them. After a year had elapsed, however, some patrons complained of the absence of critical reviews, and it was feared that the Choral might suffer from the lack of publicity. In early 1958, therefore, a committee member was deputed to discuss the matter with the editors, and the Press resumed its regular and usually admirable commentary.

Even before the war, Sargent had embarked on overseas tours. These continued to some extent, even during the war, and then, in the early 1950s, after something of a hiatus, they began again, and continued until the year of his death. There were few countries or major cities that he did not visit during his long and active career, very occasionally alone, but usually with either the BBC Symphony Orchestra or the LPO. The Huddersfield Choir accompanied him when choral voices were needed. Everywhere he was enthusiastically welcomed, and everywhere he worked at every available moment, and made friends whose affection lasted a lifetime. The remarkable thing is that he was also able to carry on such a full and active life at home in London and in the northern cities.

Sargent's increasing involvement with so many musical societies at home and abroad, as well as his commitment to the Promenade Concerts every summer season meant that, for very many concerts of the Welsh Choral, Guest Conductors were necessary. It has been suggested that Sargent began to lose interest in his large choirs in the latter part of his life, but the choirs themselves would deny this vehemently. Welsh Choral members, of course, appreciated the generosity of Sargent in giving them so much time and attention, but they were not averse to the practice of rehearsing all the basic work of a concert under the care of Dr. Jarvis, and then enjoying perhaps the new and fresh approach of a guest conductor. Of these, John Pritchard and Charles Groves were the most constant visitors, with David Willcocks chiefly for the Bach works. Myers Foggin was also a popular guest, conducting a variety of concerts. Among the other guests were two Welshmen, both the sons of well-known Welsh musicians. These were Owain Arwel Hughes, son of the composer, Arwel Hughes, and Wyn Morris, son of Dr. Haydn Morris, known for his compositions in many fields of music. Owain Arwel Hughes was to continue to conduct the Welsh Choral on occasions into the 1970s and 1980s.

From 1950 to 1967, there was no scarcity of fine soloists to succeed the roster of the 1940s. Among sopranos, Elsie Morison came here most frequently, with Jennifer Vyvyan a close second. Among contraltos, Kathleen Ferrier, of course, had died in 1953, but there was a succession of excellent contraltos: Gladys Ripley, Norma Procter, Constance Shacklock, and, most popular of all during this period, Marjorie Thomas. Among the men, Norman Walker continued to appear frequently, but other first-class soloists were: William Herbert, Hervey Alan, John Cameron and Owen Brannigan. Heddle Nash continued as the standard Gerontius, though Richard Lewis occasionally played the role. The list of fine singers who sang with the Welsh Choral is, of course, far too long to mention them all, but seldom was the choir or audience disappointed in the choices made.

During much of 1965 and 1966, Malcolm Sargent was suffering from ill-health, and in December, 1966, underwent a serious operation. Yet he would not give in. He was due to conduct a concert of the Welsh Choral in February, 1967, and requested that the work should be Elgar's *The Kingdom*. The oratorio could hardly have received a better prepared and better executed rendering. The Choral, it was remarked, showed a deeper understanding of the work then ever before, singing with faultless expressiveness and diction, and rising to impressive heights in the Pentecostal music and the Lord's Prayer. The critic concluded that the choir might well be proud that Malcolm Sargent chose this occasion for his return to the concert platform. It was his last and 65th appearance with the choir. Of this final concert, Sir Malcolm Sargent himself wrote to his secretary, "I will not easily forget the kindness shown to me by the Choir, Orchestra and audience. The Choir excelled themselves. I have not heard finer singing of *The Kingdom* ever."

Those of us who were fortunate enough to be watching the Last Night of the Proms in 1967, are not likely ever to forget it. That was on September 16. Life had not stood still for Malcolm Sargent after the Welsh Choral Spring concert in Liverpool. He had been on yet another foreign tour, ending with a performance of Sibelius's *Second Symphony* at Ravinia, Chicago's summer venue. When he returned to London, his wasted appearance shocked his friends. Yet he continued to plan for the future. He was booked to conduct eighteen concerts at that summer's Proms. For five days he struggled to rehearse the orchestra, while Colin Davis stood by to take over, but he was then rushed off for an emergency operation on July 28. While convalescing at home, he had time to plan his own Memorial Concert.[30] He was still determined, however, that he would appear at the Albert Hall for the Last Night of the Proms. With the help of his doctors and a series of glucose and saline injections, he carried out his wish, and appeared at the concert's end, straight-backed and sprightly on the podium. He ended his speech with the words, "Next year the Promenade Concerts begin on July twentieth. I have been invited to be here on that night." A pause, and then, "God willing, we all meet again then."

Knowing that he was mortally ill, Sargent then methodically took leave of his friends, calling them one by one to his bedside. On the evening of October 2, his doctor called at 11:00 p.m. to see him. As soon as he had left, Sargent telephoned his devoted secretary to say, "I am slipping away peacefully. God bless you. Good night and Goodbye". By midnight he was in a deep coma, and died the next day.

---

[30] He hoped, if there were to be a memorial service, that Colin Davis would conduct it. He selected a programme of music by British composers, naming the slow movement from Elgar's *Serenade for Strings*, Holst's setting of Whitman's *Ode to Death*, Parry's arrangement of *Jerusalem* and his own arrangement of the Dead March from *Saul*.

CHAPTER SEVEN:
MAURICE HANDFORD

News of the death of Malcolm Sargent was a cause of sorrow for each of his choirs, but it was not an unexpected blow. During that summer of 1967, few of the members of his many choirs and orchestral organisations can have been unaware that, despite Sargent's dogged determination and courage, and his insistence on personally conducting the rehearsal of the opening Prom concert, weakness and pain had eventually forced him to give up any idea of conducting the sixteen Promenade concerts on his summer schedule. Most of his admirers would also have been looking in when he made his farewell to the Promenaders in late September. His death in early October was therefore no surprise to them. From their home in Liverpool, Welsh Choral members were able to take pride in the fact that they had, for so many years, enjoyed Sargent's leadership and his sympathy and practical help. For more than twenty years he had been the Choral's guide in all things musical.

On Wednesday, November 14, the Choral held its Annual General Meeting, chaired by Alderman D. J. Lewis, and with its President, Mr. H. Humphreys Jones, present, as well as a large representation of the Choral members. The President and Chairman paid moving tributes to the late Malcolm Sargent, and they and the Chorus Master, Dr. Caleb Jarvis, in his annual report, made particular reference to the very fine performance of *The Kingdom*, conducted by Sargent in February, and to the excellent concert of Memorial Music that had taken place on November 11. On that occasion, David Willcocks had been the conductor of the performance of Elgar's *Dream of Gerontius*, preceded by the orchestral playing of the *Serenade for Strings,* also by Elgar, and followed by the *Hallelujah Chorus* and the *Amen* from Handel's *Messiah.* The concert was, in its entirety, planned by Malcolm Sargent himself.

The programme for the November 11 concert features the following tribute:

THE LATE SIR MALCOLM SARGENT
D.Mus. (Oxon, Dunelm), F.R.C.M., LLD., F.R.S.A.,
F.R.C.O.

Before Sir Malcolm died, he dictated to his Personal Secretary, Miss Sylvia Darley, some of his wishes for Memorial Music for his friends.

He hoped that The Liverpool Welsh Choral Union would consider the following programme:

The Dream of Gerontius
followed by a few minutes standing in silence with the audience on their feet and, with the audience still standing:

THE HALLELUJAH CHORUS
AMEN
from Handel's "Messiah" as he wanted
everyone to go home happy
(as he put it).
Hallelujah! for the Lord God Omnipotent reigneth.
The Kingdom of this world is become
the Kingdom of our Lord and of his Christ, and
He shall reign for ever and ever, King of Kings,
and Lord of Lords,
Hallelujah.
Amen.

In the same programme is found a tribute to Sir Malcolm by Caleb Jarvis, who had for so many years worked in close harmony with the Master:

Sir Malcolm Sargent brought many things to the Liverpool Welsh Choral Union. His unusually high standards of performance, his obvious joy in handling choirs and his infectious enthusiasm and sincere feeling for all that he did, were an inspiration which is still with us and will be for many years to come.

He was not a man who could be content with growing old gracefully, and his last great act of courage in appearing at the last Promenade Concert was wonderfully in character with the man as we knew him.

With equal determination and courage, we must continue his work.

CALEB JARVIS

A further tribute, a sonnet by M. Doris Humphreys, is also included in the Memorial programme:

His final bow is taken: ne'er again
Will choir or orchestra give back the strain
Of mighty music at his baton's call.
He makes his exit – mourned, beloved by all.

In halls which once re-echoed with applause
For this great music maker, now they pause
In silent tribute to his memory:
And poignant music makes his elegy.

We shall remember him, conductor, friend,
His smiling face, his courage to the end.
Of his rich melodies we took our fill;
These we have loved, these shall we long for still.
Life's concert ended, and the last notes died,
While trumpets sounded on the other side.

M. DORIS HUMPHREYS

The Executive Committee felt no urgency to proceed to the question of choosing a new permanent conductor. Two prominent British musicians, who had on many occasions conducted the Welsh Choral, could be counted upon for advice, whenever it might be needed. Sir David Willcocks and Sir Charles Groves were old friends by this time, and there was another who had already offered valuable support to the Welsh Choral. When there had been doubt in early 1967 as to whether Sir Malcolm would have recovered sufficiently to conduct the February performance of *The Kingdom*, the Co-conductor of the Hallé Philharmonic Society, Maurice Handford, had stood by ready at a moment's notice to take over the conducting, should it prove necessary. When, in the Autumn of 1967, members of the Executive Committee planned the concerts of the Welsh Choral for the 1967-1968 season, they were anxious to show their appreciation of Maurice Handford's gesture, and, after some discussion, the Committee passed that Handford be invited to conduct their next *Messiah*. This performance took place on December 9 of that year.

Interestingly, the critic, Stainton Taylor, in his review of the *Messiah* concert remarked on a resemblance in appearance and manner between Maurice Handford and Malcolm Sargent. Whether this was a purposeful imitation is not known. Another critic pointed to Handford's innovatory treatment of dynamics, and praised a robust and vital performance.

During the years 1968 to 1971, the Choral performed well-known works during their concerts, and only one "new" conductor came to the fore to take charge of some performances. That was Christopher Robinson. Otherwise all performances were conducted by Charles Groves, David Willcocks or Maurice Handford, with, of course, Caleb Jarvis remaining Chorus Master and Ernest Pratt, the Accompanist. The most unusual work performed in this period was perhaps Malcolm Sargent's concert version of Verdi's *Aida*. This was done altogether three times under Maurice Handford's baton, the first time in the Philharmonic Hall in Liverpool in November, 1968, and then, as part of the Hallé Summer Proms, in June, 1969. The performance in Manchester was judged to be a rich, ripe reading. Obviously, it was well received by audiences, and in July, 1971, the performance was taken to Birmingham, with the City of Birmingham Symphony Orchestra.

During the bombing of World War II, records of the Welsh Choral, dating from before 1940, were lost to the Society. The first extant Book of Minutes runs from 1940 to 1954. The entry for December 11, 1971, brings to an end the Second Minute Book. After that date comes a serious gap, a gap of over ten years' duration. Whether the story told is fact or fiction, the tradition is that, in some unexplained way, Choral records for the years from 1972 to 1984 were, most unfortunately, left on a Liverpool bus, and were never recovered by the Choral Union. We are fortunate, however, that the years 1970 and 1971 were particularly full ones in the history of the Welsh Choral, and that the Honorary Secretary, Mr. D. ap D. Jones, was meticulous in his recording of the Minutes of the period.

By December, 1969, the question arose of whether to appoint Handford as the new Permanent Conductor, but, after an inconclusive discussion, the matter was postponed. One who seemed opposed to the appointment was Caleb Jarvis, and his views carried weight in the Committee. As a democratic society, which the Welsh Choral had been since its inception, the Executive Committee was anxious that the initiative and the management remain in its hands, and did not pass into those of any conductor, however highly thought of. To ensure that its views should be clearly understood, a resolution constituting eight clauses was drawn up by the Executive. The resolution follows:

That we invite him (that is, Mr Maurice Handford) to be the conductor of the Liverpool Welsh Choral Union subject to his acceptance

1 that no specific period of years be agreed upon;
2 that if appointed he be offered a minimum of three of our normal four concerts per season;
3 if these terms are acceptable, that he be publicly and officially known as the conductor of this Choir;
4 in the event of calls from other societies compelling him to relinquish this post, that this Society be notified no later than September of any year;
5 likewise, should the Liverpool Welsh Choral Union wish to make a change in conductorship, that he be informed as soon as possible, and no later than September as in paragraph 4;
6 the above conditions will not apply where the Choir are invited to sing outside of the Philharmonic Hall locally, nor when invited to sing for other societies who have their own conductors, wherever that may be;   ·
7 fees to be paid after each concert on terms to be mutually agreed upon;
8 should agreement on the above points be reached, the Executive Committee, on behalf of the Choir, agree to give every support to him for the betterment and advancement in every sense of our musical standard.

This resolution on conductors and conductorship was proposed, seconded and carried in the Executive Committee by a majority vote of 15 to 6. Mr Handford having accepted the terms proposed, the following announcement appeared in the printed programme of February, 1970: "This Society has pleasure in announcing the appointment of Maurice Handford as its own conductor, and wishes him every success."

The death of Malcolm Sargent and subsequent appointment of Maurice Handford as Permanent Conductor was the first major alteration in the leadership of the Welsh Choral for over

Maurice Handford
Principal Conductor of the Liverpool Welsh Choral Union
1970 - 1982

twenty years. But in the early 1970s came a series of changes, initiated in 1971 by the death in May, at the age of 93, of the President, Mr. H. Humphreys Jones. The announcement of his death appeared in the Choral Concert programme of November 6, 1971. The Tribute read:

H. HUMPHREYS JONES, Esq., F.R.I.C., M.A., J.P.

President of
THE LIVERPOOL WELSH CHORAL UNION, 1934-1971

The death of our much loved President Mr. Humphreys Jones in May this year brought to an end his long and close association with the Liverpool Welsh Choral Union which dates back to 1903.

We feel his loss deeply, for to us, he was no mere figurehead but a warm hearted friend who inspired, encouraged and uplifted us. His welcome presence at many of our rehearsals was always a joyous occasion, and his lively wit and infectious good humour promoted a wonderful sense of happiness and enthusiasm throughout the choir.

He will be greatly missed, but we feel privileged to have had his wise and friendly leadership for so many years.

B. A. C.

Mr Humphreys Jones's death made necessary the choice of a new President. Two names in particular emerged, and in December the selection was made. The two candidates, Dr. Emyr Wyn Jones and Alderman D. J. Lewis, each offered to withdraw in favour of the other, but the matter was amicably resolved in a most satisfactory way. The announcement was made in the concert programme of February 12, 1972. The President was to be Dr. Emyr Wyn Jones, O.B.E., M.D., F.R.C.P., D.P.H. Alderman David J. Lewis, J.P., A.R.I.B.A., Chairman since 1948 of the Liverpool Welsh Choral, would remain in that position.

Dr. Emyr Wyn Jones,
President of the Liverpool Welsh Choral Union
1972-1986

CHAPTER SEVEN: MAURICE HANDFORD

Dr. Emyr Wyn Jones was born in Waunfawr, Caernarfonshire in 1907. He was educated at the County School, Caernarfon, and later studied Medicine at the University of Liverpool. He spent most of his professional life as a cardiologist in Liverpool, but made his home in Llansannan, though in retirement he moved to the Llŷn Peninsula. His contact with Wales, its people, culture and history, remained strong throughout. He wrote extensively on medical, historic and literary topics. He served on many national bodies, including the British Cardiac Society, the Welsh Language Medical Society, and the National Library and National Museum of Wales. At one time he acted as President of the Court of the National Eisteddfod. For his services he was awarded the honorary degree of LL.B. of the University of Wales.

With the account of the Annual General Meeting in November, 1971, the Second Book of Choral Minutes comes to an end. The Minutes, in the clear hand of Mr. D. ap D. Jones, confirmed the choice of President and Chairman. Other officers mentioned were those of Mr. B. A. Coppack as Vice-Chairman and Mr. Maurice E. Helliwell as Honorary Treasurer. Mr. Helliwell proposed a non-member but faithful attender, Mr. Berwyn Morris, as Deputy Secretary, and these appointments, as well as those of Auditors and Librarians, were confirmed by the general meeting.

A further change in the early 1970s was caused by the death of the Honorary Secretary, Mr. D. ap D. Jones, who had served in that office since 1963. He died in August, 1972. A tribute to him appeared in the concert programme of November 11, 1972.

> The Officers and Members of the Liverpool Welsh Choral Union heard with deep regret of the sudden death in August last, of their devoted and dedicated Honorary Secretary, Mr. D. ap D. Jones.

He joined the choir in 1930 in the Tenor Section and in 1954 was appointed Assistant Secretary and in 1963, Secretary. His work as Secretary has been outstanding, marked by indefatigable zeal and sustained by his love of music and his burning desire to promote the interests of the Liverpool Welsh Choral Union. We mourn his loss and will ever be grateful for all he has done for us.

B.A.C

With so many changes taking place, it must have been reassuring, for the time being, that the Chorus Master, Dr. Caleb Jarvis, and the Accompanist, Mr. Ernest Pratt, continued their faithful service to the choir. In the Executive meeting on November 10, 1971, it was decided that gifts should be presented to Dr. Jarvis to celebrate 25 years as Chorus Master, and Mr Pratt for 26 years as Accompanist. The presentation was made in the Annual General Meeting of December 8, 1971.

Naturally much of the choir's success was attributable to the meticulous work of preparation carried on under their Chorus Master, Caleb Jarvis. The critics were not slow to recognise his work and to mention it in their critiques. Sometimes we find a special passage mentioned as admirable, as in February, 1972, when, in a performance of *Gerontius*, the Demons' Chorus was praised as particularly convincing, whereas in former years it had been criticised as "too gentlemanly".

The retirement of Jarvis was not, unfortunately, a totally happy occasion. Five years had elapsed since the presentation of gifts to him and Pratt after their long service to the Choir. The Executive Committee may have anticipated an announcement of his retirement within a year or so of the presentation. But none came. It is acknowledged by most that retirement, contemplated in the abstract, looks attractive, but when the time arrives, it is tempting to postpone the crucial moment. And so it was not until he had been Chorus Master for thirty years that Caleb Jarvis retired. It is possible that some members of the Welsh

Choral had been aware for some time that there was, waiting in the wings, as it were, a very suitable successor for their retiring Chorus Master. That was Mr. Edmund Walters, already Chorus Master of the Philharmonic Choir.

Mr Walters was born in Milford Haven in West Wales. He had attended the Grammar School in Milford Haven, and then, having taken a music degree in the University College of Wales, Aberystwyth, and spent some years in the R.A.F., he had returned to teach music in his old grammar school, and had organised and conducted a successful choir in the town. In 1960 he had moved to Liverpool to take up a teaching post and to conduct the College Choir at the I. M. Marsh College. In 1967 he had taken over the Philharmonic Choir, and amongst his other Liverpool appointments was the conductorship of the University Gilbert and Sullivan Society. He was obviously interested in a choir of Welsh origin, and gladly accepted the post of Chorus Master of the Liverpool Welsh Choral when, in 1976, it was offered to him. Very soon the Liverpool music critics noticed in his work a freshness of approach which they welcomed, though Walters tended in many ways to follow in the steps of Jarvis. He was, like his predecessor, an Elgar enthusiast. The work of Jarvis was not forgotten, and after his death in early 1980, the February concert was dedicated to his memory, and Elgar's *Enigma Variations* played as a tribute to him.

Naturally, as the years went by, there were inevitably other changes in the leadership of the Choral. In 1976, Alderman D. J. Lewis, who had until then served as Chairman, joined Dr. Emyr Wyn Jones as Joint President, and continued in that position until his death in January, 1982. In 1976 Alderman Lewis's place as Chairman was taken by Mrs. Eileen Morris, who remained in that position for four years, to be followed by Mr. Ifor Griffith. Mr. Maurice Helliwell served as Treasurer for two years, after which he became Honorary Secretary until

1980, when Graham Connolly took his place. For the years of 1973 and 1974, Mr. T. J. Leith Gratton served as Treasurer, and was succeeded by Miss Eileen Vaughan, who served for the remainder of Mr. Handford's conductorship. Miss Vaughan has herself left a memoir of this period in her life, when she worked indefatigably and happily for the Welsh Choral. Naturally, too, at each Annual General Meeting, new members were elected to the Executive Committee, members who would eventually become the leading spirits of the Choral.

The main function of the Executive Committee during Maurice Handford's term of office remained the preparation of concerts, including the choice of works to be performed, and of soloists to take the necessary roles in each work. During the years 1970 to 1982, there were far too many new faces to make it possible to identify them all. Naturally, some of the popular singers of the 1950s and 1960s had withdrawn from the concert field, but others remained. The most constant guest soloist was Marjorie Thomas, who led the lists during Malcolm Sargent's day, and continued to do so throughout the 1970s. Among the men were some favourites too, who appeared repeatedly with the Welsh Choral: Brian Rayner Cook, Raimund Herincz, David Johnston, Duncan Robertson, Michael Rippon and Philip Ravenscroft each sang more than five times in concert with the Choral. Some new names appeared among the women soloists: Jean Allister, Barbara McGuire, Wendy Eathorne, and especially Felicity Lott became favourites, and several nationally known singers appeared occasionally: Norma Burrowes, Alfreda Hodgson and April Cantelo. A few Welsh singers, Eiddwen Harrhy, Kenneth Bowen, Wynford Evans and Richard Lewis, made appearances from time to time, and many of these retained their popularity into the 1980s and 1990s.

Though it was obvious that the reputation of the Welsh Choral would be maintained by the Committee and the members, the same financial problems continued to plague the

D. J. Lewis
Chairman of the Liverpool Welsh Choral Union,
1948 - 1976,
Joint President of the Liverpool Welsh Choral Union,
1976 - 1982

choir. It was apparent that fees, especially for the hire of the Royal Liverpool Philharmonic Orchestra, were continuing to rise. As early as 1968 it had been found necessary to announce a new scale of admission charges, as follows:

PRICES OF ADMISSION (All Seats Reserved)

	SERIES	SINGLE
	£ s d	£ s d
Boxes (to seat 6)	16 16 0	4 4 0
Boxes (to seat 6)	15 12 0	3 18 0
Boxes (to seat 6)	14 8 0	3 12 0
Centre stalls	2 6 0	11 6
Side stalls	2 0 0	10 0
Front two rows	1 6 0	6 6
Third & fourth rows	1 14 0	8 6
Upper stalls	2 6 0	11 6
Front Balcony	2 2 0	10 6
Upper Balcony	1 18 0	9 6
Upper Balcony	1 12 0	8 0
Back two rows	1 6 0	6 6

In later years, admission prices continued to increase gradually. There was, of course, always the possibility that an increase in ticket prices might lead to smaller audiences, but it was not until late in 1971 that a monetary loss, due to unsold tickets, was serious enough to provoke comment.   An entirely different reason for rising costs, however, was unprecedented in the experience of the Choral, and important enough to impel immediate action. Perhaps in ignorance of the Choral Rules, some guest conductors, without reference to the Executive Committee, had made arrangements for the engagement of additional soloists and instrumentalists. The Committee immediately took steps to prevent the repetition of such an action. The Committee, it declared, must be consulted before a guest conductor took the initiative in such management matters. At the same time, it was passed in committee that no one person, even the Chorus Master, should invite another body of musicians to join in concert with the Welsh Choral unless the possible joint appearance had previously been discussed and passed in committee.

Various internal matters occupied a good proportion of time in committee meetings. The question of regular attendance at rehearsals was troublesome. Caleb Jarvis raised the matter at the AGM in 1969, but the situation was no better in 1970, when it was reported that the number of active members had fallen to 180, with the average attendance at 150. It was to be hoped that more students could be recruited to the choir, especially in the male sections. A positive publicity effort in 1971, with attractive posters and brochures, was effective in bringing in a few new members, but yet more young voices were needed.

Another perennial question for discussion was that of dress, chiefly that of the women, of course. The problem of the varying lengths of ladies' dresses was discussed in November, 1967, but postponed for further discussion when there would be a better female representation. Four years later, steps were taken to obtain written views on the matter from the women of the choir, and a report was said to be available "soon". Since the second volume of minutes ends with the matter unsettled, it is not possible to know what the finished report recommended at this period in the choir's history. Indeed, whether much progress at all was made during the 1970s is open to question. Some decisions on the nature of women's dresses may indeed have been made. However, in a concert review printed on December 8, 1979, Joe Riley, the *Echo*'s usual critic, had this to say: "On a fashion note, my companion observed that the long, brilliant white dresses of the ladies of the Welsh Choral not only dazzle the eyes, but look like shrouds. I had to agree."

While internal matters occupied the greater part of the Committee's time, it was also concerned with related musical affairs. Helping the National Eisteddfod in its Flint gathering in 1969 was an effort adopted with enthusiasm. The Welsh Choral gave an *Elijah* performance, the proceeds of which went to support the Eisteddfod's expenses. Then in January, 1970, the Choral accepted the B.B.C. invitation to record hymns for the *Songs of Praise* programme, and this broadcast was transmitted in February.

Prior to this, in 1968, it had been decided that the Welsh Choral should join the newly-formed Merseyside Arts Association. The chief purpose in joining this association was to become eligible for grants. The decision to join, however, would necessarily involve some revision of the rules of the Welsh Choral. In the 1970s the Executive Committee embarked on a very thorough revision of the Rules of the Society. Work on this extended over some years, and it was not until 1977 that it was possible to publish the revised Rules.[1]

Were the years of Maurice Handford's conductorship successful ones for the Welsh Choral? Certainly there was no drop in attendance at concerts, and there was enthusiastic audience reception for each concert in turn. In the absence of Choral Minutes, we are, of course, forced to rely on the reviews of the critics.

Early in the period, while the critics were still referring to Handford as a 'new' conductor, one wrote, "The future looks bright for the city's Welsh Choral Union." Several times during the next twelve years, commentators remarked on the choir's special relationship with the works of Elgar, as well as the Choral's reputation from the early 1900s for bringing Elgar's works, for the first time, to Merseyside. They refer particularly to the choir's special affinity and affection for *The Dream of Gerontius*. Often complimentary comments are made on the artistry and vocal brilliance of the singing, the zeal and warmth

---

[1]A copy of the Rules of 1977 is to be found in Appendix II

of the voices, and the burning sincerity that shines through their work. Towards the end of the 1970s, one critic remarks on a concert's being a wholly satisfying one, and another that concerts by the Welsh Choral are always hard to match. Leece, a well-respected critic, tells us that in 1979, the Choir is "as good as I ever heard it."

What of Handford's personal share in the Choir's successes? It is interesting that there is a progamme in the files, obviously one having belonged to a choir member. He, or she, has written on the cover of the *Messiah* programme of December, 1969, the comment: "Maurice Handford, whose remarks at the final rehearsal about Choruses 22 and 24 I will remember every time I sing them (Lovely!)" Leadership of this kind must certainly have been appreciated by the Choral members. Mr. Handford was praised by the critics for well-planned and well-performed concerts, for inspiring eloquent singing and orchestral playing, for capturing the style and spirit of the works of each composer in turn, and for instilling dignity and expressiveness, especially into new works or those not previously heard in Liverpool. His conducting was especially praised in opera or works that had in them elements of the operatic, like Rossini's *Petite Messe.*

In a Liverpool Welsh Choral programme of the early 1980s, Maurice Handford's career was described in the following way:

> Mr. Handford has one of the largest repertoires of any British conductor. This is the result of considerable experience which began with studies at the Royal Academy of Music in London, where he is now Conductor of the First Orchestra and a Fellow. Michael Kennedy, critic and leading authority on Elgar, has described him as "an Elgarian conductor of the utmost distinction". Soon after his debut with the Hallé, he started to make frequent guest appearances with this and other orchestras, and in 1964 he was appointed Barbirolli's Assistant and soon after Associate Conductor of the Hallé. In this capacity he was responsible for introducing and maintaining

many new and major works to Hallé audiences, in addition
to directing the popular Industrial Concerts. Over many years
Mr. Handford has broadcast literally hundreds of concerts
for the B.B.C., has appeared on B.B.C. television and has
broadcast for almost every radio station in the many countries
he has visited. His American debut was made in 1971 with
the Houston Symphony in concerts which included Walton's
Belshazzar's Feast, and his particular skill with choirs, allied
with his sympathy for music of most periods, has won him
popularity and acclaim from audiences and critics. He is
Permanent Conductor, and only the third (actually, the fourth)
in its long history, of the Liverpool Welsh Choral Union. His
conducting of such works as Elgar's *Dream of Gerontius, The
Apostles,* and *The Kingdom,* and the Berlioz, Mozart and Verdi
Requiems has received most enthusiastic reviews and ovations.
So have his stage and concert performances of many operas,
including Verdi's *La Traviata, Aida,* and *Nabucco,* Mozart's
Don Giovanni, Marriage of Figaro, and *Magic Flute,* Wagner's
Meistersingers and Berlioz's *The Trojans.*

Maurice Handford has received official recognition
of his eminence as a conductor. In 1967 he was awarded
the coveted Arnold Bax Memorial Prize. More recently, he
received the medal of the City of Le Havre on behalf of the
Royal Philharmonic Orchestra after conducting this orchestra
in a concert described as "Pas seulement un evenemente, un
pur regal". In 1971 a panel of Manchester's leading citizens,
including the Lord Mayor of Manchester, named Maurice
Handford "Man of the Year" for the way, following Sir John
Barbirolli's death, he had "held the Hallé together over a
difficult period in their history".

In 1981 he accompanied the Hallé in its Far East Tour to
great acclaim.

How many Welsh Choral members are familiar with the
Welsh expression, *Cythraul Canu* or *Cythraul y Canu*? To our
shame, most of us brought up in Welsh Chapels will have heard
the expression from early childhood. It can be translated as

'The Devil in the Singing', and signifies a devilish spirit that infiltrates an otherwise friendly singing association, and brings about disagreement or, worse, a permanent failure to work in harmony. It is usually to be discovered among people who care very much about music-making, but are convinced that one approach rather than another is the only reasonable one. For three-quarters of a century, until the 1970s, the Welsh Choral seems to have been immune from attacks by this Devil, but Maurice Handford's time with the Choir was not so harmonious as appeared at first. Perhaps some of the friction was caused by an imperfect understanding of the Rules, dating from the time when Handford was first appointed to the postion of Conductor.

By 1980, Handford had conducted an unusually large proportion of the concerts that had recently taken place. This circumstance may have given Mr. Handford the impression that he, and he only, was in sole charge of the Choral. The Executive Committee naturally felt uncomfortable by the threatening loss of control over the organisation of the Choral, and were wary of allowing Mr. Handford too much leeway. In 1981, Mr Handford conducted none of the Welsh Choral concerts. Then, after a concert in early 1982, in which the choir was described as tired, there appeared in the *Daily Post* an extraordinary article, headlined "Rumpus as Choir Chief Quits", and followed by the statement, "'I've quit', conductor tells choir." One long-standing matter of dispute had been the question of who was to have the final say on the works to be performed. Such disagreements had not been unknown in former years, but they had always been settled on the understanding that the Executive Committee chose the works, 'with the advice of the Conductor and Chorus Master'. It was obvious in this case that Mr. Handford and the Committee could no longer work together in harness, and a somewhat bewildered choir was told, during the following rehearsal, that Mr. Handford was no longer their Principal

Conductor, though he might return from time to time as Guest Conductor. The situation was unfortunately exacerbated by the outspoken comments of some choristers who had equally failed to comprehend the nature of the Choral's constitution, and were not sufficiently conversant with its Rules. The decision was irreversible. It had been taken, after all, by their democratically elected Committee, a committee that had invariably striven for the ultimate good of the choir.

In spite of harsh words spoken in the heat of the moment, it is obvious that Mr. Handford's services to the Choral were still held in high regard by all the officers and members, and the concerts directed by him were almost without exception reported favourably by the Liverpool critics.

Some years later, the Welsh Choral programme of April 11, 1987, was dedicated to the memory of Mr. Handford who had died on December 16, 1986. The dedication reads:

This Concert is dedicated to the memory of

MAURICE HANDFORD

Principal Conductor of The Liverpool Welsh Choral Union
1970-1982

Maurice Handford, who died on 16th December, 1986, was Principal Conductor of the Liverpool Welsh Choral Union from 1970 to 1982. During that period he gave exceptional service to the Choir, striving at all times to achieve the highest standards of musical excellence.

Maurice Handford was a gifted choral conductor, and we recall with pleasure numerous thrilling performances under his baton. He was a noted exponent of the works of Sir Edward Elgar, and it was particularly fitting that in 1970 Maurice Handford should conduct THE DREAM OF GERONTIUS in memory of his own mentor, Sir John Barbirolli.

In similar vein, The Liverpool Welsh Choral Union

dedicates tonight's performance of THE KINGDOM to the memory of Maurice Handford.

With the departure of Maurice Handford, it was resolved to return to the practice followed before his appointment, that is, to invite guest conductors for each Choral concert in turn, and to take plenty of time to consider the situation further. A new generation of able and ambitious young conductors was growing up in Britain, and there would be no difficulty at all in obtaining the services of one or other for each of the Welsh Choral concerts. In this ninth decade of the Choral's existence, the future continued to look bright.

CHAPTER EIGHT:
AN ERA OF GUEST CONDUCTORS

It is unfortunate that the continuing absence of Choral Minutes makes exhaustive enquiry into the history of the Welsh Choral in the early 1980s utterly impossible. However, the Executive Committee undoubtedly continued its thorough and increasingly demanding labours, and the successful concerts of the period 1982-1984 testify to the fact that there was no decline in enthusiasm on the part of the choristers or of the audience.

Naturally, the schedule for the 1982-1983 season had been arranged before the departure of Maurice Handford. On November 6, 1982, a Gala Opera Concert was held. Owain Arwel Hughes was the conductor on this occasion, and the choir was joined by soloists from the Welsh National Opera. The Choral was commended for its fine singing, in Italian, of the closing chorus from Puccini's opera, *Turandot.* Howard Williams led the Choral in its Christmas *Messiah.* It was deemed a muted and subdued performance, and the critics, for the first time, questioned the wisdom of offering the oratorio every Christmas. The audience had certainly seemed less warmly enthusiastic about their annual fare than in past years. Perhaps it might be time to give the *Messiah* a rest.

In February 1983, the choir returned to an old favourite with a performance of *Gerontius* under the baton of Sir David Willcocks. It was, said one critic, an impressive performance, with a charismatic conductor. Another commented, however, that the singing, though commendable, was not exactly riveting. It was, nevertheless, a presentation of delicacy and exactitude, the enunciation of the Choral as admirable as ever. A new Gerontius, Maldwyn Davies, had come to the fore.

On St. George's Day in April, 1983, the Choral presented an English evening, featuring music by Tallis, Parry, Vaughan-

Williams and Tippett. This was a novelty for the choir, a fresh venture into more contemporary English choral literature.

The November event was a colourful concert, a performance of Verdi's *Aida*, the version of an hour and three-quarters length, devised by Malcolm Sargent for the use of his choirs. There were, it was remarked, some lapses in ensemble in this presentation, but it was exciting. Robin Stapleton led a performance that was not flawless but certainly never dull. Indeed, it might be called over-exuberant. During the evening, the traditional retirement present, a clock, was presented by the Treasurer, Miss Eileen Vaughan, to the long-serving Accompanist, Ernest Pratt.

Despite the criticism of the previous year, the Welsh Choral put on its usual *Messiah* at Christmas, 1983. Sadly, seldom could the Choral have been given so poor a press reception. It was a generally unconvincing performance, prone to error and fluffed leads. The conductor, Martin Merry, and the orchestra were often at variance over tempi and dynamics, and the orchestra itself was obviously not fully committed to the work. The excuse offered was that of confusion deriving from varying versions of the work.

It must have been a relief to return to safe ground in late February 1984, with a Welsh Festival to celebrate St. David's Day. Owain Arwel Hughes was once more the conductor, and the concert was enjoyed by a large audience.

June brought the fiftieth anniversary of the death of Elgar, when Sir Alexander Gibson led the Choral in a performance of *The Apostles*, part of a three-week Liverpool Festival of Elgar's music. The Welsh Choral was joined in this concert by the Liverpool Cathedral Choir and the choir of Worcester Cathedral. The singing of the oratorio brought nothing but praise for conductor and choirs, even though it was acknowledged that it was difficult to negotiate the acoustics of the large body of singers in the Cathedral. It was judged to be an impressive reading, noble in overall feeling.

The Liverpool Welsh Choral Union at the Liverpool International Garden Festival, 1984
Edmund Walters conducting

For several months during the summer of 1984, Liverpool was celebrating a very successful International Garden Festival. Though it was not customary for the Welsh Choral to hold concerts during the summer months, the Choral contributed three evening programmes of light music to the Festival.[1] Edmund Walters conducted on these occasions, and Mr. Ifor Griffith acted as compère.

In the Autumn of 1984 came the resumption of Choral Minutes, and naturally, of discussion concerning many matters that arose perennially to demand solution. An important meeting of the Executive Committee was held in November 1984. It is obvious that what most concerned the Committee was the fact that Edmund Walters, who had been Chorus Master since 1976, should have indicated his intention to retire in 1985. Consequently, during late 1984, the Committee had placed advertisements for a Chorus Master in the journal, *Classical Music*, and in the *Daily Telegraph*. The high standing of the Welsh Choral is evidenced by the many letters received, indicating interest in the post. All who had written in response to the advertisement received a one-page summary detailing the nature and history of the choir, and inviting formal applications, to be sent along with the Curriculum Vitae of each applicant, and the names and addresses of two referees. A sub-committee of the Executive Committee was appointed to consider these applications and to report back with recommendations. Four criteria were to guide them in their work:

1 Advice should be sought from Sir David Willcocks and Sir Charles Groves.
2 The Secretary should write to each applicant offering an interview, with expenses paid to cover travelling costs, and briefly stating salary terms.
3 Candidates should supply the names of two referees (with addresses).

---

[1] Photographs of the Choir on this occasion can be found in the LWCU's Archive Picture File.

4 The closing date to declare an interest in the post was 31/12/84.

Eleven applications remain in the Choral archives, and make very interesting reading. Six of them were from relatively local candidates, and the other five came from the South of England. Most applicants were in their thirties or forties. Some had advanced degrees from the Royal Academy or Royal College in London, or from the Northern School of Music in Manchester. Some had had further training under well-known conductors, and several were school teachers or college lecturers. More than one had had experience abroad. One stands out as especially well qualified, having been an organ scholar at Queens' College, Cambridge, and having conducted the choir there, before spending three years at the Royal Academy studying piano and harpsichord. Later he had joined the staff at Glyndebourne, and established choirs in several southern towns. Unfortunately he was resident in High Wycombe, whose distance from Liverpool probably counted against him.

By the time of the Committee Meeting in early February 1985, the process of selection was well advanced. Nine candidates were considered, and their C.V.s and references circulated among Committee members. Important decisions were taken by the Executive Committee:

1 A contract should be issued for one probationary year only.

2 Those short-listed must be made aware that the Chorus Master, when appointed, must be present **every** Wednesday evening.

3 It must be understood that it was a Chorus Master **only** that was being sought, and not a Permanent Conductor. It was the Policy of the Welsh Choral to use conductors of national repute, though the Chorus Master might conduct a concert occasionally.

4 Auditions for the position would be based on verbal interviews by the sub-committee, and then followed by the candidate's conducting a rehearsal.

5 An outside musical assessor, probably Sir Charles Groves,
   would be asked for an opinion.
6 It was essential that **all** the sub-committee have a chance to
   interview and be present at the projected rehearsal.
7 The sub-committee and assessors would then meet the full
   Executive to put forward recommendations. It was hoped to
   have a short-list of three, with one reserve.
8 If several were assessed to be equal, then the full Executive
   Committee would decide on behalf of the Choir.

Appropriate interviews and meetings took place during
February and March, after which there was lively debate. It
was eventually determined that an invitation be extended to
Mr. Anthony Ridley of Bebington, to be Chorus Master and
Musical Director for the 1985-1986 season, subject to a possible
extension to a three-year term. Mr. Ridley had, early in 1984,
as it happened, made independent enquiries about the post of
Chorus Master, and, by the time of the interview, he was booked
to conduct one Welsh Choral concert. Mr. Ridley's C.V. was
impressive. In a 1988 Welsh Choral programme, the following
account of Ridley's background was printed:

> Anthony Ridley was a former leader of the National Youth
> Orchestra of Great Britain and a graduate of Oxford University
> where he was the President of the University Music Society.
> For eight years he was a violinist with the Royal Liverpool
> Philharmonic Orchestra. During this time he gained
> much valuable experience conducting first rehearsals of
> contemporary works and preliminary rehearsals for Sir Charles
> Groves and various guest conductors which led gradually to an
> increasing conducting commitment. In 1973 he left the RLPO
> to concentrate on a conducting career. After the first Liverpool
> Seminar for Young British Conductors he was invited to
> participate in a series of masterclasses with Rafael Kubelik
> at the Brighton Festival. In 1975 he deputised for Sir Charles
> Groves at two hours' notice in two performances with the

RLPO in Manchester and Liverpool. In 1977, at the personal invitation of Sir Yehudi Menuhin, he appeared with the Berlin Philharmonic with such critical acclaim that he was invited back in 1979. In 1983 he made a highly successful debut in Leipzig in East Germany with the renowned Gewandhaus Orchestra. He has since conducted many of the major British orchestras, including broadcasting from the Royal Festival Hall with the Philharmonia Chorus and Orchestra, and has worked extensively with various BBC orchestras. He is at present Musical Director of the Chester Music Society Choir, the City of Chester Symphony Orchestra and the Halifax Symphony Orchestra, together with youth orchestras in both the Wirral and Warrington areas.

While engaged in selecting a Chorus Master, it was possible for the Committee to settle another matter. One of the remaining applicants for the Chorus Master's post had been Derek Sadler, on whose behalf Ian Tracey, the Cathedral organist, had spoken. Mr. Sadler had stated, in his application, that his chief interest lay in teaching and rehearsing, rather than actually conducting. As a consequence, therefore, he was invited to become the Choral's new Accompanist, a position he accepted to the general satisfaction of Committee and Choir.

The Executive Committee had, as usual, already chosen the works to be prepared during the 1985-1986 season, with conductors and soloists selected for each work. In order not to make too many demands on the new Chorus Master, four comparatively familiar favourites had been selected for the winter's concerts: *Elijah, The Messiah,* a Carol Concert, and Brahms's *Requiem.*

Anthony Ridley's probationary year with the choir proved entirely satisfactory. In the performance of *Elijah* in November, 1985, critics mentioned the choir's accuracy and wealth of colour contrasts, as well as its articulate rhythms and vigorous singing, much of which could be attributed to rehearsal under Ridley.

Three Chorus Masters of the Liverpool Welsh Choral Union

Caleb Jarvis, 1946 - 1976

Edmund Walters, 1976 - 1985

Anthony Ridley, 1985 - 1989

This performance was followed by a Brahms *Requiem* concert, conducted by Owain Arwel Hughes. On this occasion, critics spoke of the rarified beauty of tone, pointing to painstaking rehearsal training. After the extension of Ridley's contract to the end of the 1987-1988 season, choir and Chorus Master could be assured that the usual high standard of preparation still prevailed.

On the other hand, when Ridley made a rare appearance as conductor, there were some less complimentary remarks. It was pointed out that there was sometimes an imbalance in the resulting performance, not always due to the severe scarcity of tenors, or to the difficulty sopranos were experiencing in obtaining pure tone on the high notes, but, more seriously, to Ridley's habit of permitting the orchestra to drown the singers with its too raucous playing. By early 1988, however, better press reviews were emerging, and it was remarked that Ridley had infused new confidence into a choir of great traditions whose morale and performing standards had lately been sagging alarmingly.

In our consideration of the period, of course, praise and blame alike must be shared between Chorus Master and the guest conductors selected by the Committee. During the period 1985 to 1989, Martin Merry made several appearances with the choir, and so did Anthony Hose. Edward Warren conducted only once, a performance of *The Creation* in 1989, but this concert was noteworthy in that Bryn Terfel was heard as soloist here for the first time. He had, in 1988, won the Kathleen Ferrier Memorial Scholarship. He showed, it was reported, impeccable technique and an impressive stage presence.

The most frequent and most popular guest conductor during this era was Sian Edwards, the first woman conductor in the experience of the Welsh Choral. She conducted the Choral on four occasions during the 1980s. Her first appearance was in December 1985, when she conducted the Christmas *Messiah* performance. The programme for that occasion gave an account of her career up to that point.

> Sian Edwards came of a Pembrokeshire family, was born in West Sussex and grew up in Oxford. She attended the Royal Northern College of Music, where she found herself conducting concerts while still a student. Later, she won a place on the Conductors' course at Hilversum in the Netherlands, and later still, a British Council Scholarship to study at the Leningrad Conservatoire in Russia. In 1984 she had won the first Leeds Conductors Competition, and was, in 1986, due to conduct the City of Birmingham Symphony Orchestra, the Liverpool Philharmonic, the Scottish National Orchestra, and the BBC Philharmonic, as well as the Royal Philharmonic at the Barbican in London. This appearance with the Liverpool Welsh Choral was only one of several appearances she was to make on Merseyside.

For the opening concert of the 1986-1987 season, the Committee had chosen Orff's *Carmina Burana,* again conducted by Sian Edwards. Much useful publicity attended the preparation of this concert. Miss Edwards was interviewed on the local BBC Radio Station, and, partly for this reason, and partly because of the nature of the work, the November concert was sold out. The *Echo* reported that the audience was rapt at the singing of the "loud, dirty" songs! All the critics were unanimous in their praise, and pointed particularly to Sian Edwards's enthusiasm, skill and determination. Indeed, special skill was needed, since the Welsh Choral had been augmented by the boys from the choir of the Liverpool Anglican Cathedral, as well as six tenors from the Royal Northern College. The orchestra, too, though announced as the Royal Liverpool Philharmonic Orchestra, was actually a blended one, in which some of the regulars were replaced by extras.

A year later, in November, 1987, while still only 28 years

Sian Edwards
Principal Guest Conductor of the Liverpool Welsh Choral Union
1987 - 1989

of age, Miss Edwards conducted an operatic programme, after which she was named the Principal Guest Conductor. She drew a standing ovation from the enthusiastic crowds for the unrivalled perfection of the evening's performance. The fourth of Sian Edwards's concerts took place in April 1989. It was a performance of the Fauré *Requiem*, dedicated to the victims of the Hillsborough disaster, and this was followed, after the Interval, by *Belshazzar's Feast*, in which the Choral and the RLPO were praised for their dramatic power.

The 1986 Annual General Meeting that took place on November 12 was unusual in its extensive changes of leadership. The Chairman, Richard A. Wynne Williams resigned at the end of his term of three years, as well as the Vice-Chairman. The Treasurer, Miss Vaughan, resigned after ten years' service, along with the two ticket secretaries. The Joint Librarians, John and Pat Ward, resigned after a period of fifteen years' devoted service. Also, most importantly, after fifteen years in that position, came the resignation of the President himself. For several years, Dr. Emyr Wyn Jones had been Co-President with Alderman David J. Lewis, who, however, had died in May 1982. For the major part of the fifteen years Dr. Jones had served alone. In his farewell speech made that evening, Dr. Jones expressed the pleasure he had taken in his association with the Welsh Choral, and his pride in the high standards maintained by the Choral. He spoke of his certainty that, under Anthony Ridley and Derek Sadler, these standards would persist. A new President, who had for years taken an interest in the choir, Judge John Edward Jones, was chosen, and was warmly welcomed. There could not have been a more appropriate choice. One of the most prominent members of the Welsh community on Merseyside, he was born in Liverpool of Welsh parents, the elder of two brothers. A diligent worker with a highly-trained mind, he had a brilliant career in the legal profession, making his name as a barrister in the North-West. In 1969, he had become a Circuit

His Honour, John Edward Jones
President of the Liverpool Welsh Choral Union
1986 - 1998

CHAPTER EIGHT: AN ERA OF GUEST CONDUCTORS

Court Judge. He married a Liverpool Welsh nurse trained at the Royal Infirmary, and two children were born to them, both following their father into the legal profession. His interests were widespread. He had served as a deacon in Heathfield Road Chapel since 1947, was a correspondent to the Welsh local paper, and was, in 1987, writing a book on the Liverpool Welsh. He was a strong advocate of peace and temperance movements, and was for years a leading spirit in the Liverpool Red Cross. His other interests included travel to all parts of Britain and abroad, and, more recently, doing research in Welsh history, learning calligraphy, and becoming familiar with computers and their uses.

It would have been an unusual decade in which the Welsh Choral did not find itself struggling with financial problems, and, perhaps, having to resort to strange and original ways of dealing with them. The 1980s were no exception to this general rule. The costs of producing a concert were naturally rising, year after year, as inflation took its toll. More frequently than in former years, the Committee had to forego the pleasure of using the RLPO, and found it necessary to plan less costly programmes, and to use smaller supporting groups or brass bands. The rising fees of nationally known singers had also to be considered, as well as the fees of the conductors. The Committee was reluctant to increase, to the public, the cost of tickets, and made every effort to avoid this. Small economies such as finding new, less expensive printers of tickets were considered, and the cost of printed programmes had to be carefully balanced between making them too elaborate and therefore too expensive to be purchased by the patrons, and yet attractive enough to encourage sales.

Members of the Choral were aware of the money problems and took them to heart. The Treasurer urged the covenanting of subscriptions. The 100 Club was formed, which brought in fresh membership subscriptions, and many members devised new ways of raising funds, like sponsored swimming events. Badges were available for purchase, and at concerts, small items were set out for sale, Choral sweat shirts and articles of stationery. Even so, at the end of the decade, in June 1990, the concert account showed a loss of over seven thousand pounds, though other accounts were in better shape.

The most troublesome problem confronting the Committee durng these years was the one of recruitment. More than once, critics had referred to depleted numbers, and especially to the weakness of the tenor section, and the Choir itself was well aware of the necessity of adding to its numbers. Mr Ridley, too, while conducting auditions, had remarked on the imbalance. Suggestions made to remedy the situation included that of offering prizes to those who might discover possible new members, but this brought little response. Neither did advertising campaigns add significantly to the choral numbers. Moreover, ranks were thinned by too ready a tendency to absenteeism among the members, and to neglect of the rule that choristers must attend 'obligatory' rehearsals or face dismissal.

New members, on joining the choir, were warmly welcomed. Towards the end of the decade, it became customary for them to receive, along with their music and a book of rules, a letter of welcome, of which the following is an example:

CONGRATULATIONS on passing your audition and WELCOME to the Liverpool Welsh Choral Union.

NOW you are a member you may find the following information useful.

1. ATTENDANCE: Regular attendance is essential. If absence is unavoidable, you should contact the Leader of your section:
SOPRANOS Carol Edwards
ALTOS Beryl Hemphill
TENORS David Williams
BASSES Ifor Griffith

If you know that you will be unable to sing at a concert, you should inform either the Registrar (John Howard) or the Secretary (Alun Jones)

2. SUBSCRIPTIONS: Owing to our current financial difficulties the annual subscription has been increased to twenty-five pounds, and the voluntary weekly contribution to fifty pence. Please see the Treasurer (Megan Billinge) about your subscription; see also Eileen Vaughan about covenanting the subscription. While you are thinking about money, why not ask Joan McMinn about the 100 Club.

3. MUSIC: can be hired or purchased from the Librarian (Shelagh Francis)

4. UNIFORM for concerts

5. OTHER NAMES you might find useful

Chairman	David Mawdsley
Vice-Chairman	Janet Lomax
Ticket Secretary	Arthur Miller
Concert Secretary	Graham Connolly
Chorus Master	Anthony Ridley
Accompanist	Derek Sadler

Nevertheless, there was good news to report in several fields. At last, after very many years of confusion and uncertainty, a scheme of seating, with numbered seats, had been devised for both rehearsals and concerts, and a more orderly method of processing to places on the platform had been adopted and standardised. This latter change was so startling that it was remarked upon by the press reporters, and, perhaps even more exceptionally, by the Philharmonic Choir, who thought it such an improvement that its choir followed in the footsteps of the Welsh Choral. We who are used to the present professional appearance of the Welsh Choral have cause also to compliment the 1980s Committee for ensuring that music henceforth should be held in identical neat black folders, making for uniformity of appearance on the platform.

To all outward appearances, and to the loyal followers of the Choral, all must have seemed to be flowing smoothly. In spite of all their efforts, however, the officers of the choir were once more finding difficulties in their way, and that chiefly in the matter of the relationship between Committee and Chorus Master. Although the Committee had made it clear when appointing Mr. Ridley as Chorus Master in 1985 that it was the Choral's policy to engage guest conductors for most concerts, he had continued to press for an opportunity to conduct more concerts than the Committee would have wished. A compromise had been reached, which resulted in Mr. Ridley conducting a number of concerts in the second and third years of his three year contract.

As the expiry of that contract approached, the Committee made it clear that it was only prepared to renew the contract on the basis that Mr. Ridley reverted to his original role as Chours Master only, leaving the Choral free to engage guest conductors for all concerts. This unfortunately led to a growing feeling of ill-will between the Committee and Chorus Master, who ultimately agreed to continue in that reduced role for only one more season, that of 1988-1989. As Mr. Mawdsley pointed out in his report to the Annual General Meeting on December 5, 1989, however, Mr. Ridley had to his credit faithfully fulfilled his obligations to the Choral during that final season, when there had been no perceptible change in the quality of the work done, or in his attitude to the choir.

The Carol Concerts at Christmas 1988 were conducted by Mr. Gwyn L. Williams, a Welsh musician from Anglesey. So successful had those concerts been that Mr. Williams was invited to accept an appointment as the Choral's Director of Music, a position which he took up from the start of the 1989-1990 season.

Gwyn L. Williams
Director of Music, Liverpool Welsh Choral Union,
1989 - 1999

In one way hitherto not mentioned, the 1980s differed from all the decades that had gone before. There is a bulky file of correspondence from the period. Some is of a business nature, but much of it consists of personal letters, sometimes between members of the Committee, sometimes from 'ordinary' choir members to the Committee, but sometimes too from members of the public to the Choral. There are some delightful letters of congratulation, and, inevitably, others of criticism. The most interesting date from the late 1980s and refer to the approaching 90th anniversary of the Choral's founding. With this milestone in mind, the President, Judge Jones, wrote in 1988 to St. James's Palace, to request the patronage of the Prince of Wales for the Choral Union. The reply he received, although disappointing, indicated that the request had been seriously considered:

ST. JAMES'S PALACE
LONDON SW1A 1BS

From: The Deputy Private Secretary to H.R.H.
The Prince of Wales
1st March 1989

Your Honour,

Thank you for your letter of 22nd February in which you asked whether The Prince of Wales would be able to take on the Patronage of the Liverpool Welsh Choral Union.

His Royal Highness has now had time to consider your request but has decided, sadly, that he is unable to accede to it.

The problem is that His Royal Highness only takes on positions of this nature if he feels that he will be able to give at least some time to the organisation or event concerned and he is so heavily committed at the moment that he is having to turn down many worthy applications of which yours is, sadly, one.

I am sorry to have to send you a disappointing reply, but

His Royal Highness much appreciated your kind thought in asking him.

Yours sincerely,

David Wright

Despite this disappointment, the Welsh Choral members were able to start the 1990s in optimistic mood. They had a strong, forward-looking President, one who had an intense appreciation of the Choir, past and present, as a vital Welsh element in Merseyside social and artistic history. A Welsh musician from Anglesey, Mr. Gwyn L. Williams, who had more than once conducted the choir and was already active and involved in various aspects of Welsh choralism, had been appointed as the new Director of Music from the start of 1989 - 1990 season. The Choral's officers included men and women of ability and experience, who worked together in harmony, and the Liverpool Welsh Choral had, in another decade, a very significant anniversary to which to look forward, its CENTENARY.

CHAPTER NINE:
GWYN L. WILLIAMS

The Welsh Choral began the Season of 1989-1990 in fine fettle under its new Musical Director, Gwyn L. Williams. Mr. Williams was the first Director for many years to have been born and brought up in Wales, and to have continued to make his home there. His school days over, he became a student at the University College of North Wales, Bangor, from which, after graduation, he progressed to the Royal Academy in London to study composition and to play the trumpet. In London he had the opportunity to play with several orchestras, including the London Philharmonic and the English Chamber Orchestra. In 1976 he returned to Bangor as a lecturer, and was also responsible for the direction of the University Chorus and the University College Singers. In 1980 he joined the BBC Music Department in Cardiff, but again returned to North Wales as Music Producer for the BBC in Bangor, later to become Senior Music Producer for the Welsh Region. Since 1983 he had conducted the Welsh male voice choir, Côr Y Traeth, based in Anglesey, and was soon also to become conductor of Cantorion Menai.

When Mr. Williams became LWCU's Director, he had already well-formulated aims and ambitions for the choir he was now to direct. These aims he set out for all to hear at his first Annual General Meeting. He could see a need for improvement in the singing tone of the choir. He expressed agreement and pleasure when he understood that the officials of the Choral expected him to audition all candidates for admission to the Choir, and re-audition all members, in order better to determine the best voices for a semi-chorus. It was perhaps significant that Mr Williams was taking over the directorship in the same period that the new Rules for the Choir were being discussed, passed and brought into force, and everyone was made aware that discipline in general was to be more positively enforced. No-one could ever accuse the Committee of allowing itself to become complacent. Throughout its existence, the Committee members had always been ready to look for specific causes when anything unforeseen had occurred to disturb the smooth running of the organisation, as had happened towards the end of the 1980s. The Committee would now correct or improve existing rules or bye-laws, and, if necessary, construct new ones. There were three stated reasons for rule changes in 1989. The Committee wished to encourage 'new faces' on the executive, and this could be best achieved by limiting the terms of office of Chairman, Vice-Chairman, and the rotating members. Some few officials with special responsibilities were not to be restricted by these limits, however, because of the importance of retaining their expertise. Secondly, new functions had emerged since 1977, when the last rule change had taken place. It was necessary by 1989 to have a Publications Officer to be responsible for the Newsletter and the concert programmes. Thirdly, in order to keep the total number of the Executive Committee members within bounds, it was thought wise to reduce the number of ordinary members from 12 to 8, and to reduce the number of voting officers. It was felt that these changes would not diminish the democratic control exercised by the Choir over the Committee. The Committee would still number 16, more than 10% of the current choir, and the Committee would remain answerable to the choir. The rules were carefully devised and framed, and at the AGM on October 25, 1989, they were read, discussed and passed unanimously.

The concerts of the first season had, of course, been planned before Gwyn Williams became Director, and he set to work at once with the auditions and rehearsals. The opening concert was Bizet's *Carmen*, conducted by Anthony Hose; the second a performance of the traditional *Messiah*, which Gwyn Williams conducted himself. Next came participation in a *Cymanfa Ganu* at the Anglican Cathedral. There followed a concert in Wales, at

*The Liverpool Welsh Choral Union at the Philharmonic Hall, 1990
William Mathias conducting.*

the Mold Parish Church, a Variety Concert that Gwyn Williams again conducted. The final event of the season was the Choral's Ninetieth Birthday Concert. The opening section consisted of well-known, established Handel and Elgar classics, but then came the special feature, a work by William Mathias, *This Worldes Joie,* conducted by the composer himself, the first time in the Choral's experience that this had happened. It was by no means an easy work to perform, but it was accomplished with credit. Critics referred to the sense of excitement generated, and, most unusually, they discovered in the work a sense of fun!

The success of the William Mathias performance was such that, at the Choral's Executive Committee of July 1990, the question of inviting him to become the choir's Patron was discussed, and all approved the motion with enthusiasm. A formal invitation was sent to Doctor Mathias, and his acceptance was greeted with pleasure by the Choral. Doctor Mathias's name appeared among those of the officers in the programme for November 3, 1990: PATRON: William Mathias, C.B.E., D. Mus., F.R.A.M.

William Mathias was born in 1934 in Dyfed. At a very early age, he showed an interest in composition, and determined on a career in music. He attended the University College of Wales, Aberystwyth, from which he graduated with first-class honours as a Bachelor of Music. He entered the Royal Academy in London on an open scholarship. In 1965 he became a Fellow of the R.A.M. and in 1966 a Doctor of Music of the University of Wales. From 1970 until 1988 he held the post of Professor and Head of the Music Department at the University College of North Wales, Bangor. In 1988 he resigned in order to give more time to composition. He remained, however, the Artistic Director of the North Wales Music Festival that took place periodically in St. Asaph. Apart from the composition of choral works, he made significant contributions to the field of organ music and also had several operas to his credit. His name was

William Mathias
Patron of the Liverpool Welsh Choral Union
1990 - 1992

known beyond the shores of Britain, and he had been honoured in America at the Westminster Choral School in Princeton, New Jersey. In 1985, in the New Year Honours, he had become a C.B.E.

Unfortunately, members of the Welsh Choral had but a very short time to become acquainted with their distinguished Patron. In September 1991, the Minutes record Dr. Mathias's illness, and we learn that the Choir sent him flowers and a message. In 1992 he died. There had been an interchange of letters in the months before his death, in one of which Dr. Mathias sent encouragement to the Choral to continue with its interest in modern music. Up to the end, he was looking ahead, full of his invariable enthusiasm.

The Welsh Choral's Ninetieth Birthday Season had also been a successful first season for Gwyn Williams, though his own expressed opinion was that, for the time being, it might be well if the Choral avoided opera presentation. He had not much enjoyed working with the choir on *Carmen*. After such a promising start to his choral training, the November concert of 1990 must have been a disappointment to Gwyn Williams, to Brian Wright, the guest conductor, and to the Choir. It was a performance of *Elijah,* which met with a very poor reception from the critics. So dismal indeed were the critiques that a suggestion was made that the *Daily Post* critic, at least, not be given tickets thereafter for concerts of the Welsh Choral.

Early in 1990, the LWCU learned that the Royal Liverpool Philharmonic Orchestra would be unavailable for concerts during the 1990-1991 season. Even more of a disruption loomed in the offing, as for a period of some months the Philharmonic Hall would be closed for alterations and decoration. It would plainly be necessary for the Welsh Choral to do some serious thinking about alternative venues for its concerts. In Liverpool, the only places suitable for a large choir were the two cathedrals and St. George's Hall. There might be difficulties about each, problems with acoustics and the arrangements for audience seating. There would also be the question of finding suitable orchestras to accompany the choir. As so often occurs, the closure of the Philharmonic Hall was several times postponed. It was actually closed early in 1994. The Welsh Choral had hoped to be back in the Hall for the 1994 Carol Concert, but, as it happened, it was December, 1995, before the LWCU was able to resume its concerts there, and 1997 before their former partnership with the RLPO was restored.

During the closure of the Philharmonic Hall, the Choral sang in other Liverpool venues, once at the Halewood Town Sports Centre, once in the Kirkby Suite in Knowsley. These concerts, while altogether satisfactory, did not draw newspaper reviews. A different matter altogether was the Choral's cooperation with the Chester Music Society Choir and the Chester Sinfonia, a music society known to the Choral for several years. On one occasion, the two choirs joined to present Berlioz's *Grande Messe des Morts,*' and a year later to present a concert based on themes having to do with the Sea. Of the first it was remarked that once again "Big is Beautiful", and the sheer volume of sound in Chester Cathedral was impressive. The sea concert did not win universal praise. It was apparently an overlong evening's programme, with too big a choir for the works performed. There was, it seems, a lack of focus and of verbal and tonal clarity. Nevertheless, the experience in Chester was enjoyed by the choir, and the Chester singers later came to Liverpool for a return visit with the Welsh Choral.

Whether or not it was the advent of a Welshman as Musical Director, there is no doubt that the connection between the Welsh Choral and Wales itself was re-established during this decade. As early as the Welsh Choral AGM of 1989, reference was made to the participation of members of the Wrexham and District Choral Society in two concerts held during the previous season. The Wrexham Society was pleased to have had the opportunity to unite with the Liverpool choir, and friendship had been established. Some years later, when the Wrexham Society was dissolved, it sent a monetary gift to the Liverpool Welsh Choral, along with expressions of hope for its continued success.

A long-lasting association began in 1989 between the Welsh Choral and Cantorion Menai, a mixed choir of approximately fifty members, based at the Pritchard Jones Hall of the University College at Bangor. Very soon after Gwyn Williams became Musical Director, the LWCU initiated a series of concerts in Bangor. The Choral was joined from 1993 to 1996 by Cantorion Menai. In all, eight concerts were given in the Pritchard Jones Hall, seven of them performances of *The Messiah,* the earliest of these taking place in December 1989, and the last in 1997. On the whole, these events ran smoothly, though it was never an entirely easy relationship. On most occasions the Bangor choir was supportive, but now and again audience numbers were rather low, since the Bangor choralists had sold too few tickets to please LWCU's officials. Once, at the request of Mr. Williams, a small orchestra was hired to accompany the oratorio, but this resulted in a financial loss for the Welsh Choral. At another time, the cost of hiring a harpsichord was judged excessive.

It is probable that those Choral members who retained strong Welsh connections found much to please them in these visits, but some complaints arose from the non-Welsh elements. The Bangor Concerts, after all, came at a busy time of year, and the rehearsals for the Bangor *Messiah*, so near to those for the Liverpool Carol Concerts, took too much precious time. The cost of transport to Bangor was another sore point. A further objection was harder to counter. Though Choral members did not actually relish the practice of being re-auditioned, they took pride in being an auditioned choir, and felt it somewhat demeaning to be asked to sing with unaudition groups, and with choirs that were not required to follow the Choral's rule for compulsory final rehearsals. This objection of theirs, of course, was not confined to the occasions when the Choral sang in Bangor, but to other cooperative ventures as well. Nevertheless, satisfaction with the Bangor association was strong enough, so that once, in 1994, Cantorion Menai joined the Choral for a Gala Concert at the Philharmonic Hall, a charity concert in aid of the Wirral Hospital Trust.

A charity concert was by no means a rare occurrence in the Welsh Choral's calendar. Some charities to which they gave their help included Wirral Holistic Care, The Women's Unit of Wirral Hospital, Leukaemia Research, Action Research, the Post-graduate Education Centre of Arrowe Park Hospital, and the Clatterbridge Hospital League of Friends. Generally, on such occasions, the charitable trust would take charge, and would be responsible for the expenses of programmes and tickets, as well as of allocation of boxes at the Philharmonic Hall, and other business matters, leaving the Welsh Choral the freedom to concentrate on its music.

During the Nineties there were many programmes centred on specific themes, others that were dedicated to the memory of persons they wished to honour, and yet others celebrating the work of one particular composer. Three times there were popular Viennese evenings, twice American evenings, and once a French night. On two occasions there were programmes calling to mind Liverpool's connections with the Sea. Two programmes of Mozart music proved very popular with audiences, one of these sung in memory of Mr. Ernest Pratt, for forty-one years the Choral's Accompanist. A Puccini programme of opera music followed by a mass was an unusual combination. Orff's *Carmina Burana* was again received with delight, as had happened in the 1980s. The Verdi *Requiem* was twice performed in the 1990s, once in the Autumn following the death of Diana, Princess of Wales. A very important occasion was the performance of *The Dream of Gerontius*, on a date coinciding with the ninetieth

The Liverpool Welsh Choral Union at the refurbished Liverpool Philharmonic Hall, 1995

birthday of their former conductor, Sir Malcolm Sargent. Perhaps in view of Gwyn Williams's disapproval of concert versions of opera, only once was one attempted, *Cavalleria Rusticana,* in 1998.

The Liverpool audience was no longer offered a Christmas performance of *The Messiah* by the Choral, although the Philharmonic Choir routinely continued to sing performances of *The Messiah* in the Springtime. For the Welsh Choral, as close to Christmas as possible, an annual Christmas Carol Concert was instituted. It must have been a challenge to the Executive Committee to devise a new name each year for the concert. The concerts were variously called: *A Christmas Concert, Celebration of Christmas, A Christmas Fantasy for All the Family, Christmas Spectacular,* and *Christmas is Coming.* The Christmas concerts were in the hands of Gwyn Williams, and the Choral was usually joined by a children's choir, more often than not conducted by Ifor Griffith, a Welsh Choral member of long standing. Generally in the 1990s the Northop Silver Band accompanied the choir, and the evening was distinct from other concert occasions in that it had a compère, who provided continuity, and who was officially allotted twenty minutes for his part in the proceedings.

During the 1990s the critics maintained their coverage of Welsh Choral concerts, most of which were conducted by either Edward Peak or Nicholas Cleobury, two conductors who had long been associated with the Choral. Interestingly enough, newspaper criticism dealt less with the standard of the choral singing, praiseworthy or otherwise, and more often, with analyses of the music chosen. Now and again, though, a critic would allow himself a subjective response, and would call a performance thrilling or uplifting.

The soloists during this period tended to be local ones, many having studied at the Royal Northern College of Music in Manchester. Only once, in a performance of *Elijah* in

1994, were all the soloists born in Wales. Partly because of the increasing cost of using the Royal Liverpool Philharmonic Orchestra, and partly because, with a shrinking choir, a less full orchestra was more appropriate, several smaller ensembles were used, the Manchester Camerata, the Liverpool Sinfonia, and the Philharmonic Concert Orchestra. On occasion, too, brass bands were the accompanying ensembles, such as the Northop Silver Band already mentioned.

In telling the true story of the 1990s, there is one subject impossible to avoid, the matter of UNIFORMS. Over a period of five years, from early 1992 to 1997, the subject was aired, according to the Minutes, in almost thirty Executive Committee meetings, and in five AGMs. There is nothing more traumatic in a mixed choir than the vexed subject of uniforms.[1] Although it is of supreme interest only to the ladies, the whole choir is drawn into the decisions on colours, sizes and styles, as well as other associated questions.

It is obvious from early photographs that the Welsh Choral had required its ladies to be dressed in long white dresses. There does not seem to have been any rule as to style. Older members recalled that evening dresses, wedding dresses, and a variety of afternoon dresses were worn, all white, of course. Critics in the audience, in a bad moment, were known to have referred to the choristers as milk bottles. Other kinder people called them angels. One press reporter even remarked that the singers reminded him of shrouds. The choice of epithet may have depended on how well the choir was judged to have sung.

During the 1960s the idea of a more uniform dress style had been mooted. Progress towards such conformity was championed and organised by Eileen Morris (later to become the first female chairman), and her sister, Doris Cook. New members in the 1970s were required to purchase a chosen pattern and white polyester material for the making of their dresses.

---

[1] The greater part of the information on uniforms was supplied by Rhiannon Liddell, Chairman in 2000.

CHAPTER NINE: GWYN L. WILLIAMS

By the 1980s, following in the footsteps of other well-known choirs, it was decided that the Choral should again make a change in its appearance. The choir adopted a black skirt and cream blouse with a bow at the neck, a mode of dress likely to suit all sizes and shapes. This was the uniform that can be seen in photographs of the Choral at the International Garden Festival in 1984.

Attempts to change the uniform again surfaced in March 1992. It was then decided to retain the black skirt, and to concentrate on the question of new blouses. Blouse designs were ordered initially from the usual suppliers, with samples of materials to accompany them. Not all were happy with the design submitted. Some, of course, saw no urgent need for any sort of change, but were persuaded to submit to the prevailing will. At least there was general agreement on the colour, an attractive apricot gold.

When the blouses arrived in late 1992, there was widespread dissatisfaction with the quality of the work. Many blouses did not fit properly. Others were badly put together with seams coming apart. The sleeves of many were wrongly inserted. The Committee decided that the entire consignment must be rejected.

Throughout 1994 and 1995 the matter remained in abeyance, despite the hard work of a specially appointed committee. Not until 1996, under the leadership of Gladys Morris, was the work re-assigned to a Birmingham company, which contracted to be responsible for supplying blouses, all made to individual measurements. In January 1997, the blouses were promised for early delivery at a cost of £30 each, and by that summer they had at last arrived. General approval of the choir's changed appearance was expressed at the next concert, and praise for the untiring work of the committee appears in the Minutes of the 1997 Annual General Meeting. The photograph of the Choral taken at Liverpool Cathedral in Centenary Year 2000 suggests the Battle of the Blouses had reached a happy conclusion.

To the dismay of the choir, however, early in the new century, the manufacturer ran out of material and was unable to source any more. Since there was no surplus for newly-joined members, new tops had once again to be considered. It was determined this time to settle for a black tunic top with a facility to use scarves for ornamentation, an advantage since colours could be varied by having differently coloured scarves for different occasions. This plan has served the Choral well, and, at this time of writing (2006), the matter remains in the hands of the wardrobe mistress, Pat Mitchell.

From the time of his election as President, Judge Jones had made it his business always to be present at the Annual General Meeting of the Society. His speech to the assembled choristers invariably reflected his sense of optimism as to the choir's future. From 1994 onwards, however, one important matter occupied him above all others and he never failed to impress on his listeners his concern about it. He felt that the Choral was being negligent in failing to record the brilliant past achievements of its society. Judge Jones was anxious that the documents of the past should be assembled, sorted by an archivist, and eventually deposited in a safe place, such as the Liverpool Record Office. In his 1994 speech Judge Jones expressed his thanks to one former choir member, then living in Cumbria, who was equally troubled about the lack of action in this matter.

A collection of letters exists, starting in May, 1994, between Judge Jones and Commander Ashmore, who also urged the appointment of an archivist, and revealed that he himself had a collection of programmes and other documents, dating from the period when his father had been Secretary, which he would gladly hand over when he was assured that they would be cared for by an officially appointed archivist. This active correspondence continued until Judge Jones's death. Within the last few years, after the death of Commander Ashmore, his wife has continued her husband's work, and has sent some relevant papers that she has come across in Commander Ashmore's collection.

Judge Jones's plea of 1994 was repeated in 1995, along with a hope that someone might be found to work on the choir's history. When no immediate response came, and because he himself had a deep interest in the subject, he embarked on the writing of a history, and this he reported to the choir in 1996. It is interesting that, from first starting on the work, Judge Jones obviously considered that the account must begin long before the Year 1900, the traditional Eisteddfod starting point for the Choral. He felt that the history of the Liverpool Welsh in the early days must be chronicled and that the efforts of such people as John Ambrose Lloyd in the 1800s must be celebrated. In April 1996 Judge Jones made known to the Committee that he would like a meeting specifically to discuss the nature of a choral history, and, at the same time, he hoped that someone would come forward to take over this heavy task. By October 1997, the Judge was expressing concern over the scarcity of documents, on which to base his writing.

Sadly, the next year brought an interruption to all these plans. The Judge had been in poor health for some years, and throughout the year 1998 he became increasingly unwell. His death came on June 28, 1998, peacefully, and surrounded by his loving family.

In the Welsh Choral programme of November 21, 1998, the following obituary was published.

HIS HONOUR, JOHN EDWARD JONES

It is with great sadness that we record the death on 28th June 1998 of our President, His Honour, John Edward Jones – or 'the Judge' as he had for many years been affectionately known to members of the Liverpool Welsh Choral Union.

As one of the most prominent members of the Welsh community on Merseyside, the Judge had numerous calls upon his time. It was accordingly a great honour for the choir when he accepted an invitation to become our President in 1986. Having done so, he never failed to give his unstinting and enthusiastic support. He rarely missed one of our concerts, whether in Liverpool or further afield. The courtesy and good humour with which he conducted our Annual General Meetings will long be remembered by members of the choir.

In common with the numerous other organisations in which the Judge took an interest and played an inspirational role, the Liverpool Welsh Choral Union has lost a good friend and will be the poorer in consequence. With great affection we dedicate this evening's performance of *The Music Makers* to the Judge's memory, and extend our deepest sympathy to the members of his family.

D. H. M.

At the Annual General Meeting in November, the Choral's choice of a new President was confirmed. Professor Huw H. Rees is a native of the village of Bwlchygroes in North Pembrokeshire, and is a fluent Welsh speaker. Having attended Cardigan Grammar School, he proceeded to the University College of Wales at Aberystwyth to read Biochemistry. His undergraduate days were followed by a period as a research student, after which he was, in 1966, awarded a Ph. D. degree. He next joined the Department of Biochemistry at the University of Liverpool, first as a Postdoctoral Fellow and then as a lecturer in Biochemistry. Except for a period in 1973, spent at Beltsville, Maryland, in the United States, he has remained at Liverpool University, where, since 1987, he has been a Professor. From the time of his childhood in Wales, Professor Rees has had an interest in music, and, after his move to Liverpool, a growing interest in the Welsh Choral in particular.

With the death of Judge Jones, it was obvious that no complete history could be hoped for by the time of the Centenary, though the new President, Professor Huw Rees, as well as Chairman Rhiannon Riddell, both wrote excellent summaries of the chief milestones in the Choral's history. Judge Jones's family, after his death, made a donation to the Welsh Choral in his memory, and it has been suggested that perhaps this gift might be used to help defray the expenses of such a publication as the Judge would have wished. In recent years, at last, there is a Choral member who is, by profession, an archivist, and is ready to collect and arrange documents for eventual deposit in the Record Office.

In 1989, it will be recalled, Amendments to the Rules and Regulations had been discussed and passed. Not all of these were followed so scrupulously as those who composed them would have wished. The Committee had to ask its Music Director, Mr. Gwyn Williams, on more than one occasion, to remind the choristers of the rule about attending a minimum of rehearsals in preparation for each concert, and, even more frequently, it had to be made clear to the assembled singers, that the rehearsals on the final Friday evenings and on Saturday afternoons were compulsory ones.

By 1995, for a variety of reasons, it was decided by the Committee that it was time again to consider some of the rules. A sub-committee was set up to look into the matter, and was given plenty of time to make sure that all questions had been fully aired. The Executive in 1996 was presented with the sub-committee's report, and had time to study the proposed changes. By January 1997 all was ready. The Amendments were accepted by the Committee, and the decision taken to print the Rules and to present them to the full Choir for acceptance. Mr. David Mawdsley was given the task of phrasing the new Rules. Some members of the choir were not completely happy with the rule concerning compulsory attendance, but after it was agreed that extenuating circumstances could be recognised, the Rules were presented and accepted at the 1997 AGM. It was decided that each member should have a copy, possibly in booklet form,

Professor Huw Rees,
President of the Liverpool Welsh Choral Union,
1998 - present

and ideally combined with a membership card. The Rules[2] are actually dated November, 1997, but it was noted in the Minutes that, by the end of 1998, the Rules had not yet been printed. It is to be hoped that no reconsideration will now be found necessary for many years to come.

During the decade, the same problems were confronted by the Executive Committee as had troubled it in the past, chiefly questions of finance and discipline. The procedure of organising and managing concerts had become almost routine, and was always successfully achieved. Naturally, as time went on, the expenses of concert planning and presenting rose constantly, and the reduced number of choir members struggled to make ends meet. The costs of orchestra, conductor and soloists escalated rapidly and alarmingly throughout the decade. Inevitably, the cost of tickets had to be increased, but the LWCU was still reluctant to charge prices as high as those of the Philharmonic choir and orchestra.

Side by side with financial problems there were, within the choir, disciplinary matters: behaviour during rehearsals and on the concert platform; questions of absentees and late-comers, and the troublesome one of seating. Several times seating plans had been drawn up and seats numbered, followed by the frustrating work of implementing the plan. Perhaps with the realisation that the Centenary was so near, members were readier than formerly to commit themselves to making sure their performances were well planned and executed. In one particular way, the Choral's efforts were superb. Members were asked to consider ways of raising funds for the very special celebrations ahead of them. Their efforts bore fruit. Members who threw themselves into one project or another drew closer in friendship, as they worked towards their common aim.

It was in June 1995, that we find the first reference to the Centenary in the Minutes of the Executive Committee. It was suggested then that, if there were any intention of commissioning

[2] A copy of the Rules of 1997 is to be found in Appendix III.

a new musical work for the occasion, it was high time to make enquiries as to whether a grant might be forthcoming from one of the organisations of which the Welsh Choral was a member. In the Annual General Meeting of that year, it was pointed out that the Choral no longer had a Patron, and that the appointment of an influential Patron might help the Choir towards a worthy celebration. But who should be invited? Several names were suggested, but none who were likely candidates. It was not until years later that the association of Karl Jenkins with the Welsh Choral began.

Still, that was no reason not to begin preparation for the Centenary. In late 1995, working groups with varied objectives were set up. One group carried on investigating the possibility of commissioning a work of music, and of obtaining funding for it. They found, however, that no funding would be available from any Millennium or other funding group unless the choir had a specific project in mind. One suggestion considered by the Committee was that John Rutter be asked to write a carol for the choir, but of course, if this were achieved, the Executive Committee wanted to be assured that the Welsh Choral would have the right to give its first performance. By the end of 1996, the Choral was no nearer deciding on a commissioned work; and it was not until July 1999, that the Choral's new Musical Director, Graham Jordan Ellis, was asked to write and to score a secular piece, to last about four minutes in performance. This he did, and it was ready by the Autumn, to be sung at a Centenary concert. The Choral had its commissioned work!

Naturally, the Executive Committee as a whole discussed the works the Choral should perform in its Centenary year, and the Committee was anxious that the conductor of the Centenary Concert, at least, should be a distinguished Welshman or a Liverpudlian. It was hoped that the main concert could take place at the Philharmonic Hall between April and June of the Year 2000. A tour was considered, to Manchester, London and

Cardiff, and, if possible, to Dublin. However, it was obvious that the idea of a tour was not attractive to everybody, especially to older members who would not find travel easy.

During 1997, it was decided that the concerts of the year 2000 should all be of music known to be popular with audiences. The Year 2000 would also mark the 100th anniversary of the composition by Elgar of *The Dream of Gerontius,* so closely associated with the Welsh Choral in its early days, and therefore an appropriate work for presentation. At the AGM of 1997, Graham Connolly and David Williams, the Chairman at that time, were asked to prepare a Curriculum Vitae of the Choral, for inclusion in the programme. It was settled too, that there should be a celebratory dinner with short suitable speeches by the guest speakers. The question of whether any other choir should be invited to join the Welsh Choral for a centenary concert was discussed, but left in abeyance.

As time went on, the Choir was kept fully informed of the progress being made in Committee, and many members of the Choral suggested projects for the raising of funds, and also for the creation of publicity. A sponsored walk along the Wirral Way was organised, a raffle was to be held, and an entirely original project, the making of a Welsh Choral quilt, was well in hand by early 1998.

By the decade's half-way mark, some suspicion arose that Gwyn Williams was beginning to lose interest in the Welsh Choral. There were occasions when he was not able to be present at rehearsals, and it was Derek Sadler, the official Accompanist, who was left to take charge. When in 1995, the Executive started to make plans for the coming Centenary, Mr. Williams failed to come to one essential planning meeting. It was, nevertheless, assumed that he proposed, in the Year 2000, still to be Musical Director. In January 1998, Mr. Williams was invited to be Visiting Professor for a year at an American university, and he requested a sabbatical leave from his Choral responsibilities during the 1998-1999 season. The Executive Committee could not do less than grant his request. At the same time, the Committee asked that Mr. Williams's plans for 1999-2000 should be made clear to them. For the remainder of the 1997-1998 season, rehearsals and concerts continued as usual, and the Committee arranged with Mr. Williams that, after the Centenary year, in the usual way, a rolling system of auditions and re-auditions should be reinstated.

Naturally plans had to be made for a Chorus Master for the 1998-1999 season. As it happened, that did not prove difficult. Two musicians declared themselves interested in the part-time post, Steven Roberts and Graham Jordan Ellis, and a Job Description for the position of Chorus Master, a description newly drawn up by David Williams and Graham Connolly, was sent out to each, a document that made amply clear what were to be the main duties.[3] Both men signed and returned contracts. After discussion, it was agreed that the post should be shared between the two candidates for the duration of the year, after which the matter would again be open to discussion.

Steven Roberts had graduated in 1991 with a first-class honours degree in Music from Leeds University, and won the Special Award for a high standard of musical achievement in the same year. Since graduating, he had conducted many choirs throughout the United Kingdom, including the Huddersfield Choral Society. More recently he had won the British Federation of Young Choirs Award for a Choral Conductor. Mr. Roberts was in demand as musical director of choral days and workshops. He had conducted choirs in North and South America as well as on the Continent of Europe.

Graham Jordan Ellis was born and educated on the Wirral, and was an honours graduate of Liverpool University. He had studied organ with both Caleb Jarvis and Noel Rawsthorne, and later achieved a considerable reputation as a freelance conductor of choral and orchestral music. The Liverpool Sinfonia, an

[3] A copy of the Job Description is to be found in Appendix IV.

Graham Jordan Ellis
Director of Music, Liverpool Welsh Choral Union
1999-2003

orchestra of professional players, was founded by Mr. Ellis in 1990, and had several times accompanied the Welsh Choral in concerts. With the Chapel Choir of Birkenhead School, Mr. Ellis had undertaken successful tours on the European Continent. Since 1996, Graham Ellis had been Music Director of the Chester Music Society, and with its choir, had performed a wide range of standard and of modern works.

By the end of January 1999, Gwyn Williams had not yet let the Executive Committee know his plans, and there was still no news from America by the end of March. It was realised that, in fact, Mr. Williams's contract would in any case terminate on July 31 of that year. The Chairman wrote to alert Mr. Williams to this fact, and when there was still no reply, Mr. Williams was given notice that the contract had lapsed. So that there should be no misunderstanding among the ordinary choir members, a special meeting of the LWCU was called, at which the Chairman explained in detail the actions of the Committee to the assembled members.

The concert year passed relatively smoothly. Graham Jordan Ellis and Steven Roberts shared the Choral's Musical Directorship, and press reviews of the concerts were encouraging. At the Annual General Meeting in the Autumn of 1998, Professor Huw Rees had taken up the Presidential reins where Judge Jones had left off, and there was no perceptible alteration in direction. At the season's conclusion Mr. Ellis emerged as the more suitable conductor to be offered the usual three-year contract, the more important this time since the period would include the Centenary Year.

It became known that, on Mr. Williams's return from America, he took up a post as Director of Theatr Ardudwy in Harlech. From there he moved in early November, 2001, to become the first ever Chief Executive of the Llangollen International Musical Eisteddfod. In that post he was responsible for the day to day running of the Royal International Pavilion at the Llangollen Eisteddfod.

Members of the Executive Committee of the Welsh Choral re-assembled in the Autumn of 1999, aware that only a few months remained before Centenary Year would be upon them. But they were ready. What strikes the reader of the Minutes of this period is the sense of self-confidence that emerges. It was not complacence, but the knowledge that the Choral was fully prepared for its celebratory year, with only a few matters outstanding to be dealt with. The Committee, for instance, was not yet certain of a children's choir for the performance of *Carmina Burana.* Still, within a few weeks that, too, was settled. The Philharmonic Youth Choir would be available and pleased to take part.

With so much in hand for the year 2000, the Committee found leisure, in fact, to discuss plans for years ahead, and the result was a comprehensive schedule of works, conductors and possible soloists for the next three or four seasons. These concerts, it was hoped, could be at the Philharmonic Hall. It was decided that each season should, as usual, consist of four main concerts: a light-weight one in the Autumn, the Christmas Carol Concert in December; a charity concert about March, and a major serious concert to end the season. So far as *The Messiah* was concerned, the Choral would plan to give a performance in alternate years, but at another venue. A suggestion enthusiastically proposed was that, as the Choral was scheduled to sing *Gerontius* in 2000, the year of the work's centenary, might it not be possible also to sing Elgar's other oratorios, *The Apostles* and *The Kingdom* each in its centenary year?

The 1999 Annual General Meeting served to confirm the arrangements made by the Committee. Mr. Graham Jordan Ellis was welcomed as the new Director of Music, and replied with his thanks to the choir. It was further announced that Mr Ellis would conduct all the concerts of the Centenary year. As anticipated, Mrs. Rhiannon Liddell was welcomed officially as the new Chairman. The retiring Chairman, Mr. David Williams was thanked for his work, and then presented his valedictory address.

In his report on this vital season's work, Mr. Williams expressed his gratitude to all those who had worked so untiringly to ensure the financial strength of the Choral: those who had run the 100 Club, the shop, the coffee sales, and the Quilt makers, workers on the Newsletters, the raffles and the socials. He was less complimentary when he came to speak of the matter of loyalty to the Choral's commitments. He was disturbed to report that some members persisted in picking and choosing their concerts. On the other hand, he suggested a reason for this when he thanked those members who had sung at all **ten** events of the season. Ten events must have entailed a considerable amount of dedication and sacrifice, not easily accomplished by the most devoted follower.

In the last Committee Meeting, it was reported with satisfaction that there had been 17 recent applications for membership. Five new members had been accepted, but four of the other applicants had failed the audition. It was obvious, though, that membership in the Welsh Choral remained desirable, and certainly, hope for success was running high. As 1999 drew to a close, the Welsh Choral could go forward into the future with confidence, and could look towards the Year 2000 with pleasurable anticipation.

CHAPTER TEN:
THE CENTENARY

The Year 2000! The concluding year of the Second Millennium! A Year of Celebration throughout Britain and in all parts of the world, however distant!

But, for the Liverpool Welsh Choral Union, something else in addition, its Centenary! It causes one to wonder whether, a hundred years ago, Harry Evans ever envisioned such an event. Indeed, somewhat nearer our time, could Hopkin Evans or Malcolm Sargent have thought that, in the year 2000, members of the Welsh Choral would still be singing *The Dream of Gerontius*, and others of their old favourites? But so it was.

In some ways, there was nothing exceptional about the manner in which the year began. Nine members of the Executive Committee met on January 5, 2000. Their chief purpose, of course, was to make absolutely certain that all was in place for the concerts of the Centenary, the first of which would take place in early March. It was gratifying to know, as the year began, that their Treasury was in a healthy state, and that the Carol Concert of December, 1999, had, as usual, yielded a good profit. Some arrangements remained to be finalised with regard to an additional concert at the Mossley Hill Parish Church in May, but the chief concern of the Committee at the moment, one that had troubled the Welsh Choral for years, was that of recruitment. So urgent did the Committee consider this question that an open meeting was called for January 26, 2000, specifically to discuss the matter, and the following Committee meeting in February considered the problem of sufficient importance that methods of recruitment became their main topic of discussion then and, indeed, at intervals throughout the year.

There were suggestions made to establish contact with mature students at the Liverpool universities; to hold Come

Three accompanists of the Liverpool Welsh Choral Union

Stephen Hargreaves,   *Ernest Pratt, 1941 - 1983*
2002 - present

Derek Sadler,
1983 - 2002

and Sing Evenings at various venues, preferably in April; to appeal to interested singers through advertisements in *The Echo* and *Mersey Mart*; and to approach other choirs for possible recruits. Hope University was kind enough to offer its rooms for use in recruitment. Each appeal brought some success. In April there were twenty-eight applicants, of whom fifteen were accepted. It was thought vital to recruit as many young voices as possible, especially in the higher ranges, the sopranos and tenors. Problems could, however, arise with regard to young university members. One new young recruit, for instance, asked permission to be absent from rehearsal for several weeks during the university holiday, but it was felt vital to refuse such a request as it contravened the Choral Rule regarding attendance at a given number of rehearsals.

The most immediate need was for additional tenors to sing in the *Messiah* concert, and, on this occasion, it was thought essential to reinforce the tenor section by the addition of choristers from the Chester Music Society, a group well-known to the Welsh Choral, and, more importantly, one conducted by the same conductor, Graham Jordan Ellis.

Since 1996 the specially appointed Centenary Concerts Committee had been working diligently towards making the concerts of the year 2000 noteworthy. Out of about thirty possible programmes considered, the Committee had eventually reduced the number to four, all of them works familiar to the majority of the Choir, and favourites of theirs, as well as of the audience: *The Messiah, The Dream of Gerontius*, the Verdi *Requiem*, and the Carol concert. Their choice received the blessing of the full Executive Committee.

The designers of all four programme covers deserve to be highly congratulated. All were attractive, in excellent taste, and worthy souvenirs of a most special year. The contents of the programmes were thoughtfully conceived, and each programme in turn deserves our equally careful attention.

The first of the year's main concerts was an early March performance of *The Messiah*. The outer cover was designed to suggest the oratorio's Easter message, a background of chiaroscuro blues, setting off a plain cross of light as its centrepiece. The concert was announced as an introduction to the Centenary Celebratory Year. Page 2, the inside cover, listed the Officers of the Welsh Choral Union, including the names of Vice-Presidents, but not, on this occasion, all the Committee members. The Honorary Members, numbering twenty-five; were listed, with an acknowledgment of their financial support. On page 3 appeared the announcement of the items of the evening, along with the names of the conductor, the orchestra and its leader, and the four soloists.

The double spread of pages 4 and 5 contained a foreword by the Society's President, Professor Huw Rees, a message from the Chairman, Rhiannon Liddell, and a short account of the current work of the Liverpool Welsh Choral Union. Professor Rees gave a condensed history of the Society since its inception in 1900. Photographs of Professor Rees, Mrs. Liddell, and the assembled Choral and Orchestra were also reproduced here. On pages 6 and 7 were printed photographs of the night's conductor, Simon Robinson, and of the four soloists, along with a brief account of the background of each.

On page 8 was an excellent article by Sir Malcolm Sargent, his notes on the performing of *The Messiah*. It was introduced in these words by Sir Malcolm: "It is my sincere hope that many will receive pleasure and be spiritually uplifted by this masterpiece, which will remain one of the world's 'wonders', so long as there is music." The performance was dedicated to the memory of Sir Malcolm, one of the Choral's former conductors. Pages 9 and 10 contained the words of the oratorio, divided into Parts I and II, according to Sargent's division rather than Handel's.

On the inside back cover the names of the singing members

of the Welsh Choral were listed, accompanied by a photograph of Graham Jordan Ellis, the Chorus Director. The outer back cover contained notices of the remaining concerts of the year, coupled with the announcement that the LWCU was recruiting new singers, especially Tenors and Basses, for its Centenary Season. A nice humorous touch was the statement: "P.S. You don't need to be Welsh!"

It would not be surprising if the Welsh Choral were somewhat disappointed with the *Daily Post* coverage of this first Centenary Year concert. Its review was not written by the usual music critic. What we had here was an article on the life and career of Simon Robinson, the conductor. It told us of his childhood in Liverpool, his training abroad, and his present life in Maribor, Slovenia, a province of the former Yugoslavia. In the article, Mr Robinson was said to take pleasure in his association with the LWCU, and with the Philharmonic Hall and Orchestra. The *Echo* review was an improvement, so far as the Welsh Choral was in question. Joe Riley gave the concert a rating of "a rousing 4-star". He spent the greater part of his space in reviewing the choir's background, and describing the nature of the *Messiah* version heard at the Saturday night concert. He hailed it as "a beefier, more ponderous, and certainly louder interpretation than is the norm today." He mentioned that the organ was used rather than a harpsichord, and that Sargent, who arranged this version, had called for trombones, formerly used in Mozart's day, and used by the present orchestra to good effect. Mr. Riley obviously appreciated and enjoyed the performance, and commented that the Choral, "despite a dearth of men's voices", provided a thrilling fortissimo.

A feature of the *Messiah* evening was the display, for the first time, of the Centenary Quilt. Its history is an interesting one. Fund-raising, of necessity, was always an integral aspect of the choir's life. Appeals had been made to choir members for money-raising ideas in the years running up to the Centenary, and several members, skilled in embroidery, had responded by organising the Quilt project. Choral members had been encouraged each to take a four-and-a-half inch square of the material provided, in green, peach or lemon fabric, and, leaving approximately half an inch as a border on each, to embroider the square with their names and any other chosen device. Almost a hundred members had responded, chiefly women, but also some brave men, each member aiming to raise about £5 in sponsorship. 120 squares were, in time, returned to the organisers. Pat McCoy, the venture's chief instigator, set the squares in a pattern of ten across and sixteen down, and, aided by other talented colleagues in the choir, supervised their joining together. A centerpiece showing the name of the choir and the dates, 1900 to 2000, was embroidered by Pat Mitchell, a City and Guilds qualified embroiderer. The embroidery was done in satin stitch with gold couching. The whole quilt, measuring approximately 70 by 40 inches, was framed in one-and-three-quarters inches of dark green fabric. Lastly, a five-and-a-half inch border of background fabric was placed all around. The final quilting, incorporating the reverse side, was done by a group in West Derby, the Liver Birds. When shown to the assembled Choral, the quilt met with enthusiastic applause. In addition, the venture had succeeded in raising over £1000 for the Welsh Choral Centenary Fund. The quilt was displayed at the Philharmonic Hall on the mezzanine floor during the *Messiah* concert. Where its ultimate destination will be is still under consideration.

Not only did the quilt meet with much interest and admiration by all who saw it, but it is evident that the participants had thoroughly enjoyed their project, so much so that when, in the year 2005, the Welsh Choral travelled to sing in Germany, they took with them a second quilt as a gift to the Cathedral in Cologne. It is understood that this quilt was even more handsome than the first, for, of course, all the choral embroiderers had had some practice. To ensure its superior appearance, the second quilt was quilted professionally by a long-armed quilter.

Back in the year 2000, the chief concerns of the Executive Committee, from March to May, were the evolving plans for the *Gerontius* programme, to take place in the Anglican Cathedral in June. Sponsorship was still sought, but difficult to secure for the LWCU, with so many conflicting local and national claims based on its being Millennium Year. A grant of £3000 was promised by "Awards for All", but a part of that had to be set aside for the transport of youth groups. Bishop Eton School, whose choral singing was of a high standard, was engaged to join the Welsh Choral and the Chester Music Society to sing in *Gerontius*. The two senior choirs between them would number 300 voices. This performance could be counted upon to draw a good audience, but it was obvious that it would still be an expensive concert. There would inevitably be a loss on the cost of music hire for such a number. Since the RLPO would not be available for the concert on this occasion, the fortunately less expensive Philharmonic Concert Orchestra would be the ensemble of the evening. Rehearsals during these months were going well, and loyalty to the Choral was perhaps given a timely boost by the fact that Mr. Ellis was re-auditioning the choir, and had, by the middle of May, already heard ninety people.

The concert on June 3, 2000 was technically the concluding concert of the 1999-2000 season, and the high point of the year to many, for whom *Gerontius* was an all-time favourite. As one would expect, the cover of this programme was a restrained one, artistically speaking, chiefly a painting, in browns and sepias, of angels. The soloists were named on the front cover, along with a list of the other participants, the Philharmonic Concert Orchestra, the Choir of the Chester Music Society, and the evening's conductor, Graham Jordan Ellis. We were also informed that the concert was supported by the Millennium Festival Awards for All, and by the Friends of Liverpool Cathedral. Inside the

The Liverpool Welsh Choral Union at the Liverpool Anglican Cathedral, 2000
Conductor: Graham Jordan Ellis

cover, the Officers and Honorary Members of the Welsh Choral were named. At the foot of the page was an invitation to join the Cathedral Friends.

Page 3 contained three brief articles, one on the background of the Liverpool Welsh Choral Union, one on the Chester Music Society Choir, and the third on the Philharmonic Concert Orchestra. On page 4 were photographs of the conductor, Mr. Ellis, and of the three soloists, Harriet Williams, Geraint Dodd, and David Kempster, with a short summary of the previous achievements of each. Page 5 contained the names of the singers in both adult choirs. It is interesting to notice that the numbers in each were almost exactly matched; that each choir had a large number of sopranos and a moderate number of contraltos. Each choir remained somewhat short of tenors, but had a strong body of basses to provide a firm foundation.

On page 6 appeared a short article on Elgar's association with the Welsh Choral in its early days, followed by a facsimile of the *Liverpool Echo* critic's comments on a performance of *Gerontius* in 1908, under Harry Evans. The following page consisted of programme notes on the work, and an analysis of its parts.

The next four pages, 8 to 11, contained the words of *The Dream of Gerontius*, words written, of course, by Cardinal Newman. The back page was almost a repeat of the back cover of the *Messiah* programme, and prominently advertised the Gala Centenary Concert, to take place in November.

It is difficult to understand the attitude of the *Daily Post* to this concert. The performance was, in fact, utterly ignored by the newspaper. It is almost incredible that a major concert of the Choral, one in which the oratorio, *The Dream of Gerontius*, was being presented on the centenary of its composition by Elgar, and a concert in which the local choir was joined by the fine choir of Chester Cathedral, - incredible that such a concert should have received no press mention. And why? Because precedence was given to reporting on one of the many concerts of the RLPO. Surely this was a surprising choice! It can be assumed, nevertheless, that the concert was an unqualified success. Never had the singing of *Gerontius* been less than a triumph for the Welsh Choral, always commended by the critics, from the occasion of Elgar's own congratulation to the choir until the present day.

Shortly after the *Gerontius* concert came the Choral's own personal Centenary celebration. It was planned and organised by the choir's Social Committee, led by Eryl Dooling, and took the form of a dinner, held at the Riverside Marina on June 10, 2000. Seventy-five people were present at the event, of whom thirty-six were members of the Choral. The President, Professor Huw Rees, gave the address, and musical entertainment was provided. Graham Connolly, the Concert Administrator, had written a song for the occasion, and he himself sang it, to the general acclaim of the gathering. Meryl Langford, who was to join the Choral as soloist at the forthcoming Gala, sang a selection of Welsh songs, which gave much pleasure to her audience. Thus the 1999-2000 Season ended, but, of course, half the Centenary Year was still to come.

The Executive Committee resumed its meetings at the end of July, and met three times before the Gala Concert. The Committee was ready to grapple with final arrangements for the concert, and with the anticipated difficulties. Early in the year invitations had been issued to many friends and patrons of the Society, to attend the Gala Concert in November. Throughout the Spring and Summer, replies had been coming in, some letters addressed to the Chairman, Rhiannon Liddell, some to the head of the Gala Concert Committee, and some to Graham Connolly, the permanent Concert Administrator. Many accepted the invitation with thanks, but some, inevitably, regretted their inability to be present. Among these were Sir David Willcocks and Marjorie Thomas, the contralto.

Sir David's letter contained the following passage:

> I have very happy memories of conducting the Liverpool Welsh Choral Union on a number of occasions when Dr. Caleb Jarvis was Chorus Master and Organist. I send warm congratulations to the LWCU on its distinguished contribution to British Choral Music over the one hundred years of its existence, and my good wishes for continuing success in the years ahead.

Marjorie Thomas, who appeared first as a soloist with the Welsh Choral in 1950, wrote:

> Please convey my warmest wishes for a very special evening, and please renew all the happiest memories I enjoyed over the years as contralto soloist with the choir.

Two letters of response may be of exceptional interest. The first, written on November 7, 2000 came from the Chief Clerk in Buckingham Palace. The final sentence of the letter reads: "Her Majesty was pleased to receive your message and sends her warm good wishes to you all for an enjoyable and successful occasion."

The second reply came from St. James's Palace, from Stephen Lamport, Private Secretary to H.R.H. The Prince of Wales. Stephen Lamport acknowledged the letter sent to the Prince, inviting him to write a message of support for the Liverpool Welsh Choral's Gala Concert. He explained, however, that the Prince received so many requests of this kind that he had to limit acceptances only to those organisations to which he was already committed. The Prince of Wales nevertheless "sends his very best wishes to all the members of the choir in its centenary year."

While there would be no Royal presence at the concert, it was remarked, with satisfaction, that there had been twenty-seven acceptances to the invitations. The Concert Committee, however, decided that plans must be made for the entertainment of as many as seventy guests. Choral members had to be appointed to welcome these guests, and others to see to the provision of refreshments to be served during the concert interval. It was agreed that choir members and honorary members might, if they wished, share the buffet at a minimum charge. The Lord Mayor would be officially received by the President, Professor Rees, and stewards and ushers would be on hand to provide a warm welcome to all who attended the concert

For the smooth running of the Concert, it was customary to have a presenter whose comments would link all parts of the programme into an effective whole. This time Canon Frayling, Rector of Liverpool, was to serve in that capacity, and a suitable script must be prepared for him. Dress for the concert would be the one recently devised for the ladies, black skirts and the peach coloured blouses, with normal evening dress for the men. Space backstage, the Choral had to be warned, was expected to be at a premium, since there had to be provision for fifty to sixty costumed artists to join the choir in the *Aida* section of the programme. However, by early November, the Committee could rest easy, knowing that all was as ready as possible for the big day.

Apart from the arrangements for the Gala Concert, there were still routine matters to be decided by the Committee. For instance, it was agreed that the Choral could not undertake a concert for Claire House before Christmas, though by March 2001, it would be possible to stage a concert for the School for the Blind. A proposed concert with the Chester Society was also given a favourable reception. Though the financial report showed the Choral funds to be in rather low waters, this had been anticipated by the Treasurer, and she had every hope that a well-attended Gala, followed by the usual popular Christmas Concert, would redress the balance.

While all four Centenary year programmes were a triumph

of careful planning and artistic inspiration, the Gala Concert programme outdid all the others. It was labelled a Souvenir Programme, and was certainly one to be treasured by all who were present that evening. The front cover was itself beautifully designed, and cleverly indicative of what was to be revealed inside. The layout at once suggested celebration: a huge blaze of celebratory bonfire, in muted browns and orange, with the pictured heads of the five composers of the evening incorporated into the pattern. Practical details such as the date and time of the concert were clearly given, along with the names of the conductor, the orchestra and the venue, and, naturally, the full title of the choir.

Inside the front cover, a great deal of information was to be found. On the left-hand side of the page was a complete listing of the Society's Officers, the sponsors of the concert, and acknowledgments to persons and societies that had contributed to the evening's success. On the right was a message from the Chairman, information on how to join the Choral, and an invitation to become a Friend of the Choir.

It was good to find on page 3 a recent photograph of the Choir, along with a listing of the names of the members. Below the photograph was an acknowledgment of the vital part played by the Royal Liverpool Philharmonic Society, and especially of the Orchestra, in the life of the Choir. At the opening of the concert's second half, a short ceremony took place on stage, when gifts were exchanged between the RLPS and the LWCU. The President of the Welsh Choral, Professor Huw Rees, spoke on the Choral's behalf.

On page 4 the Centenary Concert Committee explained its selection of music for this particular concert, and made clear the reasons for the choice of the night's composers: Elgar, Bach, Mendelssohn and Verdi, with Bernstein included as a modern favourite of the evening's conductor. In the right-hand column could be read the names of members of the Choral's officers,[1] from its start in 1902 to the end of the century.

[1] See Appendix V

Pages 5 and 6 set out the programme of the evening. Included was a new composition, *Degrees of Joy* by Graham Jordan Ellis, set to words written by Rhiannon Liddell, Chairman of the Society. As the concert had opened with the British National Anthem, in Elgar's arrangement, it was brought to a close with the singing of the Welsh National Anthem.

Pages 7 and 8 offered photographs and biographies of the soloists of the evening, Meryl Langford, Diana Palmerston, Leah-Marian Jones, Nicholas Burton, Glenville Hargreaves, and John Noble, and of the conductor and the stage director, Elsie Kelly. On page 9 was an exact repetition of Professor Huw Rees's article that had first appeared in the *Messiah* programme. This time, however, it was entitled *A History of the Liverpool Welsh Choral Union.* At the foot of the page appeared a grateful acknowledgment of the important part in the work of the Choral played by Derek Sadler, the Organist and Accompanist.

What else might one want to know about the choir? Page 10 gave us photographs of the Choral's past Conductors and Chorus Directors: Harry Evans, T. Hopkin Evans, Sir Malcolm Sargent, Maurice Handford, Gwyn L. Williams, Caleb Jarvis and, most lately, Graham Jordan Ellis. In the middle of the same page was a photograph of the Welsh Choral as it was in 1923 in the Queen's Hall, London. Below that, we were reminded of the Choral's most recent achievements in its issuing of the Christmas CD, featuring the LWCU, and joined by the Rudston Junior School Choir.

The crowning feature devised by the Concert Programme Committee appeared on pages 11 and 12, a chronology[2] of the Choral performances for the entire century, from 1900 to 2000, along with the composer of each work. What a daunting task it must have been to put together such a list!

Pages 13, 14, and 16 contained advertisements by sponsors and supporters, and page 15, notices of the remaining three concerts of the Liverpool Welsh Choral Union in the 2000-2001 Season.

[2] See Appendix VI

*Four recent Chairmen of the Liverpool Welsh Choral Union at the Liverpool Anglican Cathedral, 2000
David Mawdsley, David P. Williams, Rhiannon Liddell, Ifor Griffith*

The Gala Concert was, of course, planned to be the climax of the Centenary Year. That, indeed, it proved to be. A magnificent Concert in its own right, it was acknowledged to be a triumph by all who were present at the Philharmonic Hall that night. The audience included, this time, the *Daily Post* critic. His praise, unfortunately, was only luke-warm. He suggested that the choir was recovering from a particularly bad crisis of artistry, and that any merit was almost entirely attributable to the efforts of the new conductor. The review of the Gala concert was decidedly patronising in tone.

Perhaps this review of a "far from bad" concert, as it was called, falls into its proper place, when set against the comments in numerous letters received on this occasion by the Choral. Some of the writers had been present in the hall. Others wrote of their appreciation of the work of the choir throughout the years. Following is a selection of comments from some of these letters:

> We thought your programme was very well chosen to suit the occasion. It really displayed the wide repertoire the choir has built up over the last one hundred years and showed you are not afraid to try something new. It was obvious that the choir were enjoying themselves, and, as a result, so was the audience. Your spectacular finale was a fitting climax to the evening. It was brilliantly colourful, both visually and musically.

> *Lawrence Albrighton,*
> *Chester Music Society Choir.*

> I want to thank you for a memorable evening – both for the quality of the performance and for the personal arrangements.

> *Mark Featherstone-Witty,*
> *Principal and Chief Executive of LIPA,*
> *The Liverpool Institute for Performing Arts.*

Wonderful Gala Centenary Concert. The variety of the work was most interesting and the quality of the singing was superb.

William Fulton, JP, DL,
High Sheriff of Merseyside.

I felt the Celtic blood coursing in my veins and was so proud to know that Liverpool from its Welsh community could produce such a glorious sound. Such high standard, and so beautifully organised!

The Rt. Rev. Dr. James Jones,
Bishop of Liverpool.

My Consort particularly enjoyed being associated with the 'Welsh' Choral Union, although we left the land of his birth many years ago. It was a joy to hear and see the spectacular triumphal scene from Aida.

Councillor Mrs. Wendy M. Jones,
Mayor of Sefton.

It was a most splendid occasion and a real credit to the Liverpool Welsh Choral Union.

Professor Philip N. Love, CBE, DL,
Vice-Chancellor of Liverpool University.

A splendid occasion. Not only was the choir in tremendous voice and the soloists excellent, but the whole performance was quite magnificent.

Michael Reddington,
former Chairman of LWCU
and Chief Executive of the City

On behalf of Northop Silver Band I would like to send our congratulations to the Liverpool Welsh Choral Union in celebrating their Centenary. To have sustained the musical excellence and international esteem over a hundred years shows tremendous enthusiasm, endeavour, skill and supreme organisation, - all in all – a magnificent feat. The union is blessed with a fine tradition and a strong management team, which will surely cement not just the immediate future but over the next hundred years.

Graham Williams,
Chairman of Northop Silver Band.

Between the Gala and the Christmas Carol Concert came the Annual General Meeting of the Society. The meeting was opened with an address by the President. Naturally congratulations were in order for all who had had a part in the Centenary Gala Concert, and he wished to add his personal praise for the efforts of the Chorus Master and Accompanist. He mentioned most especially the composition by Graham Jordan Ellis, *Degrees of Joy*, written to words by Rhiannon Liddell, Chairman of the Choral. The work was enjoyed and appreciated by all who heard it. Indeed, Professor Rees felt that the feed-back from the entire concert had been phenomenal. At the same time, he had to express his regrets for the non-productive criticisms in the *Daily Post*, and his disappointment with the lack of the promised support by the local media.

The Treasurer, Irene Lockwood, as anticipated, reported losses on the concerts, but she stated that the choir's financial situation was still sound. Thanks were due to the many stalwarts who ran the shops, at rehearsals and concerts, and provided coffee and other good things on a weekly basis. The Chorus Master reported improved standards of music and choral discipline, and thanked all for making the re-auditioning as painless as it had been.

Interestingly, the question of recruitment did not arise at this meeting. During the year, thirty-three applications for membership had been received, twenty-six of whom had attended auditions, and twenty of whom had been accepted. A happy ceremony that evening was the awarding of long service medals. The presentations were made by Rhiannon Liddell, with special attention drawn to the work of Graham Connolly, the Concert Administrator, who had given service to the Choral in more than one capacity.

The Chairman, as was customary, gave her review of the year, on the whole a very positive and optimistic summary, though, as all would admit, the choir still had room for improvement. One plan for the immediate future was a scheme to reform the method of seating the singers. A proposal was made that seating should be organised into blocks, and Eileen Charnock, a long-serving Choral member, was, the following month, to lead a discussion of a plan that had met with success elsewhere. Rhiannon Liddell concluded by adding her own thanks to all officers, helpers, and 'ordinary' choir members who had made the year such a pleasant one for the Welsh Choral and its many supporters.

The front cover of the Christmas Concert programme used the traditional reds and greens of the season, in the form of a tree, suggesting the carol, "On the First Day of Christmas", and showing one pear and one turtle dove. On the inside of the cover was the usual list of Officers and Honorary Members, and opposite this, the announcement of the concert, with its conductor, orchestra, school choir, and organist listed, as well as its presenter, Nicholas Frayling, the Rector of Liverpool.

On page 4 were the portrait and career details of Graham Jordan Ellis, the conductor, and below, directions for joining the choir, or becoming a Friend. Page 5 listed the members, and, below, was reprinted the same recently taken photograph of the choir. Page 6 listed the items of Part I of the programme, and page 7, of Part II. On pages 8 and 9 were printed the carols in which the audience was invited to join, six in all.

Many in the audience would show exceptional interest in page 10, where the names of the choir of Our Lady's Bishop

Eton School were listed, accompanied by a brief history of the choir. Below this account was another of the Liverpool Sinfonia, the orchestra of the evening. Its founder was the conductor of the evening, Mr. Ellis.

The back cover was an attractive conclusion to the year's set of programmes. It announced two future concerts of the LWCU, one in March and one in May, 2001, and once again the choir's photograph was shown, this time in attractive gold tints. The page concluded with a reminder that the Welsh Choral continued to recruit new members, especially tenors and basses.

The final Committee Meeting of the year took place in early December. On this occasion, thirteen were present, a distinct improvement over the usual eight or nine. Several of these were, of course, newly elected committee members, and these were warmly welcomed. At the conclusion of such a memorable year, thanks were in order, from the Choral to several other organisations. Messages expressing the Choral's gratitude were sent to the Chairman of the RLPO, and to the Honorary Members of the Welsh Choral Union, in appreciation of the loyal support they had always shown, and continued to show.

So the long-awaited Centenary Year came to an end. In the year 1900, the leading members of the National Eisteddfod Choir had been positive in their determination that the group should not disintegrate, but remain as a permanent body to represent the Welsh choral tradition, and to form a long-lasting and distinctive singing society in Liverpool. In the year 2000, that determination was no less strong, and the organisation firm, well-experienced, and forward-looking. The Liverpool Welsh Choral Union had an unshakable trust that there would be yet further achievements possible in the twenty-first century.

EPILOGUE: AFTER 2000

In November 1986, as already recorded, Judge John Edward
Jones had become President of the Liverpool Welsh Choral
Union. It is likely that, at that point, his chief preoccupation was
the steering of his book, *Antur a Menter Cymry Lerpwl* (The
Enterprise and Endeavour of the Liverpool Welsh), through the
final stages of its publication. In that book's first chapter Judge
Jones traced the history of the Welsh people of Liverpool back
to the days of King John, before, in the second chapter, he wrote
of the religious roots of the Welsh in the city.

Perhaps it was the work of research he had done in this
connection that caused him, early in the 1990s, to become aware
that nobody had yet ventured to look into the role Welsh people
had played in the musical life of Liverpool. He was troubled
to realise that, apparently, there was no substantial record of
the participation of the Liverpool Welsh in the music-making
of the city. It was not long before he began his own research,
and he became increasingly conscious of the fact that, among
the membership of the Liverpool Welsh Choral, there was no
archivist responsible for gathering together a record of the
activities of the choir, and of ultimately seeing that such records
found a home, preferably in the Record Rooms of the Central
Library in the city. He made mention of his concern, year after
year, in his annual speech at the society's AGM.

When there was no immediate and positive response, he
determined, in the middle 1990s, himself to make a start on
collecting material for a history of the Choral, and he began
to write about Welsh participation in music in the days that
followed the influx of people from North Wales to the city,
during the Industrial Revolution. He made every effort to keep
the Welsh Choral fully informed of the progress of his work. In
his speech of 1996, he went still further, requesting the calling

together of a special meeting to discuss the means by which a history could be prepared, perhaps in the hope of a partial publication by the year 2000, the year of the Centenary.

Unfortunately, Judge Jones's indifferent health and subsequent death in 1998 made impossible the fulfilment of this project. For the Centenary programme, the new President, Professor Huw Rees, wrote a brief informative account of the choir's history, and the Chairman of the time, Mrs. Rhiannon Liddell, wrote more than one paper, some in Welsh, about the choral establishments in the 19th century and the groups ultimately uniting to form the Welsh Choral Union. The present book owes much to the efforts of Professor Rees and others, as well as to the notes of Judge Jones on the early period of history. He would have been pleased to know that now there is to be an account that takes us through its Centenary Year of 2000.

As we are often reminded, Time marches on. "Nae man can tether Time or Tide", remarked Robbie Burns. Today there is still a need for a historical record of the choir in the present century, the twenty-first, to be begun as soon as possible. It is important that there should be a recorder, who would be responsible, year by year, for the collection of current documents to add to the archive. The Liverpool Welsh Choral is fortunate at present in having among its membership a trained archivist, Felicity Jones. However able and willing, though, she will need help in setting up an archive worthy of its subject matter. A historian should also be found, preferably among the singing members of the Choral, who would write the history of the new century. Such a historian would be fortunate, for, in the first years of the century, there has been no shortage of material. Several interesting enterprises have already taken place, ripe for recording. The present Epilogue will give only a glimpse of these early events of the Choral's second century.

The first of these events came in 2003. Early in that year Graham Jordan Ellis had indicated his wish to retire, at the end

Keith Orrell
Director of Music, Liverpool Welsh Choral Union
2003 - present

of the current season, from his position as Musical Director. The Committee and David Mawdsley as its Chairman wasted no time before seeking a replacement, who would take up the post from the start of the new season in September. The vacancy was made known to musical circles, among which was the Royal Northern College of Music in Manchester, some of whose personnel had for some time worked closely with the Liverpool Welsh Choral. A copy of the Job Description was dispatched on April 1 to Jacqui Dale of the College. Seven candidates in all wrote to express an interest in the post. Among them was Keith Orrell, who wrote to Mr. Mawdsley as early as April 17, enclosing his Curriculum Vitae, and who was highly recommended by the Manchester Royal College.

By May 21, the Executive Committee was ready to create a short-list of three applicants, who, after individual interviews, could be invited to conduct an "audition" rehearsal during the summer break. At the end of the evening, it was hoped to take a ballot of those Choral members who had attended the rehearsal. This procedure was followed as planned. When, at the end of the evening, a vote was taken, an overwhelming majority nominated Keith Orrell as their first preference. As a result, Keith Orrell was appointed Musical Director of the choir from the start of the new season in September, 2003.

When Keith Orrell came to the Welsh Choral, his former achievements were by no means negligible. Born a Lancastrian, Mr. Orrell, a graduate of Liverpool University, had studied choral directing with the late Simon Johnson, and piano under Martin Roscoe. Formerly a school teacher, he went on to work free-lance as a conductor, choral trainer, and choral workshop leader. He had, at the time of his appointment, conducted several other choral societies, including the Hallé Choir, for whom he was Chorus Master for nearly seven years. In that capacity, he had prepared concerts for conductors Kent Nagano, Leonard Slatkin, Owain Arwel Hughes and many others. He was the founder/director of a chamber choir, the Beaumaris Singers, based in Shropshire, and the conductor of the Staffordshire Youth Choir.

Members of the Welsh Choral believe that Keith Orrell's appointment as Musical Director is one of the best decisions the choir has made in its long and distinguished history. Not only has the standard of the choir's singing improved dramatically since 2003, but so has the members' enjoyment of the weekly rehearsals. His musical ability is beyond doubt. Just as important perhaps is his ability to communicate with and inspire members of the choir. He always arrives at rehearsals prepared to obtain the best possible response from the choir, and is able to convey his wishes in a good-humoured way that has endeared him to all the members. In fact, "rehearsals are such fun!" Throughout his time as Musical Director, Keith Orrell has enjoyed excellent relations both with the choir's professional accompanist, and with the choir's Executive Committee by which all administrative and financial decisions are made. He has been eager to have the choir expand its repertoire and has encouraged the members to take upon themselves new ventures.

An innovative scheme was made known to the choir and conductor during the summer of 2005. The Association of British Choral Directors, the ABCD, to which the LWCU is affiliated, had instituted a plan to make available several year-long apprenticeships for young fledgeling conductors, the chosen candidates to be supervised by conductors of experience, and to work within the existing choral framework, with the purpose of further developing choral conducting techniques. Such an appointment was to be implemented in the year 2006. Keith Orrell and the Executive Committee expressed their enthusiastic approval of the scheme, and their readiness to participate in it.

The young conductor appointed to the Welsh Choral, Aled Phillips, was himself a Welshman from Rhosllanerchrugog. He had graduated with honours from the University of Wales,

Bangor, specialising in performance, conducting and composing. He had been successful in many choral competitions, including the winning of the Chief Choral Competition at the Welsh National Eisteddfod, and becoming a finalist of the BBC Radio Wales choral competitiion in St. David's Hall, Cardiff.

Aled Phillips had a profitable year with the Welsh Choral, conducting, under Keith Orrell's tutelage, some part of several concerts, especially those compositions sung in the Welsh language. The Welsh Choral appreciated his commitment, and he, in turn, was grateful to the choir and to Keith Orrell for their wonderful support and encouragement throughout the apprenticeship year.

Since the conclusion of the Centenary programmes, the Liverpool Welsh Choral has continued to give concerts of a high calibre, but none more distinguished than the performance on the evening of Saturday, May 7, 2005. On that occasion, the LWCU, joined by the Wigan Choral Society, the Royal Liverpool Philharmonic Orchestra, four excellent adult soloists, and a young performer, Ahmed Hussein, presented, in the second half of the programme, *The Armed Man: a Mass for Peace,* composed and conducted by Karl Jenkins. The *Mass* was preceded, in the first half of the evening, by a work by Edward Elgar, *Sospiri,* Opus 70, and by the Five Negro Spirituals from *A Child of Our Time* by Michael Tippett, both conducted by Keith Orrell. For the performance of *The Armed Man,* the stage certainly came to life. The RLPO, with its own percussion department, was augmented by three specialised percussion players, who regularly work with Karl Jenkins. The audience obviously loved the work, with many on their feet at the end of what had been one of the Welsh Choral's greatest successes. The Philharmonic Hall was sold out, and people had been turned away at the box office.

Karl Jenkins was born in South Wales. As a child he studied piano and oboe, becoming principal oboe in the National

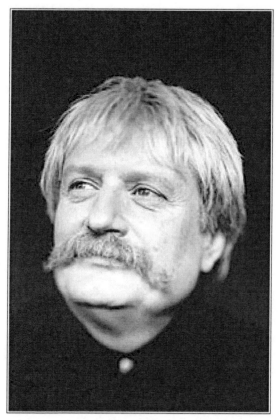

Karl Jenkins
Patron of the Liverpool Welsh Choral Union
2005 - present

Orchestra of Wales. He then read music at the University of Wales, and at the Royal Academy of Music. He has composed several works that have found enormous popularity world-wide, including some commissioned by His Royal Highness, the Prince of Wales, and others by the BBC Proms and BBC Television. It was indeed an honour for the LWCU to have Karl Jenkins conduct a work of his own in one of their concerts.

After the concert, a reception was held in the Green Room, at which Chairman David Mawdsley was able to announce that Karl Jenkins had graciously accepted an invitation to become the Choral's Patron, a position which had remained vacant since the untimely death of William Matthias some years previously. Present at the reception also was the former Treasurer of the choir, Eileen Vaughan, who had been a member of the choir for over sixty years and was, a few days later, to celebrate her one hundredth birthday. In every way, the evening had proved to be a friendly as well as a triumphal occasion.

Next day a review by Glyn Môn Hughes appeared in the *Daily Post*:

> It was a special occasion at Philharmonic Hall this weekend. The Liverpool Welsh Choral Union joined with Wigan Choral Society to perform *A Mass for Peace* by Karl Jenkins. The composer conducted – not that unusual in these parts – but LWCU Chairman David Mawdsley later revealed Jenkins is to become patron of LWCU. A sold out hall listened with rapt attention. In some ways it was highly derivative, an attraction for many. After all, Jenkins got to eighth position in Classic FM's Hall of Fame, beating off competition from the likes of Beethoven, Mozart and Bach. There were things people recognised, which made it a comfortable experience: plainsong, English partsong, French romanticism, Anglican hymns, Bach Chorales. *The Agincourt Song* was in there, as well as *L'Homme Armé*, a 15th century French song often used by composers. For some, me included, it became over-repetitive, with the same ideas done almost to death, making even Ravel's *Bolero* sound

CYF. 27. RHIF 2   GORFFENNAF 2005   40c

CYNGERDD KARL
gan Dr. John G. Williams

Yr Athro Huw Rees (Llywydd), David Mawdsley (Cadeirydd), Keith Orrell (Meistr y Côr) a Karl Jenkins
(tynnwyd gan Bob Metcalf)

Braint oedd cael gwrando ar gampwaith y cyfansoddwr Cymraeg Karl Jenkins 'The Armed Man: a Mass for Peace' yn cael ei pherfformio gan Undeb Gorawl Cymry Lerpwl o dan arweiniad y cyfansoddwr ei hun. Mae'r testun yn amserol iawn. Gyda chymorth Côr Wigan a cherddorfa y 'Phil' llwyddwyd i greu awyrgylch unigryw iawn. Braf oedd cael gwybod fod y cyfansoddwr byd enwog wedi derbyn y gwahoddiad i fod yn un o Noddwyr y Côr. Dymunwn pob llwyddiant i'r Côr ar ei ymweliad i Cologne yn yr Almaen yn niwedd mis Mai.

Llongyfarchiadau i Eileen Vaughan, un o selogion y Côr ers 1930, ar achlysur ei chanfed penblwydd ar Fai 25ain. Cyflwynwyd anrheg iddi gan David Mawdsley ar ran y Côr.

KARL'S CONCERT

by Dr John G. Williams

It was a privilege to be able to listen to the composer Karl Jenkins's masterpiece 'The Armed Man, a Mass for Peace' in its performance by the Liverpool Welsh Choral Union, the composer himself conducting. The subject is very timely. With the help of the Wigan Choir and the Philharmonic Orchestra, he succeeded in creating a uniquely fine atmosphere. It was good to know that this world famous composer had accepted the invitation to be one of the Choir's Patrons. We wish every success to the Choir on its visit to Cologne in Germany in late May.

Photograph above:
Professor Huw Rees, President, David Mawdsley, Chairman, Keith Orrell, Choir-Master, and Karl Jenkins.

Right:
David Mawdsley and Eileen Vaughan on her birthday

David Mawdsley ac Eileen Vaughan ar y penblwydd

Report of Karl Jenkins concert, May 2005
Yr Angor - Merseyside Welsh paper

interesting. Overly derivative, few new ideas. But, if it works, so be it. As a composition technique, it's nothing new, and if popularity for the genre ensues, who are we to criticise? What was notable was the splendid voice of the chorus. LWCU has had rough times in recent years, but Keith Orrell's excellent direction is paying off. With Wigan colleagues, they were disciplined, powerful and their observance of the conductor was exemplary. Jenkins's mass began a little strangely with the choir marching in situ, which made them look like an American Gospel Chorus. There were some excellent unisons from the men: movement four, for instance. And an excellent choral tutti in the *Hymn Before Action* and a folksy finale – *Better is Peace*. Least successful was *Charge*, where sustained high passages for the women showed, as they wilted and flattened. The soloists felt a little ineffective. Catherine May – a wonderful soprano voice often lost in the mêlée. Rachel Smith, contralto, was most effective in *Now the Guns Have Stopped*, while tenor Stephen Davis and bass Michael Wallace performed reasonably, though without much drama. The Royal Liverpool Philharmonic Orchestra supported and accompanied excellently. There was a highly effective, shapely and well co-ordinated performance of the Five Spirituals from Tippett's *A Child of Our Time* and a breathtakingly soporific, emotional and charming performance of Elgar's *Sospiri* by the orchestra's strings. Brave programming and, from a standing ovation, something which worked well.

The Association of British Choral Directors is only one of several beneficent organisations to which the LWCU is affiliated. Business in the Arts: North West (BIA/NW) is an organisation which "brings skills to the arts in ways that are beneficial to both business and the arts." One of the ways in which it does so is through the Skills Bank which matches the expertise of managers in business with cultural organisations in need of specific skills. The Welsh Choral made an application for assistance in March 2003, and was put in touch with Mike Edwards, the Joint Managing Director of Kaleidoscope ADM

Limited, with a view to producing an action-based marketing plan designed to improve the use of publicity materials.

Mike Edwards assisted the LWCU over a period of almost three years, chiefly on the problem of the formulation and distribution of publicity material. The most important contribution made by Mike, however, was to review the branding of the choir, which ultimately led to the design (at no expense to the choir) of a new logo incorporating the Welsh Dragon and Liver Bird. This is now used as the basis of all publicity material, including concert programmes and the cover of this book.

BIA/NW and its sister organisations hold an annual awards ceremony for the various categories of advisers, including the Skills Bank adviser. Mike Edwards was nominated by the Welsh Choral for an award, and he was selected as one of the three finalists. At the Lowry Centre in Manchester on March 22, 2006, Mike won the Haden Freeman Award for the Business in the Arts: North West Skills Bank Adviser of the Year, 2005, and he and David Mawdsley were presented with certificates to mark that achievement. In addition, Mike was entitled to donate a prize of £750 to a charity of his choice. This he graciously gave to LWCU.

You may perhaps recall that in 1914, in the final weeks of the life of Harry Evans, the Welsh Choral's first conductor, he was looking forward to a visit with his choir to Germany. Edward Elgar, always a good friend to the Choral, had invited the choir to accompany him to the Continent, where he had scheduled a performance of his work, *The Dream of Gerontius*. Sadly, this was not to take place. Even had Harry Evans continued to live, the outbreak of war in August would have made a continental visit quite impossible.

Whether Hopkin Evans or Malcolm Sargent ever considered such an expedition is not known. The Choral minutes make no mention of such an enterprise. Those presently in the choir can remember no serious consideration of a trip abroad until the idea surfaced at an Executive Committee Meeting in June, 2003, during the very weeks when the appointment of a new choral conductor was the matter of primary importance. By the time of the 2003 November AGM, it had become obvious that a foreign tour would meet with considerable interest. In March, 2004, after further discussion, David and Ruth Honour undertook detailed research, which led to more serious consideration. The possibility of one or more joint concerts with a German choir, perhaps centering on Cologne, the city with which Liverpool is twinned, was certainly an attractive notion, but it depended on the ability to find mutually convenient dates. Ultimately the idea of a joint concert was abandoned, but concerts were planned for the Welsh Choral alone. The choir settled on half-term week in late May and early June, 2005, as the best possible time to go, and in September, 2004, when rehearsals were resumed after the summer break, members were asked to sign up if interested. Seventy singing members with a number of friends and relations signed up, and the venture was accepted as a positive future engagement.

All are aware of how much energy and detailed planning is involved in even a family trip abroad. How much more time and dedicated work was involved in such a venture as this! Travel arrangements were not easy to sort out. There had to be coaches from Liverpool to Dover, coaches that would travel with the choir on the cross-channel ferry to Calais, and then on to the Hotel Weinlaube in Koblenz. Plans for the concert venues, Koblenz, Marienburg and Wiesbaden, had to be finalised, and a full music repertoire compiled, from which items would be selected for each concert. Pat Mitchell and Pat McCoy had very early begun practical arrangements for the making of a second quilt, and it had, of course, to be made ready for a formal presentation to the Cathedral and people of Cologne, as a symbol of Liverpool's friendship and goodwill.

Those who joined in the German venture were well pleased with their reception and with the entire experience. One choral member, Roderick Owen, a tenor, wrote an account of it, in Welsh, for the local Welsh paper, *Yr Angor*. Following, in translation, is his personal impression of the German week:

> During the week of the Bank Holiday, the choir went on its first musical journey to Germany, holding concerts in various churches, and especially, in Cologne Cathedral.
>
> The Choral travelled from Liverpool in two buses. It had been decided to stay at a hotel in the lovely city of Koblenz. It is a city situated at the confluence of the two biggest rivers in Germany, the Rhine and the Mosel. The weather doing its worst, we arrived on Monday evening, utterly exhausted, yet having enjoyed a happy companionship, but for the feeble few who had taken advantage of Easy Jet in order to cut short their travel time.
>
> A good sleep, early breakfast, and a rehearsal at 8:15 each morning became the pattern of our mornings for the rest of our German visit. First, however, the weather now being excellent, we had an hour's cruise on the Rhine, seeing splendid sights, passing the Lorelei, and travelling afterwards to the pleasant town of Rudesheim to spend the afternoon there before returning to Koblenz. That evening we gave our first concert to a strong audience in the Moselweiss Church on the shore of the Mosel. The choir had prepared works by Handel, Britten, Tavener, Arwel Hughes, Hammerschmidt, Mendelssohn, Rutter and Karl Jenkins. The performance was given, of course, under the able and patient leadership of our conductor, Keith Orrell, and our accompanist, Stephen Hargreaves.
>
> Wednesday was our busiest day, and the climax of our visit. We travelled for an hour to the Cathedral of Cologne to sing in the midday Mass. To see and to be present in the most beautiful of German cathedrals was a very special experience in itself, apart from the privilege of being able to sing within it. To mark the occasion, the choir presented a quilt, of the unique handiwork of its members, to the Cathedral chapter, and this

will be on permanent display in the Cathedral, a memento of
our visit.

Concerts were also held in other churches, All Saints
Anglican Church in Marienbad and Saint Augustine of
Canterbury in Wiesbaden. Excellent additional items were
performed by a small Madrigal Chorus, presenting works by
Weelkes, and there was also a traditional penillion-singing
party under the care of Margaret Anwyl Williams. Stephen
Hargreaves showed his particular skill at the organ in his
performance of *The Arrival of the Queen of Sheba*. Neill
Jackson's sensitive viola playing of the Introduction to the
Benedictus of Karl Jenkins evoked a moving response. Indeed,
such an atmosphere was created by his performance that some
in the Choir and others in the audience were moved to tears.

Altogether our visit to Germany was truly one to remember.
We must do this again!

Roderick Owen

As a matter of fact, a further adventure abroad was already
a certainty. The idea of arranging joint concerts with a choir in
Dublin on a reciprocal basis in 2006 had first been mentioned
at an Executive Committee Meeting in April, 2004, and by
June of that year, the Welsh Choral Chairman was already in
touch with Orlagh Flood, the Chairman of the Tallaght Choral
Society, a mixed choir suggested to LWCU Chairman, David
Mawdsley, by the conductor of the Dublin Welsh Male Voice
Choir, Keith Young. He is a Welshman who hailed originally
from Pontarddulais. It took however, almost twelve months
of detailed correspondence before arrangements for the Welsh
Choral's visit to Dublin and the Tallaght Society's to Liverpool
were finally completed.

On a practical level, it was fortunate that the choir was able
to arrange the concert in Dublin on a Sunday during a Bank
Holiday weekend in the U.K., and the concert in Liverpool a
week later on a Sunday during a Bank Holiday weekend in
Ireland. This enabled the travelling choir in each case to return

home on the Bank Holiday without missing a day's work. The burden of dealing with the detailed travel arrangements fell upon Tony Leigh, who accepted it cheerfully. Both Keith Orrell and Aled Phillips accompanied the Choral to Dublin, Keith acting as accompanist in the piano rehearsal, and Aled as conductor when the choir sang the Welsh hymn, *Y Delyn Aur*, at the Ambassador's Residence.

Many choristers will have enjoyed this visit sufficiently to have written their own accounts of it. We are lucky enough to have available the version written by a long-time stalwart of the choir, and a former chairman, Mr. Ifor Griffith.

> It was most fitting that, in the "Year of the Sea", the Liverpool Welsh Choral was invited by the Tallaght Choral Society of Dublin, to cross the Irish Sea to sing with them, Giuseppe Verdi's *Requiem* at the National Concert Hall, Dublin. This concert took place on Sunday, May 28, 2006. In anticipation of this forthcoming performance, the Choir had been extremely well prepared by our musical director, Keith Orrell, ably assisted by our accompanist, Stephen Hargreaves.
>
> The Choir, supported by friends and relatives, sailed from Holyhead at 9:50 a.m. on Saturday, May 27 and arrived at Dublin Port at 11:40 a.m. From the Terminal at Dublin Port the Choir was taken by coaches to the Ardmore Hotel, Tolka Valley, Dublin, where lunch was awaiting. This hotel was modern, comfortable and welcoming.
>
> At 3:00 p.m. coaches took the choir to a piano rehearsal with the Tallaght Choral Society at Synge Street Secondary School. The Welsh Choral was given a very warm welcome by the members of the Tallaght Choral Society. We had an excellent rehearsal, taken by their musical director, Mark Armstrong. At the end of the rehearsal our choir members were presented with a gift from the Tallaght Choral Society.
>
> After the piano rehearsal, choir members, including friends and relatives, were taken by coaches to the British Ambassador's Residence, Glencairn, Sandyford, Dublin, for a Reception from 6:30 p.m. to 8:00 p.m. Glencairn is a

most impressive Residence which, over the years, has been transformed into something that looks like a Scottish Baronial Castle. The British Government acquired it as the British Ambassador's Residence in 1953. The British Ambassador, Stewart Eldon, and his wife, Christine, were gracious and generous hosts, providing us with ample drinks and finger buffet. Christine Eldon is a cousin to one of the Choir's sopranos, Barbara Mason, who was instrumental in arranging this happy event. In appreciation of this generous hospitality, the Choir gave a full-blooded rendering of *Y Delyn Aur*.

After breakfast on Sunday, May 28, the Choir left the Hotel for the National Concert Hall for an 11:00 a.m. start to the rehearsal with the orchestra and soloists. The National Concert Hall proved to be a compact hall with seating for an audience of around 800. The rehearsal went very well, with a good quartet of suitable soloists, and the orchestra, the RTE National Symphony Orchestra, was most professional. The rehearsal ended at 2:00 p.m. The afternoon was spent at leisure in this vibrant city.

We were all back at the Concert Hall at 7:30 p.m., ready for an 8:00 p.m. start to the performance. Mark Armstrong, conductor, inspired all performers to give an outstanding and emotional performance of Verdi's *Requiem*. The sound of the combined choirs was indeed powerful, as was the singing of the four soloists. The two Welsh soloists, Geraint Dodd and Camilla Roberts, gave impressive performances. Andrew Slater (Bass) was somewhat underpowered. The star of the evening, for me, was the Irish contralto, Deirdre Cooling-Nolan, with her focused, wide-ranging and mature voice. At the end of the performance the audience gave it a warm and enthusiastic reception.

Later that evening, the Choir, with friends and relatives, were the guests of the Tallaght Choral Society at "The Bleeding Horse", where we were treated to an informal supper with drinks! This was a very happy ending to a memorable evening.

On Monday May 29, we left our hotel at 10:30 a.m. to catch the 12:30 p.m. fast ferry to Holyhead. In so doing we left

behind warm, hospitable and fun-loving peopkle living in a
vibrant and beautiful city. The performance of Verdi's *Requiem*
at the National Concert Hall of Dublin will rate as one of the
most memorable experiences of my long association (45 years)
with the Liverpool Welsh Choral Union.

R. Ifor Griffith

As might be anticipated, the Welsh Choral continues to plan
for the future. One important special event planned for 2007 is
an exchange with the Edinburgh Royal Choral Union. It has, of
course, again been a long time in the planning, the idea having
been first broached at an Executive meeting in February, 2005.

As many in Britain will remember, Liverpool has been
chosen as the European Capital of Culture for 2008. The Welsh
people of Liverpool are planning a Welsh Week, to run from
March 1 to March 8, 2008. It happens that St. David's Day, March
1, falls on a Saturday in the year 2008, and it has been confirmed
that the Philharmonic Hall will be reserved to the LWCU for
their Saturday evening concert. Choral and audience will surely
be looking forward to a feast of music on that occasion.

When the founding fathers met in 1902 to establish the
Liverpool Welsh Choral Union and to draw up a suitable body
of rules, they declared in Rule 2 that "the object of the Society
shall be to cultivate and promote the practice of, and develop
the taste for high-class Musical Art." While the language of the
Rule-book has been several times revised, the general purport
remains the same. It now reads that the aims and objectives of
the choir are "the study and practice of choral music in order to
foster the public knowledge and appreciation of such music by
means of public performance." Few are likely to challenge the
contention that the Welsh Choral has striven to keep these aims
always in view and has, to the best of its ability, lived up to them.
May we hope that LWCU's second century will be as successful
in artistic terms as the first, as rewarding for its members and
audiences, and as effective in fulfilling its aims and objectives.

BIBLIOGRAPHY

Aldous, Richard, *Tunes of Glory, The Life of Malcolm Sargent* (London, 2001).

Bacharach, A. L. (ed.), *The Musical Companion* (London, 1934).
Lives of the Great Composers (London, 1935).

Bebb, W. Ambrose, *Y Ddeddf Uno*, 1536 (Dinbych,1937).

Boyce, Joan, *Pillowslips and Gasmasks* (Birkenhead, 1989).

Y Bywgraffiadur Cymreig hyd 1940 (Llundain, Anrhydeddus Gymdeithas y Cymmrodorion, 1953).

Y Bywgraffiadur Cymreig 1941-1950 (Llundain, Anrhydeddus Gymdeithas y Cymmrodorion, 1970).

Y Bywgraffiadur Cymreig 1951-1970 (Llundain, Anrhydeddus Gymdeithas y Cymmrodorion, 1997).

Cheyney, Edward P, *A Short History of England* (New York,1945).

Davies, John, *Hanes Cymru* (London, 1990).

Evans, Gwynfor, *Land of My Fathers, 2000 years of Welsh History* (Talybont, 1990).

Garnett, Ron, *Liverpool in the 1930's and the Blitz* (Preston, 1995).

Griffiths, Paul, *The Penguin Companion to Classical Music* (Harmondsworth, 2004).

Harmsworth, Alfred and Harmsworth, Harold, (eds.) *The Harmsworth Encyclopaedia*, Volume VIII (London, 1905).

Jenkins, R. T. *Hanes Cymru yn y Ddeunawfed Ganrif* (Caerdydd, 1945).

Jones, John Edward, *Antur a Menter Cymry Lerpwl. Hanes Eglwysi Presbyteraidd Cymraeg, 1887-1987* (Lerpwl, 1987).

Jones, J. R. (ed.), *The Welsh Builder on Merseyside. Annals and Lives* (Liverpool, 1945).

Lewis, Eiluned and Peter, *The Land of Wales* (London, 1949).

Lile, Emma, *A Step in Time. Folk-dancing in Wales* (Cardiff, 1999).

Owen, Ivor, *Golwg ar Gymru, ei Hanes a'i Phobl. A View of Wales, its History and People. For Welsh Learners* (Y Bontfaen, 1976)

Rees, D. Ben, *Cymry Lerpwl a'r Cyffiniau yn yr Ugeinfed Ganrif* (Lerpwl, 2001).

Reid, Charles, *Malcolm Sargent* (London, 1968).

Richards, Denis and Hunt, J. W., *An Illustrated History of Modern Britain, 1783-1964* (London, 1965).

Stephens, Meic (gol.), *Cydymaith i Lenyddiaeth Cymru* (Caerdydd, 1997).

Taylor, A. J. P., *From Sarajevo to Potsdam* (London, 1965).

Taylor, Stainton de Bouffler, *Two Centuries of Music in Liverpool* (Liverpool, 1973).

Vaughan-Thomas, Wynford and Llewellyn, Alun, *The Shell Guide to Wales* (London, 1977).

Wade, Beryl, *Storm Over the Mersey* (Rock Ferry, 1990).

Who Was Who, 1929-1940 (London, 1941).

Williams, A. H., *Cymru Ddoe* (Lerpwl, 1944).

Williams, David, *A History of Modern Wales* (London, 1950).

Williams, Gareth, *Valleys of Song. Music and Welsh Society, 1840-1914* (Cardiff, 1997).

Williams, W. Albert, "Impressions of the Eisteddfod", *Y Cerddor*, Medi, 1933.

http://www.intute.ac.uk/artsandhumanities/limelight/singingcentury.html [accessed 26/05/2007]. (Kaufman, Sarah "The Singing Century", Limelight article for *Artifact*, December 2005).

http://www.mersey.gateway.org/server.php?show=ConWeb.1201 [accessed 26/05/2007]. (Chambré Hardman Archive, *Liverpool Blitz Time*).

http://scholar.google.com/scholar?q=www.+ocean+waves+merchant+n avy+heritage+merchant+navies&hl=en&um=1&oi=scholart [accessed 26/05/2007]. *(Ocean Waves, Merchant Navy Heritage, Merchant Navies)*.

http://www.visionofbritain.org.uk/text/content_page.jsp?t_:d=Cambrensis_ Desc&C_id=15 [accessed 26/05/2007]. (Giraldus Cambrensis, "Of their Symphonies and Songs", Bk.1, Ch. XIII *A Vision of Britain Through Time*).

APPENDIX I

RULES AND BYE-LAWS

Adopted in the GENERAL MEETING, 1st September 1903, and amended in the GENERAL MEETINGS held 4th September, 1905, 10th June, 1912, 6th July, 1920, and 4th July, 1922.

RULES

1. That the Society be called "The LIVERPOOL WELSH CHORAL UNION."

2. The object of the Society shall be to cultivate and promote the practice of, and develop the taste for high-class Musical Art.

3. The Society shall consist of Guarantors; Life Members; Honorary Members; and Practical Members, whose number shall not exceed 300 vocalists. Practical Members must be of Welsh Nationality.

4. The Guarantors of the Society for the time being shall comprise all who have signed the Guarantee Bond, the liability in each case not being more than the amount signed for individually. This guarantee remains in force continuously, but any Guarantor may withdraw and have his name cancelled on the bond by giving notice in writing to the Secretary on or before the 31st of March in any year, and on payment of his proportion of any liability existing, as shown in the Balance Sheet to be produced at the next Annual General Meeting.

5. Life Members shall pay a subscription of not less than £5.5s. Honorary Members shall pay an Annual Subscription of not less than half-a-guinea, due in advance.

6. Practical Members shall pay an Annual Subscription of 2/6 for Ladies, and 3/- for Gentlemen, due in advance. The admission of Practical Members shall be under the control of the Executive Committee. Applicants for Membership must notify the Secretary or be nominated by a Member, and if after examination such applicant's musical qualification be deemed satisfactory he or she shall be admitted to membership upon signing a copy of these Rules and Bye-laws.

7. The Society shall be conducted by an Executive Committee, consisting of President, Chairman, Vice-Chairman, Conductor, Hon. Treasurer, Secretary, Librarian, Registrar, and Committee of fifteen, five members of which shall retire annually, but who will be eligible for re-election. Not less than five members of the Committee must be Practical Members. Seven to form a quorum.

8. The Executive Committee shall have power to frame Bye-laws, dispose of funds for the purposes of the Society, select and purchase all music and other properties for the Society, and generally manage and superintend its affairs. It shall meet as often as required, upon 2 days' notice being given; regulate its own proceedings, and supply any vacancy occurring in its own body, during the interval between Annual General Meetings.

9. A General Meeting of the Guarantors, Life Members,

and Honorary Members shall be held annually during the second week in June, to receive the Committee's report, pass the Treasurer's accounts, elect Officers, and five Members of the Committee to serve for three years, and transact any other business relating to the affairs of the Society.

10. The President may, by notice stating the purpose thereof, convene an Extraordinary General Meeting whenever necessary, and he shall be required to do so upon receiving notice signed by not less than twenty Guarantors, Life Members, or Honorary Members, and setting forth the purpose of such meeting.

11. The regular Session shall commence about the first week in September and terminate about the end of March in each year. Rehearsals shall be held on every Wednesday evening (or such other day as may be appointed) commencing at 8 o'clock prompt. Extra Rehearsals may be appointed to take place as often as required.

12. The Executive Committee shall have power to exclude Members deemed incompetent from taking part in any of the public performances.

13. The Executive Committee, may, from time to time, cause private re-examination of Members, and if, upon such re-examination, Members are found incompetent, they shall be required to at once resign.

14. The Executive Committee shall have power to expel any Member from the Society.

15. Any Member, Honorary or Practical, wishing to resign,

shall give due notice in writing to the Secretary.

16. All questions shall be decided by a majority of votes (by ballot if desired), every Member present having one vote, and the Chairman an additional or casting vote if necessary.

17. Two Auditors shall be appointed from amongst the Guarantors at the Annual General Meeting to audit the books of the Society annually or oftener if desired.

18. In the event of any serious financial difficulty, a meeting of the Guarantors shall be called, and if funds be not then forthcoming, the Society shall be dissolved and every Guarantor shall be required to pay his or her share in the discharge of existing liabilities.

19. These rules cannot be altered or amended except at a Special General Meeting, and at the suggestion of the Executive Committee or the formal request of at least twenty Guarantors, Life Members, or Honorary Members. The desired alteration shall be notified on the paper convening the meeting, such Meeting to be legal, must number at least half the Guarantors, Life Members and Honorary Members.

BYE-LAWS

1. The Ordinary Rehearsals shall commence punctually at 8 o'clock, at which time Members are expected to be in their places; the doors will be closed at 8:30, and admission will be refused to all who present themselves after that time, unless prevented by imperative circumstances from coming earlier.

2. The Conductor for the time being shall direct the Rehearsals of the Society, and shall have power to dictate, at his direction, to the whole of the performers, and, subject to the control of the Committee, shall have the power of dispensing with the services of any Member whenever he may think fit.

3. No stranger shall be admitted to the Rehearsals except with the permission of the Conductor.

4. No Member shall leave Rehearsal or Concert before its conclusion, without the permission of the Conductor.

5. Members absenting themselves from Ordinary Rehearsals must give reasonable notice in writing to the Secretary, and any Member absent from three consecutive Rehearsals, or from any Concert without an imperative reason shall be liable to expulsion, at the discretion of the Committee.

6. Members who may be absent from their places on the Orchestra for any Concert, at least five minutes before the time appointed for the commencement, may be debarred from taking part, at the discretion of the Conductor for the time being.

7. No Member shall be permitted to take part in any Concert who has not been present in the General Rehearsal, except by special permission of the Conductor, and no Member shall be permitted to take part who, in the opinion of the Conductor, has not taken sufficient part in previous Rehearsals.

8. No Member shall be allowed to leave the Orchestra during a Concert, unless for an imperative reason, and

with the sanction of the Conductor.

9. Any Member interrupting any Rehearsal or any other meeting, using improper language, or being guilty of any other act that may be deemed offensive, shall be dealt with, at the discretion of the Committee. If any Member shall feel aggrieved at the conduct of any other Member during Concert, Rehearsal, or Meeting, he or she shall signify the same to the Secretary to be reported by him to the Committee, who will endeavour to adjust such difference, or if expedient, they have the power to expel the offending Party.

APPENDIX II

RULES

Adopted at the General Meeting held
on 9th November 1977

1. The Society shall be called "THE LIVERPOOOL WELSH CHORAL UNION".

2. The aims and objects of the Society shall be the study and practice of choral music in order to foster the public knowledge and appreciation of such music by means of public performance.

3. The members of the Society shall comprise the Guarantors, the Honorary Members and the Choristers.

4. The Guarantors shall comprise those persons who are from time to time signatories to any guarantee given to the Society's Bankers to secure any sums due to such Bankers by the Society, the liability of the Guarantors being regulated by the terms of any such guarantee.

5. The Honorary Members of the Society who are not also Choristers shall pay an annual subscription of not less than fifty pence.

6. The Choristers shall at the commencement of each season pay such annual subscription as shall from time to time be fixed by the Executive Committee, and thereupon shall *ipso-facto* become Honorary Members of the Society.

7. The Honorary Officers of the Society shall comprise President, Chairman, Vice-Chairman, Secretary, Treasurer, Librarian, Publicity Officer, Registrar and two Ticket Secretaries, all of whom shall be elected annually at the Annual General Meeting.

8. The Executive Committee shall comprise the Honorary Officers and twelve Choristers. Each of the twelve Choristers shall serve for three years, four being elected at each Annual General Meeting. A chorister retiring from the Executive Committee by rotation shall not be eligible for re-election until the Annual General Meeting next after that at which he retires. The Principal Conductor, Chorus Master and Accompanist shall (subject to the discretion of the Executive Committee) be entitled to attend but not vote at meetings of the Executive Committee. In the absence of the Secretary, Treasurer or Librarian, the absentee's assistant shall be entitled to attend but not vote at Meetings of the Executive Committee.

9. The Executive Committee shall have the general conduct and management of the Society's affairs. In particular it shall appoint the Principal Conductor, Chorus Master and Accompanist for the time being, be empowered to dispose of funds for the purposes of the Society, select works and engage soloists, the Principal Conductor or failing him, the Chorus Master being invited to take the chair at selection meetings, fill any vacancy among the Honorary Officers or its own number, and be entitled to co-opt not more than three additional members of the Society. The Executive Committee shall meet without notice being given at 6:15 p.m. on the first Wednesday of each month during the active season and otherwise as

often as required upon two days' notice being given, ten members forming a quorum. Suggested works shall be nominated one meeting before the selection meeting.

10. An Annual Meeting of the Members of the Society shall be held at least once in each year and in no event more than fifteen months after the previous Annual General Meeting. Such Annual General Meeting shall receive the Executive Committee's Report and the audited accounts for the period ending on the previous 31st July, shall elect the Honorary Officers, Vice Presidents, four Choristers to serve upon the Executive Committee, Assistant Secretary, Assistant Treasurer, Assistant Librarian and two Auditors (such Auditors not being members of the Executive Committee), and shall transact any other business relating to the Society's affairs. Not less than fourteen days' notice of such Annual General Meeting shall be given to each member of the Society, such notice in the case of Choristers being given verbally at not less than two consecutive rehearsals. Forty members of the Society shall form a quorum at an Annual General Meeting

11. The Executive Committee may convene at any time an Extraordinary General Meeting of the Members of the Society to transact such business as is stated in the notice convening the Meeting and shall do so either in the event of any serious financial difficulty of the Society or upon the request of the Guarantors or any twenty Choristers. The provisions as to notice and quorum in relation to the Annual General Meeting shall apply to such an Extraordinary General Meeting.

12. All questions at meetings of the Executive Committee

or any sub-committee thereof or any Annual General Meeting of the Members of the Society shall be decided by a majority of votes (by ballot if required), each member present having one vote and the Chairman a second or casting vote if necessary.

13. Rehearsals shall ordinarily be held between 7:00 p.m. and 9:00 p.m. on each Wednesday during the Season which shall commence and terminate on such dates as shall be determined by the Executive Committee. At the request of the Chorus Master the Executive Committee may direct that additional rehearsals be held at any time. All rehearsals shall be under the direction of the Chorus Master, without whose permission no person other than a member of the Society shall be admitted. Two final rehearsals shall ordinarily be held prior to each concert under the direction of the Conductor for that concert.

14. Any person wishing to join the Society as a Chorister shall apply to the Secretary and if after audition by the Chorus Master the applicant is considered satisfactory such person shall be admitted to the Society as a Chorister.

15. The Executive Committee may from time to time direct that any Chorister or Choristers shall be privately re-auditioned and shall ordinarily arrange that each Chorister shall be privately re-auditioned at intervals of about three years. If on any such re-audition any Chorister's musical ability and record of attendance is not considered satisfactory by the Chorus Master, the Executive Committee may (after giving such Chorister the opportunity to be heard), require such Chorister to resign or exclude such Chorister from taking part in

any one or more of the Society's concerts. A Chorister who, for any reason (not acceptable to the Executive Committee) misses two or more concerts in any one season will be liable for re-audition before the beginning of the following season.

16. In the event of any Chorister interrupting any rehearsal or concert, or using any improper or offensive language or behaviour, the Executive Committee may (after giving the Chorister the opportunity to be heard) require such Chorister to resign, or exclude such Chorister from taking part in any one or more of the Society's concerts.

17. Any Chorister wishing to resign from the Society shall notify the Secretary. Any Chorister unable to attend a rehearsal or concert shall notify the Secretary, giving the reason for his or her absence.

18. A Chorister who fails to attend either of the final rehearsals for any of the Society's concerts shall not be entitled to take part in such concert without the prior consent of the Executive Committee which, in the event of it being impossible to convene a full meeting of the Executive Committee, may be given by the Chairman and any two other members of the Executive Committee. In addition, if at any time any Chorister's record of attendance at ordinary rehearsals is not considered satisfactory by the Chorus Master, the Executive Committee may (after giving such Chorister the opportunity to be heard and considering the reasons for the Chorister's absence from rehearsals) exclude such Chorister from taking part in the Society's next concert.

19. Copies of music lent to Choristers shall be returned within seven days after a concert, failing which the Chorister shall be responsible for any additional cost incurred by the Society.

20. If on the dissolution of the Society there remains, after the satisfaction of all its debts and liabilities any property or money whatsoever, the same shall not be paid or distributed among the Members of the Society but shall be given or transferred to another charitable institution or institutions having objects similar to the Society.

21. No alteration or amendment shall be made to these rules (including the present rule) which will have the effect of rendering the Society non-charitable at law. Subject thereto, these rules may only be altered or amended at a General Meeting of the Members of the Society at which (notwithstanding the foregoing provisions of these rules) sixty Members of the Society are present. An alteration or amendment to these rules may be proposed only by the Executive Committee or any twenty Members of the Society, and such proposal shall be notified to the Secretary not less than twenty-one days prior to the General Meeting.

APPENDIX III

RULES

Adopted at the Annual General Meeting
held on 5th November 1997

1. NAME

The Society shall be called 'THE LIVERPOOL
WELSH CHORAL UNION'.

2. AIMS AND OBJECTS

The aims and objects of the Society shall be the study
and practice of choral music in order to foster the public
knowledge and appreciation of such music by means of
public performance.

3. MEMBERSHIP

(A) The Members of the Society shall comprise Choristers
and Associate Members.

(B) Choristers shall at the commencement of each season
pay such annual subscription as shall from time to time
be determined by the Executive Committee.

(C) Associate Members of the Society shall pay such annual
subscription as shall from time to time be determined by
the Executive Committee.

4. OFFICERS

(A) The Society shall invite such person(s) to be its Patron(s) as the Annual General Meeting may from time to time determine.

(B) The Society shall appoint a President and such Vice-Presidents as the Annual General Meeting may from time to time determine.

(C) The Executive Officers of the Society shall comprise Chairman, Vice-Chairman, Secretary, Treasurer, Concerts Secretary, Publicity Officer, Fund Raising Officer and Publications Officer.

(D) The Non-Executive Officers of the Society shall comprise Librarian, Recruitment Officer, Registrar, Assistant Secretary, Assistant Treasurer and two Ticket Secretaries.

5. MEMBERSHIP OF EXECUTIVE COMMITTEE

(A) The Executive Committee shall comprise the Executive Officers and eight ordinary members. The President shall ex officio be entitled to attend meetings of the Executive Committee. The Musical Director, Accompanist and Non-Executive Officers shall (subject to the discretion of the Executive Committee) be entitled to attend but not vote at meetings of the Executive Committee.

(B) Each of the Executive Officers and Non-Executive Officers shall be elected at the Annual General Meeting and shall in the first instance serve for one year. An Executive Officer or Non-Executive Officer retiring at an Annual General Meeting shall be eligible for re-election, save that a Chairman or Vice-Chairman retiring after having served in that capacity for three years shall not be eligible for re-election in the same capacity until the Annual General Meeting after that at which he or she retires.

(C) Each of the eight ordinary members of the Executive Committee shall serve for two years, four being elected at each Annual General Meeting. An ordinary member retiring from the Executive Committee at an Annual General Meeting by rotation shall not be eligible for re-election in the same capacity until the Annual General Meeting next after that at which he or she retires. A Non-Executive Officer shall be eligible for election as an ordinary member of the Executive Committee.

(D) An Associate Member shall not be eligible for election as an Executive Officer, but shall be eligible for election as an ordinary member of the Executive Committee. Not more than one Associate Member shall be a member of the Executive Committee at any time.

(E) No member of the Society shall be eligible for election as an Auditor.

6. POWERS AND DUTIES OF EXECUTIVE COMMITTEE

(A) The Executive Committee shall be responsible for the general conduct and management of the Society's affairs. In particular it shall be empowered to dispose of funds for the purposes of the Society, to appoint the Musical Director and Accompanist for the time being, to promote

concerts and select programmes, to engage conductors
and soloists, to fill any vacancy among the Executive
Officers, the Non-Executive Officers or its own number,
to co-opt not more than three additional members of the
Society and to appoint such sub-committees (whether
comprising members of the Executive Committee or
not) as it may determine to be appropriate.

(B) The Executive Committee shall meet as often as it may
determine to be appropriate upon seven days' notice
being given, six members forming a quorum. Any sub-
committee appointed by the Executive Committee shall
meet as often as may be determined by the Executive
Committee. Any member of the Executive Committee
or of any sub-committee appointed by it who for any
reason (not acceptable to the Executive Committee) fails
to attend three consecutive meetings shall be deemed to
have resigned.

(C) All questions at meetings of the Executive Committee or
any sub-committee appointed by it shall be determined
by a majority of votes (by ballot if required), each
member present having one vote and the chairman of
the meeting a second or casting vote if necessary. The
Executive Committee shall otherwise regulate its own
proceedings and shall give such directions as it may
determine to be appropriate for the regulation of the
proceedings of any sub-committee appointed by it.

7. GENERAL MEETINGS

(A) An Annual General Meeting of the Members of the
Society shall be held at least once in each year and in
no event more than fifteen months after the previous

Annual General Meeting. Such Annual General Meeting shall receive the Executive Committee's report and the audited accounts for the period ending on the previous 30th June; shall elect the President, such Vice-Presidents as the Society may deem appropriate, the Executive Officers, the Non-Executive Officers and four ordinary members to serve upon the Executive Committee; shall appoint an auditor for the ensuing year; shall consider any resolution submitted by the Executive Committee (including any resolution to invite one or more persons to be Patron(s) of the Society); shall consider any resolution submitted by a member of the Society to the Secretary not less than 7 days prior to the Annual General Meeting; and shall transact any other relevant business relating to the Society's affairs.

(B) The Executive Committee may convene at any time an Extraordinary General Meeting of the Members of the Society to transact such business as is stated in the notice convening the meeting and shall do so either in the event of any serious financial difficulty of the Society or upon the request of any twenty Members of the Society.

(C) Not less than fourteen days' notice of any General Meeting of the Society shall be given to each Member, such notice in the case of Choristers being given verbally at not less than two consecutive rehearsals. Forty Members shall (save as otherwise provided in Rules 11 and 12) form a quorum at any General Meeting of the Society. All questions at any General Meeting shall (save as otherwise provided in Rules 11 and 12) be decided by a majority of votes (by ballot if required), each Member present having one vote and the chairman of the meeting a second or casting vote if necessary.

8. CHORISTERS

(A) Any person wishing to join the Society as a Chorister shall apply to the Recruitment Officer and if after private audition by the Musical Director the applicant is considered satisfactory such person shall be admitted to the Society as a Chorister.

(B) The Executive Committee may from time to time direct that any Chorister or section of Choristers shall be privately re-auditioned and shall ordinarily arrange that each section of Choristers shall be privately re-auditioned at intervals to be agreed by the Executive Committee with the Musical Director, who shall report to the Executive Committee upon the results of such re-auditions.

(C) Copies of music lent to a Chorister shall be returned within seven days after a concert, failing which the Chorister shall be responsible for any additional cost incurred by the Society.

(D) Any Chorister unable to attend a rehearsal or concert shall notify the Secretary, giving the reason for his or her absence.

9. REHEARSALS

(A) Rehearsals shall ordinarily be held between 7.00 p.m. and 9.00 p.m. on each Wednesday during the season which shall commence and terminate on such dates as shall be determined by the Executive Committee. Two final rehearsals shall ordinarily be held prior to each concert under the direction of the conductor for that concert.

At the request of the Musical Director the Executive Committee may direct that additional rehearsals be held at any time.

(B) All rehearsals shall be under the direction of the Musical Director or (in the case of the two final rehearsals prior to a concert) the conductor for that concert, without whose permission no person other than a Member of the Society shall be admitted.

(C) If at any time any Chorister's record of attendance at rehearsals is not considered satisfactory by the Musical Director, the Executive Committee may (after giving such Chorister the right to be heard and considering the reasons for the Chorister's absence from rehearsals) exclude such Chorister from taking part in the Society's next concert.

(D) A Chorister who fails to attend either of the final rehearsals for any of the Society's concerts shall not be entitled to take part in such concert without the prior consent of the Executive Committee which, in the event of it being impossible to convene a full meeting of the Executive Committee, may be given by the Chairman and any two other members of the Executive Committee.

10. RESIGNATION OF CHORISTERS

(A) Any Chorister wishing to resign from the Society shall notify the Secretary.

(B) In the event of any Chorister failing to pay such annual subscription as shall from time to time be determined by the Executive Committee, the Executive Committee may (after giving the Chorister the opportunity to be heard) require such Chorister to resign or exclude such Chorister from taking part in any one or more of the Society's concerts.

(C) In the event that upon any private re-audition of a Chorister his or her musical ability or record of attendance is not considered satisfactory by the Musical Director, the Executive Committee may (after giving the Chorister the opportunity to be heard) require such Chorister to resign or exclude such Chorister from taking part in any one or more of the Society's concerts.

(D) In the event of any Chorister interrupting a rehearsal or concert or using improper or offensive language or behaviour, the Executive Committee may (after giving the Chorister an opportunity to be heard) require such Chorister to resign or exclude such Chorister from taking part in any one or more of the Society's concerts.

11. DISSOLUTION

(A) The Society may only be dissolved by a resolution approved by at least two-thirds of those present and voting at a General Meeting of the Members of the Society at which (notwithstanding the foregoing provisions of these Rules) sixty Members of the Society or half of the total number of Members of the Society (whichever is the less) are present. A dissolution of the Society may only be proposed by the Executive Committee or any twenty Members of the Society, and such proposal shall be notified to the Secretary not less than twenty-one days prior to the General Meeting.

(B) If on the dissolution of the Society there remains, after the satisfaction of all its debts and liabilities, any property or money whatsoever, the same shall not be paid or distributed among the Members of the Society but shall be given or transferred to another charitable institution or institutions having objectives similar to those of the Society.

12. ALTERATION TO RULES

(A) No alteration or amendment shall be made to these Rules (including the present Rule) which will have the effect of rendering the Society non-charitable at law.

(B) Subject thereto, these Rules may only be altered or amended by a resolution approved by at least two thirds of those present and voting at a General Meeting of the Members of the Society at which (notwithstanding the foregoing provisions of these Rules) sixty Members of the Society or half of the total number of Members of the Society (whichever is the less) are present. An alteration or amendment to these Rules may only be proposed by the Executive Committee or any twenty Members of the Society, and such proposal shall be notified to the Secretary not less than twenty-one days prior to the General Meeting.

APPENDIX IV

JOB DESCRIPTION

Position: Chorus Master

Responsible to: The Executive Committee

Liaises with: Chairman, Concert Manager,
                        Accompanist, Membership Secretary

Main duties:

1. To prepare the choir for public performances to the highest vocal and musical standard possible.

2. To prepare in advance of each concert a written schedule detailing the (passages of) works to be rehearsed.

3. To liaise with and advise the Accompanist; the Chorus Master should consult the Chairman if any difficulty arises in this area.

4. To be responsible for discipline during rehearsals and to set standards for attendance at rehearsals and concerts.

5. To recommend the most appropriate and acceptable platform manner, layout and order for concerts.

6. To liaise with guest conductors as to their interpretation of the work(s) to be performed.

7. To audition prospective choristers and to accept or reject applications.

8. In consultation with the Executive Committee to audition existing choristers as appropriate and to make recommendations.

9. To conduct those concerts for which a guest conductor has not been engaged.

10. To attend rehearsals taken by guest conductors.

11. To participate in the planning of the Society's future concerts and engagements.

12. To participate in the recruitment of new choristers.

13. To make arrangements of music as appropriate.

14. To participate in the selection of new venues for concerts.

15. To assist in bringing the Society to the awareness of the community.

16. To prepare a written report for presentation at each Annual General Meeting.

APPENDIX V

OFFICERS OF THE CHOIR

PRINCIPAL CONDUCTORS

Harry Evans	1902-1914
Hopkin Evans	1919-1940
Malcolm Sargent	1944-1967
Maurice Handford	1970-1982
Sian Edwards	1987-1989

CHORUS MASTERS

Harry Evans	1902-1914
Tom Lloyd	1914-1946
Caleb Jarvis	1946-1976
Edmund Walters	1976-1985
Anthony Ridley	1985-1989

DIRECTORS OF MUSIC

Gwyn L. Williams	1989-1999
Graham Jordan Ellis	1999-2003
Keith Orrell	2003-present

ACCOMPANISTS

Maggie Evans	1902-192?
Millicent Richards	192?-1931
Edith Darbyshire	1931-1934
Oliver Edwards	1935-1938
Laurence West	1938-1945
Ernest Pratt	1941-1983
Derek Sadler	1983-2002
Stephen Hargreaves	2002-present

PATRONS

William Mathias, CBE	1990-1992
Karl Jenkins, OBE	2005-present

PRESIDENTS

William Evans	1902-1910
Robert Roberts	1911-1933
H. Humphreys Jones	1934-1971
Emyr Wyn Jones	1972-1986
David J. Lewis	1976-1982
John Edward Jones	1986-1998
Huw H. Rees	1998-present

CHAIRMEN

Robert Roberts	1902-1910
Richard J. Hughes	1911-1914+
R. Vaughan Jones	1919-1935
Hugh T. Bellis	1935-1938
J. R. Jones	1938-1947
David J. Lewis	1948-1976
Eileen Morris	1976-1980
R. Ifor Griffith	1980-1983
R. A. Wynne Williams	1983-1986
David H. Mawdsley	1986-1990
Michael Reddington	1990-1993
Edward Goulbourne	1993-1996
David P. Williams	1996-1999
Rhiannon Liddell	1999-2002
David H. Mawdsley	2002-2005
Bob Metcalf	2005-present

APPENDIX VI

LIST OF CONCERTS

Year	Composer	Work(s) / Concert Title
1903	Handel	*Samson*
	Handel	*Messiah*
1904	Mendelssohn	*Elijah*
	Harry Evans	*Hymn of Praise, German Welsh Rhapsody*
	Handel	*Messiah*
1905	Harry Evans	*The Golden Legend, Victory of St. Garmon*
	Haydn	*The Creation*
	Mendelssohn	*Elijah*
1906	Elgar	*The Dream of Gerontius*
	Coleridge Taylor	*The Song of Hiawatha*
	Handel	*Messiah*
1907	Bach	*St. Matthew Passion*
	Sullivan	*The Martyr of Antioch*
	Handel	*Samson*
1908	Elgar	*The Apostles*
	Elgar	*The Dream of Gerontius*
	Mendelssohn	*Elijah*
1909	Bantock	*Omar Khayyam*
	Coleridge Taylor	*Hiawatha*
	Handel	*Messiah*
1910	Bach	*Mass in B Minor*
	Harry Evans	*Dafydd ap Gwilym*
	Berlioz	*Faust*
	Mendelssohn	*Elijah*
1911	Handel	*Acis and Galatea*
	Bantock	*Omar Khayyam 2/3, Pierrot of the Minute, Sappho Songs*
	Elgar	*King Olaf*
	Handel	*Messiah*

1912		Concert featuring
		Dame Clara Butt
	Bach	*St. Matthew Passion*

Unfortunately, many records
from 1913 to 1930 were destroyed

1931	Bach	*Mass in B Minor*
	Handel	*Messiah*
1932	Handel	*Messiah*
1933	Hopkin Evans	*Psalm to the Earth*
	Mascagni	*Cavalleria Rusticana*
1934	Handel	*Messiah*
1935	Bach	*St. Matthew Passion*
	Verdi	*Aida*
	Handel	*Messiah*
1936	Elgar	*The Apostles*
	Mendelssohn	*Elijah*
	Handel	*Messiah*
1937	Brahms	*Requiem*
	Wagner	*The Flying Dutchman,*
		The Mastersingers, Tannhäuser
	Handel	*Samson*
	Handel	*Messiah*
1938		Works by Beethoven, Bach,
		Handel, Hopkin Evans,
		Bruch, Chopin, Edwardes,
		Lassus, Scott, Parry, Verdi
	Coleridge Taylor	*Hiawatha's Wedding Feast*
	Elgar	*The Banner of St. George*
	Mendelssohn	*Lobgesang*
	Handel	*Messiah*
1939	Bach	*Mass in B Minor*
	Handel	*Messiah*
1940	Mendelssohn	*Elijah*
	Handel	*Messiah*

1941	Haydn	*The Creation*
	Handel	*Messiah*
	Handel	*Messiah*

1942	Verdi	*Requiem*
	Mendelssohn	*Elijah*
	Handel	*Messiah*

1943	Handel	*Judas Maccabeus*
	Handel	*Messiah*
	Verdi	*Requiem*
	Handel	*Messiah*

1944	Bach	*St. Matthew Passion*
	Handel	*Messiah*
	Coleridge Taylor	*Hiawatha*
	Handel	*Messiah*

1945	Haydn	*The Creation*
	Handel	*Messiah*
	Handel	*Israel in Egypt*
	Handel	*Messiah*

1946	Berlioz	*Faust*
	Handel	*Messiah*
	Elgar	*The Dream of Gerontius*
	Handel	*Messiah*

1947	Elgar	*The Apostles*
	Handel	*Messiah*
	Mendelssohn	*Elijah*
	Handel	*Messiah*

1948	Brahms	*Requiem*
	Elgar	*The Music Makers*
	Elgar	*The Dream of Gerontius*
	Handel	*Messiah*
	Vaughan Williams	*Dona Nobis Pacem*
	Elgar	*To Women*
	Elgar	*For The Fallen*
	Verdi	*Te Deum*
	Handel	*Messiah*

1949	Elgar	*The Apostles*
	Handel	*Messiah*
	Verdi	*Aida*
	Brahms	*Song of Destiny*

	Elgar	*The Dream of Gerontius*
	Haydn	*The Creation*
	Handel	*Messiah*
1950	Verdi	*Requiem*
	Elgar	*The Kingdom*
	Elgar	*The Apostles*
	Handel	*Messiah*
	Berlioz	*The Childhood of Christ*
1951	Handel	*Israel in Egypt*
	Faure	*Requiem*
	Walton	*Belshazzar's Feast*
	Elgar	*Serenade for Strings*
	Elgar	*The Apostles*
	Elgar	*The Dream of Gerontius*
	Brahms/Sargent	*Four Serious Songs*
	Parry	*Blest Pair of Sirens*
	Berlioz	*The Childhood of Christ*
	Handel	*Messiah*
1952	Julius Harrison	*Mass in C*
	Verdi	*Aida*
	Elgar	*The Kingdom*
	Mendelssohn	*Elijah*
1953	Handel	*Messiah*
	Bach	*St. Matthew Passion*
	Faure	*Requiem*
	Walton	*Belshazzar's Feast*
	Verdi	*Aida*
	Schubert	*Symphony No. 8*
	Julius Harrison	*Mass in C*
1954	Handel	*Messiah*
	Elgar	*The Dream of Gerontius*
	Handel	*Solomon*
	Haydn	*The Creation*
	Bach	*Sleepers Awake*
	Berlioz	*The Childhood of Christ*
1955	Handel	*Messiah*
	Vaughan Williams	*Fantasia on a Theme by Thomas Tallis*
	Verdi	*Requiem*
	Vaughan Williams	*A Sea Symphony*
		Works by Handel, Elgar and Brahms

	Mendelssohn	*Elijah*
	Elgar	*The Apostles*
1956	Handel	*Messiah*
	Faure	*Requiem*
	Walton	*Belshazzar's Feast*
	Handel	*Organ Concerto No. 10*
	Mozart	*Mass in C Minor*
	Mendelssohn	*Hymn of Praise*
	Kodaly	*Missa Brevis*
	Handel	*Messiah*
1957	Bach	*St. Matthew Passion*
	Elgar	*The Kingdom*
	Verdi	*Requiem*
	Elgar	*For the Fallen*
	Handel	*Messiah*
1958	Elgar	*The Dream of Gerontius*
	Mozart	*Mass in C Minor*
	Walton	*Coronation Te Deum*
	Mendelssohn	*Elijah*
	Berlioz	*Damnation of Faust*
	Handel	*Messiah*
1959	Bach	*St. Matthew Passion*
	Haydn	*The Seasons*
	Mendelssohn	*Elijah*
	Handel	*Samson*
	Handel	*Messiah*
1960	Elgar	*The Aposltes*
	Rossini	*Petite Messe Solenelle*
	Parry	*Blest Pair of Sirens*
	Verdi	*Nabucco*
	Handel	*Messiah*
1961	Mendelssohn	*Elijah*
	Elgar	*The Dream of Gerontius*
	Verdi	*Requiem*
	Elgar	*For The Fallen*
	Handel	*Messiah*
1962	Verdi	*Aida*
	Bach	*St. Matthew Passion*
	Verdi	*Nabucco*
	Handel	*Messiah*

1963	Dvorak	*Stabat Mater*
	Vivaldi	*Gloria*
	Elgar	*The Kingdom*
	Handel	*Judas Maccabeus*
	Handel	*Messiah*
1964	Rossini	*Petite Messe Solenelle*
	Poulenc	*Organ Concerto*
	Elgar	*The Dream of Gerontius*
	Elgar	*The Apostles*
	Handel	*Messiah*
1965	Haydn	*The Creation*
	Bach	*St. John Passion*
	Mendelssohn	*Elijah*
	Handel	*Messiah*
	Handel	*Messiah*
1966	Verdi	*Nabucco*
	Bach	*Mass in B Minor*
	Elgar	*For The Fallen*
	Verdi	*Requiem*
	Handel	*Messiah*
1967	Elgar	*The Kingdom*
	Dvorak	*Stabat Mater*
	Vivaldi	*Gloria*
	Elgar	*Serenade for Strings*
	Elgar	*The Dream of Gerontius*
	Handel	*Messiah*
1968	Haydn	*Nelson Mass*
	Mendelssohn	*Hymn of Praise*
	Bach	*Mass in B Minor*
	Verdi	*Aida*
	Handel	*Messiah*
1969	Bach	*St. Matthew Passion*
	Poulenc	*Organ Concerto*
	Elgar	*Sea Pictures*
	Elgar	*The Bavarian Highlands*
	Elgar	*The Music Makers*
	Mendelssohn	*Elijah*
	Verdi	*Aida*
	Brahms	*Song of Destiny*
	Verdi	*Requiem*
	Handel	*Messiah*

1970		Songs of Praise (BBC TV)
	Haydn	*The Creation*
	Faure	*Requiem*
	Honegger	*King David*
	Rossini	*Petite Messe Solenelle*
	Vivaldi	*Gloria*
	Handel	*Messiah*

1971	Elgar	*The Apostles*
	Handel	*Israel in Egypt*
	Verdi	*Aida*
	Verdi	*Nabucco*
	Handel	*Messiah*

1972	Elgar	*The Dream of Gerontius*
	Brahms	*Requiem Mass in D Minor*
	Haydn	*Nelson Mass*
	Mendelssohn	*Elijah*
	Handel	*Messiah*

1973	Albinoni	*Adagio*
	Berlioz	*The Childhood of Christ*
	Bach	*St. Matthew Passion*
	Verdi	*Nabucco*
	Verdi	*Requiem*
	Handel	*Messiah*

1974	Faure	*Requiem*
	Honegger	*King David*
	Elgar	*The Kingdom*
	Brahms	*Song of Destiny*
	Rossini	*Petite Messe Solenelle*
	Handel	*Solomon*
	Handel	*Messiah*

1975	Elgar	*The Dream of Gerontius*
	Rossini	*Stabat Mater*
	Bruckner	*Mass in E Minor*
	Verdi	*Aida*
	Handel	*Messiah*

1976	Haydn	*The Seasons*
	Bach	*Mass in B Minor*
	Verdi	*Requiem*
	Handel	*Messiah*

1977	Elgar	*The Apostles*

	Haydn	*Nelson Mass*
	Walton	*Belshazzar's Feast*
	Mendelssohn	*Elijah*
	Handel	*Messiah*
1978	Poulenc	*Gloria*
	Poulenc	*Organ Concerto*
	Mozart	*Requiem*
	Elgar	*The Dream of Gerontius*
	Brahms	*Academic Festival Ov'ture*
	Brahms	*Song of Destiny*
	Brahms	*Requiem*
		Charity Concert *
		(Malcolm Sargent Fund)
	Handel	*Messiah*
1979	Borodin	*Polovtsian Dances*
	Vaughan Williams	*Serenade to Music*
	Orff	*Carmina Burana*
	Bach	*St. Matthew Passion*
	Elgar	*Caractacus*
	Handel	*Messiah*
1980	Elgar	*Nimrod*
	Handel	*Zadok the Priest*
	Dvorak	*Te Deum*
	Honegger	*King David*
	Vaughan Williams	*The Old Hundreth*
	Vaughan Williams	*Toward 'Unknown Region*
	Vaughan Williams	*Sea Symphony*
	Elgar	*Serenade for Strings*
	Elgar	*The Music Makers*
	Orff	*Carmina Burana*
	Handel	*Messiah*
1981	Handel	*Messiah*
	Haydn	*The Creation*
	Verdi	*Requiem*
	Brahms	*Academic Festival Ov'ture*
	Faure	*Requiem*
	Gershwin	*Porgy and Bess*
	Handel	*Messiah*
		Family Carol Concert *
1982	Handel	*The King Shall Rejoice*
	Vivaldi	*Gloria*
	Haydn	*Theresienmesse*

	Elgar	*The Kingdom*
		Charity Concert *
		(Speke Hall Appeal)
		Gala Opera Concert *
	Handel	*Messiah*
		Family Carol Concert *
1983	Elgar	*The Dream of Gerontius*
	Parry	*I Was Glad*
	Vaughan Williams	*Fantasia on a Theme by Thomas Tallis*
	Tippett	*A Child of Our Time*
	Verdi	*Requiem*
	Verdi	*Aida*
	Handel	*Messiah*
		Family Carol Concert *
1984	Handel	*Chandos Anthem*
	Arwel Hughes	*Dewi Sant*
	Handel	*Messiah*
	Elgar	*The Apostles*
	Walton	*Crown Imperial*
	Stanford	*Songs of the Fleet*
	Elgar	*Enigma Variations*
	Walton	*Belshazzar's Feast*
	Handel	*Messiah*
		Family Carol Concert *
1985	Bach	*St. Matthew Passion*
	Mendelssohn	*Elijah*
	Handel	*Messiah*
		Carol Concert *
1986	Brahms	*Academic Festival Ov'ture*
	Dvorak	*Te Deum*
	Brahms	*Requiem*
	Verdi	*Force of Destiny Overture*
	Verdi	*Te Deum*
	Orff	*Carmina Burana*
	Handel	*Messiah*
1987		Cymanfa Ganu
	Handel	*Messiah*
	Elgar	*The Kingdom*
		Gala Opera Concert *
		Carol Concert *

1988		Cymanfa Ganu
	Handel	*Messiah*
		Arias and Choruses from
		Opera and Oratorio *
	Verdi	*Requiem*
	Verdi	*Nabucco*
		Family Festival of Carols *
		"The Glory of Christmas" *
1989	Haydn	*The Creation*
	Faure	*Requiem*
	Walton	*Belshazzar's Feast*
	Bizet	*Carmen*
	Handel	*Messiah*
		Family Carol Concert *
1990		Cymanfa Ganu
	Faure	*Requiem*
	Handel	*Zadok the Priest*
	Bruckner	*Locus Iste*
	Elgar	*The Music Makers*
	Mathias	*This Worlde's Joie*
	Mendelssohn	*Elijah*
	Handel	*Messiah*
		"Celebration of Christmas"*
1991		Cymanfa Ganu
	Mozart	"Amadeus" — *Requiem* and
		other works *
		Gala Opera Concert *
		Family Carol Concert *
1992		Cymanfa Ganu
	Mendelssohn	*Elijah*
	Walton	*Crown Imperial*
	Matthias	*Let the People Praise Thee*
	Vaughan Williams	*Serenade to Music*
	Orff	*Carmina Burana*
		"American Rhapsody" *
		"Christmas Fantasy" *
1993		Gala Charity Concert *
		(Wirral Hospital Trust)
	Berlioz	*Grande Messe des Morts*
		An Evening of Popular
		Classics *
	Handel	*Messiah*

| | | Christmas Concert * |
| Handel | | *Messiah* |

1994		Gala Charity Concert *
		(Wirral Hospital Trust)
		"Celebration of the Sea"
Vaughan Williams		*Sea Symphony*
Mendelssohn		Elijah
		"Christmas is Coming" *
Handel		*Messiah*
		"Christmas is Coming" *

1995		"The Magic of Vienna"*
		(Wirral Hospital Trust)
		Grand Charity Concert *
		(Leukemia Research)
Elgar		*The Dream of Gerontius*
		Evening of Light Classical
		Music *
Verdi		*Requiem*
		Carol Concert *
Handel		*Messiah*
		"Christmas Spectacular"*

1996		Gala Concert *
		(Wirral Hospital Trust)
		"Pomp and Circumstance"*
		Summer Concert *
		Opera Highlights *
		Viennese Gala Evening *
		(Action Research)
Puccini		*Messa di Gloria*
Verdi		*Aida (Acts 1 and 2)*
		Christmas Concert *
Handel		*Messiah*
		Family Carol Concert *

1997		Gala Concert *
		(Wirral Hospital Trust)
Mozart		"Hell and Heaven" *
		Brass Night at the Proms *
		Last Night of the Proms *
		(Action Research)
Arwel Hughes		*Gweddi*
Verdi		*Requiem*
		Christmas Concert

	Handel	*Messiah*
1998		Great Choral and Brass Classics *
		"America, America" *
		"Classic Spectacular"*
		Gala Concert *
		(RNLI)
	Elgar	*The Music Makers*
	Mascagni	*Cavalleria Rusticana*
	Handel	*Messiah*
		Carol Concert *
		Family Carol Concert *
1999		"The Magic of Vienna"*
		Gala Family Concert *
		(Rocking Horse Appeal)
	Faure	*Requiem*
	Faure	*Cantique Jean Racine*
	Gounod	*St. Cecilia Mass*
	Orff	*Carmina Burana*
		Gala Film and TV Music Theme Night *
		Family Carol Concert *
2000	Handel	*Messiah*
		Mossley Hill Church 125th Anniversary Concert *
	Elgar	*The Dream of Gerontius*
		Centenary Gala Concert *
		"A Christmas Celebration"*
2001		"Totally Brassed Off" *
		"An Evening with Mozart"*
	Bizet	*Carmen*
		Family Christmas Concert*
2002	Elgar	*The Kingdom*
		"Baroque Favourites"*
		"A Celebration in Song"*
		"Tonight, Tonight" *
		Family Christmas Concert*
2003	Poulenc	*Gloria*
	Elgar	*The Music Makers*
	Sullivan	"Silence in Court" *
		"To the Glory of God" *

| | Verdi / Puccini | "Viva Italia" *
| | | "God Rest Ye Merry" *

| 2004 | | Music for St David's Day*
| | Faure | *Requiem*
| | Rossini | *Stabat Mater*
| | | Spring Prom including
| | Rutter | *Gloria*
| | Verdi | Grand March from *Aida*
| | Orff | *Carmina Burana* Suite
| | Handel | *Messiah*
| | | Family Carol Concert *

| 2005 | | "With Cheerful Notes" *
| | Tippett | *Five Negro Spirituals*
| | Jenkins | *The Armed Man*
| | Orrell | *Trafalgar Sequence*
| | Elgar | *Sea Pictures*
| | Haydn | *Nelson Mass*
| | | "Festive Fun" *

| 2006 | | Evening of Choral
| | | Favourites *
| | Verdi | *Requiem*
| | Verdi | *Requiem*
| | Mozart | *Requiem* and other works*
| | | "Carols and Brass"*

| 2007 | Mendelssohn | *Elijah*
| | | "Summer Serenade"*

*   Full details of these varied concerts are to be found in the programmes